THROUGH A SHATTERED LOOKING-GLASS

CLAY BERRY

Publisher's Information

EBookBakery Books

Author contact: michael@ebookbakery.com

ISBN 978-1-938517-77-8

© 2017 by Clay Berry

ALL RIGHTS RESERVED

No part of this work covered by the copyright herein may be reproduced, transmitted, stored, or used in any form or by any means graphic, electronic, or mechanical, including but not limited to photocopying, scanning, digitizing, taping, Web distribution, information networks, or information storage and retrieval systems, except as permitted by Section 107 or 108 of the 1976 United States Copyright Act, without the prior written permission of the author. This book is a work of fiction. Names, characters, places and incidents are the product of the author's imagination and are fictionalized. Any resemblance to actual persons, living or dead, business establishments, events, or locales is coincidental.

DEDICATION

*For Christopher Aaron Berry,
who re-emerged*

Table of Contents

PART ONE 1

    The Splendor in Her Eyes 3
    Great and Wise Aunt Tamara 13
    Coloring Life Outside the Lines 19
    The Christmas Troll 34
    Lost in the Tunnel 43
    The Sound of Shattering Glass 51
    What Those Eyes Can See 57
    Everything Will Be Okay 67
    A Walk to Somewhere New 75
    Too Many Fiends at the Party 83
    The Five C's 97

PART TWO 103

    The Catalyst 105
    The Crow 121
    An Unexpected Diagnosis 131
    Too Many Ghosts in the Room 135

PART THREE 145

    Nanna's General 147
    The Rusty Axe Lodge 155
    They're in the Lightning 161
    An Unexpected Meeting 175
    God's Under-shepherd 185
    A Rest by the River 201
    An Eternal Precipice 213
    Light in the Valley of Shadow 223
    A White Mountain Farm Breakfast 243
    Final Descent 253

Acknowledgments 262
About the author..263

A Personal Note

This story took shape as I sought to make sense of the illness that overtook our family when one member was diagnosed with bipolar disorder.

Through a Shattered Looking-glass is an impressionistic expression of an experience that defies comprehension and evades description. As the mental illness of one affected the mental health of us all, we sought: wisdom, which was illusive; clarity, which we never found; and peace of mind. That too, was rare, but came primarily through our faith in God and the support of family, church, and friends. To them, and mostly to God, I am deeply grateful.

The characters and circumstances are entirely fictional. I chose a wealthy family from New York City to illustrate that no matter how powerful you may think you are, that power becomes an illusion when set against the onslaughts of mental suffering. Indeed, power is discovered in some unexpected places, often when we are at our weakest!

Please know that my intention is not to critique the mental health profession or advocate for a particular therapeutic approach. Our family faced our illness with the help of extraordinary professionals. I strongly recommend that one seek out the care and experience of qualified therapists when necessary.

Finally, though the story utilizes Alice's looking-glass as an important metaphor (with all due gratitude to Lewis Carroll), the reader may rest assured that this is not another adaptation of the Alice saga. You should not be surprised, however, when reality loses definition in the story. For far too many who suffer mental illness, reality stopped making sense a long time ago.

Clay

"Now, if you'll only attend, Kitty, and not talk so much, I'll tell you all my ideas about Looking-glass House. First, there is the room you can see through the glass—that's just the same as our drawing room, only the things go the other way. ... now we come to the passage. You can just see a little peep of the passage in Looking-glass House, if you leave the door of our drawing-room wide open: and it's very like our passage as far as you can see, only you know it may be quite different on beyond..."

Alice
From Lewis Carroll's, *Through the Looking-Glass*

PART ONE

1

THE SPLENDOR IN HER EYES

"GOOD AFTERNOON, LADIES AND GENTLEMEN. My name is Captain Parker and I'd like to welcome you aboard Gateway Airlines flight 236 to New York City. I'm sorry to report that we will be flying through cloud cover all the way to New York, though we should make our destination on schedule. We hope you enjoy your flight."

Aimee hadn't noticed how overcast the day had become until she heard the announcement. She took one last look at the mountains that rose above the small airport just west of North Conway, New Hampshire, and felt lost among them.

The loud propellers outside her window roared, and the plane backed away from its gangway. Her husband Terrance, seated by the aisle, unfolded the Wall Street Journal and shifted in his seat. She wrapped her arms around her body, squeezed herself, then closed her eyes to refocus. It didn't work. Memories from the mountain ripped through her head. *What did any of that mean?*

As the plane ascended and all visibility disappeared, Aimee felt encased within herself. She would not get another view of the landscape until they descended into LaGuardia. *If I needed a good metaphor to describe my life, the lack of a horizon would be a good one. But not now. Stay in touch.*

Aimee settled back and studied the texture of the clouds, hoping to push away the violent images of Friday night that may have permanently redirected their lives. *I should have brought my laptop so I could get ahead of those meetings I have in the morning.*

Her daughter, Tamara, seated between her and Terrance, was staring blankly at the seat in front of her.

Or, maybe I should reschedule. I might have to be available.

The intensity in Tamara's face incited a moment of panic in Aimee. Her eyes were tightly shut, etching ridges across her forehead.

Where are you going, now? You've been disappearing into yourself ever since we left the cabin this morning. Hang on, honey. This won't take long.

Aimee turned to Terrance but he was lost in the editorial section.

I've got to figure this out, or it may be over for us. Did we just turn a page or slam the book for good?

They would not speak a meaningful word to one another during the flight home, and that silence would change Aimee forever. As the plane rapidly gained altitude, Aimee descended into a frightening new chapter of a story about a little girl who fell through a shattered looking-glass and took her family with her.

That story began fourteen years ago...

The night wind was flecked with ice and stung Aimee's face as she emerged from the subway entrance and pushed on toward Park Avenue. Granite and glass drew her brilliant blue eyes upward. She thought the city a wonder: *What a beautiful grand dame you are. A few more days like this and you're all mine.* She had been swallowed whole by the grandeur that has always been New York.

Each morning, when she stepped onto the floor of the New York Stock Exchange, Aimee marshaled inner reserves of fluid, fiery emotional power that raged long after the closing bell halted her for the day. She had just made her clients a lot of money and paused to consider the power being consolidated by that wealth. *If this is what narcotics are like... or, better, climbing free-style up the side of one these amazing buildings. So long as I don't look down!*

This dinner date, however, was sending her into a downward, bearish spiral. At the southeast corner of Central Park, Aimee looked out over the wall into the park and felt her mood sag. *Why do we have to do this tonight? There are a dozen other things Terrance and I would rather do: dinner at that new bistro or catch up with Sarah and Don over at Dominice's Wine Bar.* She looked diagonally across the park. *The Lincoln Center. Damn. We were supposed to go to the Nutcracker tonight. But when Paul Baxter barks, dutiful son Terrance rolls over.* She took a deep breath; the orange countdown taking place on the street lamp at the crosswalk told her she had that much time to re-commit herself. 8…7…6… *Poor Terrance is already trapped up there with his parents.*

She let the crossing clock run down and gazed up at those majestic pinnacles of power one last time hoping to renew her wonder. The night cast mystic spells on the skyline. Shadows were plentiful but deceptive as light from a myriad of false stars gave these giants life and locomotion. *Nothing is stationary in New York City. None of this is as solid as people down here might think. All that stone and steel becomes molten lava when you put a price on it. Up there, currents of capital move freely around the planet at stratospheric heights.* She had always dreamed of hoisting her sails up there and coursing along those currents, so far out of reach from those living at street-level where the populace imagined life meant something else.

Up there was where Aimee was going for dinner with Terrance and his father whose dissatisfaction over the direction of Aimee's life was clear. *At least Maureen will be there.* But Aimee could count on little support from her husband or mother-in-law once the clan patriarch had sidelined them, which he did all too well.

As the arctic wind bit into her cheeks, Aimee crossed the street and moved through the after-work crowd toward Atwell's on Park Avenue. There would be no neon sign at street level. She would show the doorman her card, and he would admit her into the elevator and press the button for the appropriate floor. She'd step off into a grand entryway of an exquisite restaurant that never advertised, hand-calligraphied its menus, and held its tables for those select few whose reservations were permanently secured.

On a normal evening, Aimee would be greeted, uncloaked, greeted again, shown to her seat and guaranteed an array of comforts by a host of attendants. Everyone would treat her as if it were their mission in life to see to her particular needs for as long as she graced their presence. Tonight, however, she bumped into her father-in-law as she stepped off the elevator. He was returning from the men's room and took her in hand personally.

"Mr. Baxter! I'm sorry I'm running behind," said Aimee as she sought to repair her faulty entrance.

She was still navigating the social dynamics of Terrance's family. The old moneyed mannerisms cultivated by the Baxters over the course of generations had been an aphrodisiac when she was easing her way into this thrilling new relationship. That sensation had passed.

"Here, allow me," he said as he helped her with her coat and then handed her brief-case to the attendant.

"I'll take that, actually," she said, retrieving her case. It was her only symbol of status, and she would need it later.

"As you wish," said Paul, looking over his spectacles at her.

She read his appraisal of her in the stare. She would never be able to boast of any sort of pedigree, and in these moments without sufficient time to arm herself, she felt her lack of breeding. Her family coat of arms had a Buick in one quadrant, season tickets at Yankee Stadium (right field) in another, a donkey in the political corner, and two stars representing the best they could afford on a night out for dinner. Aimee's liberal-leaning family prided themselves on being fashionably multi-cultural; Terrance's parents were multi-national, and they weren't apt to confuse one for the other any time soon.

She met his eyes and affected a smile but didn't care if he bought it. *You know good and well it's not my credentials that are up for grabs tonight, so watch your step, old man.*

Aimee had grown up in Queens; her father was a lawyer in a young, struggling law-firm. Aimee had to put herself through college. She pursued a fine-arts degree for three semesters but shifted to economics when life's realities began closing in. She interned with a brokerage firm for a semester in Chicago. There, in the futures market at the Board of Trade, she developed her craving for the fight. Her success on the trading floor and the rapport she developed with her mentors, brought her to the attention of two firms back in New York. Her position at Tristom

Securities was won by honest hard work and a forthright interview that proved her gristle, if not yet her maturity.

Seeing herself through Paul Baxter's eyes, however, was a mental exercise she wished she could abandon. She held his gaze until he blinked. *There are people of power, and then there are powerful people. Who do you really imagine yourself to be, Mr. Baxter?* Aimee had entered their world at an altitude she worried she couldn't maintain, and she fretted about falling from their graces before she had gained her foothold. *More importantly, who do I intend to be, with or without you?* She nodded respectfully in his direction. *I think we're about to find out.*

"We're over here," Paul said. She knew the way to the Baxter table but submitted to his summons with due deference.

The room was coutured to present as sharp a contrast as money could achieve to the grimy streets fourteen stories below and those that walked them. The air was bathed in crystalline light that glinted off gold-rimmed china; mahoganies and maroons were delicately balanced and did what they were supposed to do: accessorize the personalities on display.

"I'm surprised at you," said Maureen, as Aimee took her seat. Her mother-in-law often interchanged verbal castigation and encouragement as if they were the same thing; it was always well-intentioned, but usually failed.

"You should at least take a cab," she continued after pointing out how chapped Aimee's face was.

Terrance, on the other hand, thought how striking she looked with red cheeks and stray hair which she hadn't managed to tuck back into its tightly drawn bun.

"How are you feeling, dear?" asked Maureen, overly maternal toward Aimee since they'd heard the news.

"As well as one could expect, as you know, I'm sure," said Aimee.

"What did the doctor say the other day?" asked Maureen.

"Everything's right on schedule, though we still have a number of decisions to make, like…"

"About that." Paul leaned forward as if to fill all the empty space between them. He was agitated with their banter and had matters to settle, but he had lost the advantage of an opening position. Maureen grabbed his arm and shut him up.

"Let her speak, dear. She's had a long day," said Maureen.

Aimee decided on silence, instead, frustrated that her mood had darkened and resembled the wintry mix she had slogged through earlier. As an antidote, she let her eyes wander. *Tyndale... Snyder... Sorenson...* She ticked off the names of the "players" in the room and imagined the corporate-sized ulterior motives hidden within every conversation. *How many millions are at stake whenever a group of men in evening dress presume to be enjoying a night out with their wives?*

"If you will excuse me, I think I'll go freshen up a bit," said Aimee. She cast Maureen one of those knowing glances that communicated more to another woman than to the oblivious men in the company then headed toward the women's lounge. She hoped for a moment to reclaim her resolve.

"Don't fret, dear," said Maureen as she slipped into the restroom. Aimee was looking in the mirror, but she was studying her doubts.

"It's okay," said Aimee, pretending to repair her mascara.

"Paul wants what's best – for himself first, for sure – but also for you and Terrance. He has little faith in his offspring, I'm afraid. As well as Terrance has done for himself, Paul will always take the credit for it. So be careful. He wants to take his share of credit for you, too, my dear. Just be careful."

Maureen feigned a moment of care for her own appearance then left Aimee to simmer.

My aims are my own, thank you, very much. The bright spot on her horizon was the prospect of owning her own securities firm. That was no secret to Paul who, as a wedding present, all but promised his rolodex of friends and a few well-oiled assurances that she had little to worry about.

Aimee and Terrance's plan included children once their foundations were secure, but back in September Aimee's period was late, three and a half years early. She refused to think about it, dismissed the idea of a home pregnancy test and couldn't imagine why she should worry Terrance until she was certain. But she knew she had conceived, and the force of that knowledge couldn't be beaten back by any of the lies she was telling herself. When she told Terrance, however, they regrouped and had a trust established for the kid before the first trimester.

As Aimee maneuvered through the dining room back to their table, Paul was in full-throated mastery of the family dynamic.

"The moment Alford decided to transfer those shares I knew he was in trouble, and I don't want you to make the same mistake," Paul was saying to Terrance whose look of relief upon Aimee's return was palpable.

"Ah," Paul said, calling a halt to the lecture directed toward his son and gearing up for the one he had planned for her.

"I believe you had asked me a question, Mr. Baxter," said Aimee, directing the full force of her attention in Terrance's direction.

"Well. No," stammered Paul. "Not a question, precisely. I was about to let you in on a piece of advice."

"I'm listening," she said.

The waiter hovered, ready to take their order, but Paul kept everyone focused on the matter at hand. Aimee refused to look at him. His stony face knew one expression; he had trained it to intimidate, so Aimee spared herself the treatment.

"Now, when Maureen and I were married, we made sure our professional careers were well in hand before…"

"Paul was a vice-president in the bank before Terrance's older brother came along," Maureen interjected.

"Decently and in order, like it says in the Good Book," quoted Paul. It was probably the only scripture the old man knew and made use of.

"Dad. If I may --"

"What is it, son?"

The look silenced Terrance, and Aimee felt the thrust of Paul's tone in her own heart. She knew where this was coming from. Aimee's pregnancy would not have been a problem if she wasn't a professional in her own right. Terrance's father adored the idea of a traditional family, but Aimee had captured her father-in-law's attention and her aptitude for finance was a bright spot on his professional radar.

"As I was saying: Had you two ordered your lives a little more decently and given the securities firm a bit more time, then maybe you wouldn't have to cash in such a promising career so soon."

"Paul!" Maureen's intrusion into her husband's speech took the young couple by surprise. They had never seen her counter her husband in public. Terrance saw plenty of that at home, but the public face of the Baxter clan belonged to Paul. Maureen's face, and opinion, was meant to grace his at all cost.

Aimee stewed. *Had I ordered my life more decently! Or, what? Paul could have greased my skids in some wonderful ways is the implication. I'm not through here, by any means.* She bristled at the insinuation that she couldn't cut it on the Stock Exchange and was taking the maternal way out. The fact that she was this far along in her pregnancy, and there was no means of reversing course, seemed to have heightened his frustration. Furthermore, the sonograms showed it would not be a male heir, and while Paul would never so openly utter disapproval, it did seem as if the Old Man was waiting for an apology.

"If you will let me continue," he said. "I've been giving this a lot of thought." He grew agitated because he couldn't get anyone to look at him. Terrance could only gaze at the sparkle in his glass of scotch.

"So have I, sir," said Aimee, in crisp, clear tones without looking at him. Her eyes were for her husband who couldn't bear to look up, but also couldn't resist. The glint in her pupils was all he needed to rally. Without breaking the bond between them, she reached for her case, and extracted two crisp documents which she laid before him.

Terrance took them in hand and scanned them carefully. He smiled, lifted his glass and met her gaze with his own glint of satisfaction. She tucked the pages back in her case and lifted her glass.

"Very good," said Terrance.

Paul's face was ripe red and Maureen was stupefied. Aimee let the moment linger long enough to solidify her position in the conversation.

"What was that?" shouted Paul.

"That," said Aimee, "was a letter from the president of Tristom Securities assuring me of their complete support. My position in the company is secure, and I should feel free to negotiate an appropriate amount of maternity leave with a promise of a bonus if I agree not to shop my talents while I'm away. The second page was a list of post-natal specialists I have been interviewing."

"A post what - for Christ-sake?" said Paul.

"She will assist me as I work out the right balance between motherhood and career, which I see no reason to give up."

"A foreign nanny, you mean," protested Paul.

"No, sir. These are a cut above European *au pairs*. They are credentialed, bonded, and come with impeccable references. They specialize in providing care – both before and after delivery – for profession-oriented couples. I will e-mail you several web-sites so you can see for yourself. I've conducted six interviews and have narrowed the field considerably. I think I have just the person who will suit our needs and satisfy your demands."

"For how long?" he demanded to know.

"One year, renewable contract until she enters pre-K," said Aimee.

"Then what?"

"A European nanny."

"I thought so," he grunted.

Her eyes sliced into the elder Baxter. She held him as long as she dared, then she turned to the waitperson.

"I'll have the scallops," she said.

"I'll have the brazed quail," said Terrance. "He'll have the sirloin, medium rare, the beet salad for her, another of whatever it was they were drinking, and I'll take care of this tonight."

"Very good, sir."

Yes, it is. Yes, it is.

On Monday morning Aimee called Emily Eason, invited her to lunch, and offered her the job as "vice-mom."

Emily's first role was to investigate options and present her suggestions for nursery furnishings, appropriate play equipment, car seats, pediatricians, clothes, diaper services, etc. She was to be available twenty-four-seven the week of her delivery. Emily suggested they set a date for cesarean section, given the demand of the couple's busy schedules.

We're off to an excellent start! "Will you contact the obstetrician, or should I?" Aimee asked Emily.

"That is your department!" Emily laughed. "I take over once she's arrived. In the meantime, I'll get everything ready for the little princess."

2

Great and Wise Aunt Tamara

As the plane leveled off from its ascent, it dropped thirty feet and slammed its belly on the air mass below then collided with rough pockets of sky that hammered against the wings.

"Ladies and Gentlemen, we have reached cruising altitude, however, the captain has requested all passengers remain in their seats with seat belts fastened," announced the flight attendant.

That voice was shortly replaced by another. "Ladies and Gentlemen, this is captain Parker. We are skirting a storm coming from the southwest and will be experiencing severe turbulence for a little while. Our present course should avoid most of the storm, though it may add a few minutes to our travel time. As soon as the ride evens out, our stewards will come through the cabin with the refreshment cart. We are sorry for any discomfort you may be experiencing."

Aimee saw the color disappear from Tamara's face and tension replaced her placid stare. She took her daughter's hand but Tamara snatched it away and started digging through her back pack.

"What do you need, honey?" asked Aimee

"A new head," snapped her daughter.

Aimee's emotional temperature rose. *A few more bumps in the road and we're in for real trouble.*

Tamara shifted in her seat and rebelled at the confinement she suffered belted in so snuggly. Her long legs were angled back under the seat, knees pressed firmly against the seat in front of her, and there wasn't room for expansion.

She wrestled her sketch-book from her satchel and started to doodle. Random shapes with a heavy line moved over the page, but then supple squiggles and myriads of pin-point dots coalesced into a spectral figure. Crude at first, the human form evolved until its essence was no longer bound by the physical features she gave it. Soon, it emanated light and power.

"What is it?" Aimee asked.

But Tamara hesitated so long to answer that Aimee got the message to back off.

࿙

As Emily prepared to leave one evening, she placed a piece of paper on the table in front of Aimee, a list of names.

"I hadn't heard any names mentioned, so just for fun, I took the liberty of researching a few – dignified, not too trendy, and they all go well with Baxter," said Emily.

"Ugh! Not again," groaned Aimee, frustrated by this topic and the pressure from their parents to select favorite family names. She mumbled as she scanned the list: "Rosalind, Nora, Jessica, Kayla, Victoria. I don't know," she said with defeat in her voice. "I'll show it to Terrance and see what he thinks."

"Tamara," said Terrance, surprising them. He had just come home and slipped into the dining room.

"Did you say, 'Tamara?'" asked Aimee.

Emily looked warily at Terrance and buttoned her coat.

"Tamara," he affirmed, quietly.

"You're serious," said his wife. "Where in the world--"

"Tamara Esmeralda Cousins," he said, as much to himself as to Aimee. "Though, you could drop the Esmeralda!" he added quickly. "She was my great aunt on my father's side. One of the most exquisite ladies I ever knew. Of all my parents' relatives, I used to look forward to her visits more than any other. I always thought I'd like to honor her in some way. And I would love to think our daughter might emulate her instead of some of the other members of the clan."

"Tamara," whispered Aimee. Her brow furrowed. "We'll see."

"Good night," said Emily. "Just let me know what to put on her birth announcements."

After she was gone, Aimee set the list aside and pursued Terrance's suggestion.

"Tell me more about this Aunt Tamara," she said, joining him on the couch with a glass of soda water while he sipped his scotch. "Tamara. I don't think I've ever met a Tamara."

"When I was a kid, we were taught early and often that family image was everything. We represented the family name in all we did, our schoolwork, our sports, the way we dressed and behaved in public. Everything. My father was petrified of ruining his reputation. He had inherited it from his dad in a day and time when a man's name was his stock in trade. His honor was all he had among other gentlemen of their class. And a man's children were a barometer of his authority at home. You see, my family's heritage ... no, wait, we don't need to go through that again. Where Aunt Tamara was concerned, she didn't give a rat's ass about any of it. She had a different sort of confidence about life I don't think my parents ever had. And I mean life with a capital L, not life down at the bank, or life at the club, but the life we all thought we would discover once this other finally paid off. Somehow, she was the only one who comprehended what it was we were working our asses off to achieve. She could enjoy people, love them. She really loved life. At family gatherings, she was the only one you could count on to listen and care about what you were saying. She'd laugh at your jokes, and you knew she genuinely thought they were funny."

"So, you want our daughter to take after the odd-ball in the family?"

"Yes! Exactly. She was odd, no question, but she was probably one of the wisest people I ever met. I'm sorry you'll never have the pleasure of knowing her. She was an equal partner in the family business, but the truth is, she wasn't interested in financial empires or power. She served on several of the family corporate boards – more out of loyalty and wanting to be involved, though she had a lot of fun with the perks and bonuses! Anyway, she had vision, mixed with down-in-the-dirt common sense that no one else in the family shared. Very intuitive.

That sky-high confidence gave her clarity that most in the room lacked, not to mention an air of abandon no one else wanted. But they trusted her instincts. They argued with her, but seldom won her over. Once her mind was set, as people fell in line and a plan took shape, many left the room a little frightened of where her ideas would lead. Nine times out of ten, however, she was dead on the money. What set her apart for me was that she was supremely human. I could have learned a lot more from her. I wish I had."

As Aimee listened, she sat back to get a clearer view of the man talking about this woman in this fashion. *This is so unlike him.* She sensed a lonely longing in his description of her. *Was it a quality he desired for himself, a luxury he yearned for yet couldn't afford to risk? And if it's too late for him, maybe in his daughter? Interesting.*

Terrance grew introspective and looked away from Aimee.

"What is it?" Aimee asked.

"Just remembering her and how different she was from my father. He used to call me in and dress me down all the time in front of the others – public shame taught the sort of lessons that were meant to stay put: 'You are going to pay for that decision in more ways than one, young man.'" Terrance did a fair impersonation of his father.

"I was only eleven years old, standing as rigid as a jersey barrier in front of the aunts and uncles, trying for all the world not to cry – I can't remember what bad decision promised to be my ruin on that occasion; I just remember the weight of how wrong it was in my father's eyes, and the fear I felt for the calamity about to roll over me at any moment. And because he had to always be towering over me, it wouldn't do for him to go sit down. He'd exit the room as though he had to fix whatever it was that I had so thoroughly broken. No one would look at me. Then came this wise and wonderful voice from the other end of the drawing room. 'There will always be decisions that need to be made, Terrance, and your decisions will need to be made of something more than fear of your father.' Only my Aunt Tamara could have said that. It has taken me years to sort out what that means, or, how to do it."

Aimee would come to cherish Aunt Tamara stories and the way Terrance admired what she represented: her freedom and the supple way she navigated family tensions without letting it ruffle her.

"She had a wisdom no one else in the family possessed," he said. "And given the world into which our daughter is about to be born, I'd like to think she could find her way through it with as much grace and wisdom."

"Then, Tamara it is," said Aimee, feeling slight movements within her that she wished Terrance could experience too.

3

Coloring Life Outside the Lines

Feeling oppressed by the white wall outside her window, Aimee turned her attention to the image taking shape on Tamara's drawing pad. She once imagined her life as an artist and had been delighted to see those traits had emerged in her daughter. *But why are your fantasies so demonic and filled with death?* Angry and in full stride, this whatever-it-was fiercely stalked some doomed victim Aimee couldn't see. *Is this the demon that has been chasing you all your life? And is that what you saw during the storm Friday night?*

The airline's catalog was in reach, so she grabbed it to divert her thoughts. *I so enjoyed my imagination.* Her eyes drifted over the jewelry and perfumes, then she found a chess set for sale, the pieces of which resembled characters from the chronicles of Alice. *I remember landing on that field of battle as a kid, drawing my croquet-mallet sword, donning a flower-pot helmet, and joining the joust with Tweedle Dee and Tweedle Dum. Then, victorious, I set out across the board to claim my queenly crown.*

Tamara's eyes were fiery with rage. She moved to another quadrant of the page and made sharp slashing motions with her pen to add shade to the figure's cloak and severity to his face. *Is there no light in there? Where is all this ferocity coming from?*

In self-defense, Aimee looked back at the magazine. As a child, she had tagged along with Alice, down the rabbit hole and through the looking-glass. She fought red queens and tea-toasting mad hatters as she gratified her imagination again and again. One morning, her cocker-spaniel, Angel, flushed out a small mole and chased it to the edge of their yard where it dove down a hole, no bigger than a golf-ball. *If I could have thought the right thoughts and run toward the hole at the right velocity with the right faith, I could have shrunk to the size of a walnut and soared down the tunnel after the mole. There, the door-mouse would have introduced me to every sort of woodland creature seated around a beautifully appointed table all laid out for tea.*

In her periphery, Aimee saw Tamara's forearm and fist. She gripped her pen as if it were the only thing that kept her from falling into a ravine. Her muscles were taut and her knuckles were white. *Hold on, baby. Don't fall.*

Her head hurt, so Aimee shut her eyes and forced her memories back to those creative moments that gave her such relief as a child. She saw the mysterious full-length mirror in her grandmother's back bedroom. She would plant herself in front of it and get lost in those wondrous worlds behind the door at the end of the reflected room.

One afternoon, the mirror enticed her to step through. Brightly adorned guards in the castle threatened never to give her back. *After all, they needed a new queen and it was Thursday, which meant it was my turn to rule.* She was sure it wasn't a dream and insisted so as her grandma scooped her from the floor and moved her to the living room sofa to finish her nap – and her jousts with the Jabberkitty that kept nudging her.

At home, she had discovered the portal that existed through the mirror in their front hallway. It was framed by coats that hung on large hooks, and it cast its gaze backward down the long hallway that led to the kitchen and out the back door where she discovered a passage into Narnia. *Or, step through one of the doors in the hallway, and you would emerge under the front stoop on Sesame Street. In my Looking-glass house, the Salt-queen would shake herself and it would snow, the Pepper-king would sneeze and blow it all away. Then, they would launch into ridiculous spats and draft every spice-soldier in the cupboard into the fray.* She smiled and then grieved the memory. *I've gotten trapped inside that haunted world and taken too many wrong turns. When I was a kid, I could explore a landscape festooned with hidden chutes and steep ladders that took me suddenly into Candyland: I might climb onto cotton candy clouds, or slide hundreds of feet into the licorice whip forest. The aim was to get back to the queen's castle and resume my reign. There, at my decree, Ice Cream Sundays lasted a whole week before they became Milk Chocolate Mondays. Now, the aim is just to find a way out.*

The economic reports released by the White House were positive, so the Dow was up thirty-seven points at the opening bell. All the indexes climbed rapidly throughout the day in active trading. Aimee was still out of breath, but she loved going home after work feeling that sizzle. *I wonder if Terrance's day had been as profitable.* She looked forward to the nightly debrief they enjoyed over dinner.

The house grew quiet after their German *au pair* left for her evening out, but the transition was a jolt for Aimee as she heard the nanny's report: Terrance had called and would be working late, and Tamara was in a foul mood over being scolded by the housekeeper. She had strewn her toys all over the den to vent her displeasure then refused to pick them up. That was her job, Tamara had told the housekeeper who threatened to give notice. *The au pair looks like she might not be far behind. And after such an exhilarating day.* The meal was warming in the oven. Aimee poured herself a drink and looked over the mail.

Her first drink didn't help much, so she refilled her glass and moved to the living room. She heard the crinkling of paper as she sat on the couch. Under the cushion, she discovered a crumpled crayon drawing.

"Hello there," she said as she recognized Stamey, one of Tamara's stuffed bears. "And how did you find your way under there?"

Aimee admired the drawing then set aside. But the expression on the bear's face drew her eye. The likeness was simple, immature in its execution and on the surface, unremarkable. The polka-dotted vest and bow tie were delightfully rendered, but the bear's features were out of proportion. The real bear up in Tamara's room wore a perpetual smile. Its eyes always screamed, 'Don't you just love me!' The bear in the drawing, however, was placid; its eyes were half closed and the overall personality of the bear was subdued. *You're kind of cute.* The calm bear in the picture lent Aimee her own measure of serenity. *I think I like you better than your snotty doppelganger upstairs! I could use a snuggle with you right about now.*

Tamara entered the room so quietly Aimee wasn't aware of her until she had crawled onto the couch and burrowed her face into Aimee's side.

"How're you doing, monkey?" asked Aimee, as she put her arm around her daughter.

Silent, as usual. If she was lucky, Aimee might get a blank stare from her daughter. Tonight, all she got was a head full of long, tangled black hair. Tamara was a small girl; she ate little and looked out of proportion for her height. She could carry herself with perfect posture when she walked, then knot herself up into the tiniest ball of nothing when she became temperamental.

"Nice picture of Stamey," said Aimee.

There was the stare. Then, "He's sad," whispered Tamara, as she buried her face once again.

"Why would Stamey be so sad, I wonder?" mused Aimee. "He's got all a bear could ever want, not to mention a killer wardrobe. He has all those tea parties he goes to. And, he's got a great friend like you." Aimee squeezed her daughter, but Tamara pushed back and separated herself from her mother.

"I'll bet he's just waiting for an invitation to dinner," said Aimee. "Would you like to ask him to join us? You could invite Jaunt. Think he'd come? Or, are they still fighting? Anyway, dinner's ready." She patted Tamara on the thigh. "All it needs are a couple of connoisseurs to enjoy it."

"Here," said Aimee, as Tamara slipped off the couch. In her hand was the drawing, but Tamara wouldn't touch it. "Don't you want it? Or, should I hang it on the fridge?"

Tamara snatched it from her mother and carried it from the room.

The bear picture reappeared a few days later under the towels in the bathroom. Aimee found more drawings tucked in odd locations; some were hidden in places Tamara wasn't normally permitted. Scenes from a tea-party were found by Terrance in his underwear drawer. One, a rendering of their house from the street, was haunting in ways Aimee couldn't put her finger on. It had a somber essence she found deeply moving. A few were cute, others were inexplicable. The drawings had been buried then forgotten by the artist. Aimee stopped showing Tamara the drawings she found. Tamara would just snatch them away and bury them somewhere else. So, when Aimee found one she kept it safe, and Tamara never noticed they had been removed.

Clutching at these inklings of creativity, Aimee began a portfolio of Tamara's work. She relished the continuance of a dream. *How did I let that die so completely?* One morning, she held a sketch of Tamara's tea set in her hand and would not have admitted to thanking God, but her gratitude soared upward and beyond her for the direction her daughter's life seemed to be taking. *I hope she doesn't get scared of it, like I did.*

Aimee searched the web for cognitive enhancing toys, intricately illustrated story books, age-appropriate art supplies and well researched approaches to childhood engagement. As the time for Tamara to begin first grade approached, Aimee interviewed several headmasters and had her enrolled in the Sebastian Preparatory School, which claimed they could polish those latent talents in Tamara's young artistic mind. For a few years, the school did just that.

Then, her teachers began to discern a difference between artistic advances and sudden spasms of intensity which were laced with more poison than inspiration. At home, Terrance noticed how quickly his daughter's imagination, if allowed to run on un-checked, could careen out of control. Lines of reason had begun to fray, unravel, become tangled, and then grow hopelessly knotted into snarls of fantasy that couldn't be undone.

"Terrance, Tamara doesn't need to control her art yet," Aimee fired back one evening. "Her school-work, yes, that has a ways to go. But she has the spirit of an artist, and if this is really her gift then we have to grant her more leeway or we'll stifle her."

"These letters from her teachers say otherwise," he argued. "Honey, it's not just her art. Tamara is coloring her whole life outside the lines."

As Tamara began the third grade, her moods became frighteningly unpredictable. One morning, her class was making animal masks fashioned after African tribal art. "I'm going to be a mongoose," she told her teacher. "They eat snakes for breakfast." She held up a picture of a bloodied mongoose attacking a cobra. The mask she had fashioned was remarkably ferocious.

As the art period ended, however, Tamara found it impossible to store her project, switch gears, and move on to math. Three times her teacher excused Tamara from the room to go to her next class and each time Tamara reappeared, disrupting the start of the next session. She wasn't belligerent, nor did she make a scene. She simply slipped into the room and went to the art cupboard to retrieve her project. The third time she did it, the teacher felt she had to discipline her. As she took Tamara by the arm to escort her to the office, Tamara's legs collapsed beneath her; she slumped into a heap, then into a tight ball with her head between her knees. She wrapped her arms around her head, grabbed large fistfuls of hair and began twisting, pulling, moaning. Her whole body contorted with pain. The teacher attempted to lift her, but Tamara thrashed about then clawed at her.

"You snake!" shouted Tamara at the teacher. In a panic, the teacher ran out the door to get help.

When Aimee arrived, she found Tamara in a small office with the headmaster, Mr. Timrose. Tamara was coloring and didn't look up when Aimee entered. The two adults sat in silence as they watched her. *She is way beyond infantile coloring books.*

"Mrs. Baxter." The headmaster shifted his attention to look Aimee in the eyes. She didn't return his gaze for long. "I'd like to give Tamara a few days off from school. She appears to be under unusual stress in the classroom. And, I'd like you to consider professional consultation before Tamara returns to school."

"Are you suspending her?" asked Aimee.

"No, certainly not," he assured her. "I realize this is probably something Tamara is finding difficult to control."

"Professional consultation?" asked Aimee.

"Yes. I'd like you to have her screened by someone. I can give you some names, or you can find someone suitable to you and Mr. Baxter."

"Screened for what?" demanded Aimee.

"Hard to say." He tapped his pen on the desk and looked at Tamara. "Emotional development, mood disorders, that sort of thing. A good child psychologist. Take a few days to do that. Before Tamara comes back. Let's give her the rest of the week off, in fact. Is that okay?"

No, it is not okay. This is not going to happen. Yes, Tamara can take the week off and she might settle down. By Monday she should be ready to start the week fresh. But the screening is out of the question.

Later in the day, however, a darkness fell over Tamara's face that frightened Aimee for the first time. Aimee's life-coach had equipped Aimee to maintain a sense of personal mastery over herself and keep her daughter's needs in proper perspective. So, Aimee felt well-informed about moods and tantrums and what the appropriate responses should be. But a light had gone out in her daughter and Aimee didn't know where the fuse box was.

"What's the matter, honey?" Aimee asked, as she placed her hand on Tamara's forehead.

Tamara pushed her mother's hand away. She rolled off the couch, went upstairs, and lay on her bed.

"Honey?" said Aimee, as she quietly tapped on Tamara's bedroom door. Tamara turned on her and pushed the door shut, forcing Aimee back into the hallway.

For two days, Tamara was silent. She ate little and resisted being with anyone, even the stuffed animals that populated her bedroom. The two lavishly dressed bears, Stamey and Jaunt, sat at the tea table awaiting their hostess, but Tamara spent most of her days curled up on her bed.

"Don't cry, Stamey," Aimee overheard Tamara say one morning as she got ready for work. Tamara's door was slightly ajar.

"It won't hurt for much longer," said Tamara, as she carried the bear to her bed. She held it so tightly Aimee feared Tamara would dislodge the head from its body. Tamara's eyes glistened by the light of the little lamp by her bed, and then they grew dull and empty.

The darkness in Tamara had cast a deepening shadow in Aimee's mood, and she would have to climb out of it soon. *I've got too much going on right now for this. Torbert will be looking for those reports at 10:00, and I've got Shoreham Trust to deal with before him.*

Aimee slipped in to kiss her daughter and say good-bye, but Tamara forced Stamey between them and wouldn't look at her mom.

"Gretta is in the kitchen fixing your breakfast. Be good to her, you hear?"

Take a deep breath. And keep moving.

On her way home from the subway that evening, Aimee picked up a new member for the menagerie, a long, slender, purple snake with a diamond-shaped head. Aimee pulled the stuffed snake slowly out of the bag to see if she could get any reaction out of her daughter, but Tamara's eyes grew dark and morose.

"The tag says her name is Sandralina. That's kind of pretty, isn't it?" said Aimee.

"That's not her name," said Tamara, who turned away from it, and said no more.

Tamara still looked pale to Aimee as they went to school Monday morning. Aimee was to check in with the headmaster and the prospect was draining her of the vitality she would need for work that morning.

"Let's see how this goes, shall we?" Aimee said, more to herself than to Tamara as she escorted her daughter into the office. Her mind rifled through her arsenal of excuses: *There was no time. I couldn't find anyone. Terrance and I couldn't agree. God, I feel like I'm trying to explain why I didn't do my homework!* Aimee couldn't decide if she was in competition with the staff at the school, or if they were her allies in this.

"They want this to be a mental health issue, and it is not," she had told Terrance the night before. "My daughter is not going to be 'read' by professionals who justify their existence by finding demons only they can see and then magically eradicate. It's the twenty-first century version of a Salem witch-hunt! If you suspect there are demons lurking in the bushes and you are convinced you will find them, then you will. This is my daughter, not a demon."

Terrance had reminded her that the demons were not all that hidden.

"Why wouldn't you want to satisfy your own opinion about Tamara?" he asked her. "If you're sure Tamara's fine, then why not have that confirmed by a specialist?"

Because, you idiot, it's not just the possibility that Tamara might be sick, it is the clinical diagnosis that will brand her from now on. Give it a label, and that reality will channel us down a path I refuse to follow. It will re-write our lives. That's our job.

"Mrs. Baxter?" said the school secretary, jolting Aimee out of her noxious reverie. "Good morning. Right this way."

They were escorted into the headmaster's office.

"Hello, Tamara," he said.

Aimee felt a rush of confusion, or was it intrusion? She sensed her personal space being invaded the moment he spoke to her daughter.

Tamara simply looked up at him, but didn't seem nervous, or necessarily talkative, either. She just stared.

"Did you have a good weekend?" he asked Tamara. No response. He glanced over at Aimee.

"She was quiet most of the week," said Aimee, looking him in the eye, choosing an executive posture. *Don't back down. Push. And don't flinch.* "It went well."

"And were you able to make an appoint-- "

"No. I'm sorry, Mr. Timrose, but I really would like to take this very slowly if we could. I understand the school's concern, but I hope you'll give her another chance this week and see. She really did seem much better by Sunday."

"I see," said the headmaster. "All right then. We'll give it another go, but there may come a time, in the not-too-distant future, when we may have to consider some other options. Perhaps another classroom setting for starters. But for now, we'll see how it goes. So, let me spend a few more minutes here with Tamara, and I'll take her down and get her situated back in class. How does that sound?"

How does that sound? It sounds like a manipulative ploy to ease me out of the diagnostic picture so you can pass judgment on her without me in the room is what it sounds like. She felt the mother bear in her rising out of hibernation. But she also felt so far out of her element she didn't know where to gain a foothold, so she acquiesced. And the moment she did, her stomach rolled over inside her. She quickly kissed Tamara on the top of her head and strode out the door. On her way to the front door, she ducked into the girl's bathroom and wretched.

Aimee hurried to the subway and let the train ride buffer the two worlds she hoped to integrate. The twenty-three minutes back to Wall Street weren't enough to realign her, so when she exited the station, she turned up Broadway trusting the pulse of the city to bathe away the grime building up inside her. Gliding past Trinity Church, her pace slowed as she felt the gravitational pull of the open doors. *Get over it girl, and focus. You've got money to make for some powerful people in just a few minutes. What matters now is your gristle.* She dashed across the street then doubled back toward the New York Stock Exchange where, for the next nine hours, her life would make sense.

The doorman nodded at Aimee as he scanned her credentials. *At last.* She quickened her pace to the elevator and savored the ring of its bell. Only then did her breathing become steady. *Twelve minutes, then you've got to give that old knife Tomlin all you've got.* By the time she was shaking his hand and looking him in the eye she was in charge again.

Phone calls came from teachers describing violent eruptions, and some were naming names: clinical depression, ADHD, schizophrenia, mania, autism, obsessive compulsive disorder, or some form of psychosis.

"Dammit Terrance – I told the headmaster if these calls don't stop then I'm calling Fredericks," warned Aimee after abruptly ending a call with Tamara's math teacher.

"Our lawyer?"

"This is the kind of speculation that can do enormous damage," she persisted.

Then other names surfaced: denial, enablement, co-dependency, neglect. The headmaster waved all Aimee's protests aside and insisted that Tamara be screened by an independent mental health specialist. Otherwise, she could not continue at the school.

"I can give you until Friday," said Mr. Timrose.

Aimee let the deadline pass, and Terrance was powerless against her insistence that Tamara would grow out of this. So, on a Tuesday afternoon in October, the headmaster called Aimee and told her they could no longer subject the other students to such disruption. He suggested public school and the special needs services offered there. And, no, he wouldn't recommend Tamara to another private school given Aimee's reluctance to pursue psychiatric intervention for her.

"Tamara," called Aimee as she entered the house that evening. She was answered by the slam of a door upstairs. *I don't blame you, honey – I wouldn't mind a door to slam myself.* Aimee set her briefcase by the couch and checked the note left by the house-keeper. *Not good. I should go up and check in with her.* She went to the kitchen and poured herself a glass of red wine then started for the den. *First, I need a minute to figure this out.*

On the dining room table lay Tamara's sketch pad which, for Aimee, had gathered about it an iconic quality and represented everything she felt cascading within her. She set her glass on the table, cradled the notebook in her arms, closed her eyes and hugged the pad close to her breast. She rocked gently allowing her inner lament to seep into her eyes and flow over her cheeks. She should have resisted the urge to open it.

The first few pages were form, shape, and shading exercises Tamara had been working on in school. Then, an eye. A single eye filled the next page. The tonal quality of the shading opened depths on the flat surface into which Aimee couldn't help but fall. *You poor, poor soul.* Aimee struggled to focus as the dark pupil swallowed her awareness of anything but dread. *What are you so afraid of?* Reflected in the fluid depths of this eye shined the fangs of something menacing yet unrecognizable within inches of the subject's cheek. *My God. Who… or, what is after you all the time?*

Aimee's long, emotional descent began as she closed the sketch-pad and placed it back on the table. She felt the teeth penetrate her flesh and their poison sicken her body as she calculated what the ensuing week would bring for them. *I don't think we've met the demons yet, but we're about to.*

The move to the public school across town caused tremors deep in the tectonic plates of her psyche, and those tremors dredged out a subterranean sluice between mother and daughter that began to kill them both. Aimee's swelling emotions were flushing the raw sewage of her anxieties into the murky ponds of Tamara's inner world and became a cesspool that stank in Aimee's darkening mind. *It's making me nauseous just to think about it – all the influences Tamara will be exposed to, and nothing, nothing I can do about it.* Aimee's emotional sludge flowed between mother and daughter like a tidal estuary. *We're going to have to have a lot of serious talks.* These shared currents poisoned the deeper waters of Tamara's psyche and intensified the trauma surging in Aimee's soul. *If she's struggling now, how does she stand a chance against the kind of kids she's sure to meet? Whatever she's so anxious about all day, it's only going to get worse.*

Aimee's anxieties turned Tamara's nightmares into venomous spiders, snakes coiled to strike, and wolves with bright red eyes. These nocturnal fiends slithered through Tamara's nights and days, encircled any glimmers of happiness, and slashed at her with venomous fangs. Tamara's tears and tantrums, in turn, escalated Aimee's certainty that catastrophe lay ahead.

On that first Monday, Aimee rode the city bus with Tamara to check the route she would take to the new school. The bus was full of neighborhood kids (and greasy old men, nosy old women, delinquent teens and drifters, all of which she steeled herself against as she clung tightly to her daughter's hand). *Decision one: just get there and get this done. Decision two: find another way to get Tamara to school and back.*

The bus let them off at the school gate where a brightly vested crossing guard welcomed all the children onto the grounds. After wading through the waste-high currents of elementary school children, they escaped the melee and ducked into the office. The guidance counselor, Mrs. Morris, came striding through the office door with several children in tow all wagging their tails like puppies waiting for kibble. To these, Mrs. Morris offered words of encouragement then shooed them off to their classrooms. She was a large, robust woman ready with a hug for every child she met. She introduced herself to Aimee and set her instantly at ease. She told Aimee that Mr. Timrose had been in touch and sent over Tamara's files.

"What else did Mr. Timrose say?" asked Aimee, feeling her fears multiplying.

"Well, not much, but it's not hard to figure these things out, you know."

Mrs. Morris looked into Aimee's frightened eyes then rested a firm grip on her shoulder. "Mrs. Baxter, I've been working with these kids going on thirty-seven years now, and there is not a one of them that doesn't have their troubles. They all come to me at some time or other. At first, they try to hide it, but I find them out. The teachers let me know, or a parent will call with a minor thing that turns major.

"Every child is different," she continued, "and every child is special, and every child has one challenge or another that keeps them from doing their best. I know Tamara has challenges or she would be right back where she was this time last week. Let's walk Tamara to her class, and then we'll go down to my office and talk for a little while."

They walked through a hallway adorned with children's art and fall decorations to room #107 where they met Tamara's new teacher.

"This is Mr. Porter," said Mrs. Morris, introducing everyone.

"He's young," said Aimee, as they walked away.

"Yes, he's one of our newest teachers, but I think he'll be fine," Mrs. Morris assured Aimee. "If not, we have some options we can discuss, but we'll work this out."

Aimee and Mrs. Morris retired to her office, a little cubby-hole of a room. Their initial conversation was fairly mundane, especially since there was little medical history to report. Mrs. Morris wrote "behavioral" and "socialization" in the line next to "Observable Concerns" and left it at that.

Then, Mrs. Morris looked long and hard at Aimee. The woman's face had had lots of practice at drawing unruly children into her gracious sphere of influence and calming them into quiet reflection, and Mrs. Morris began having that effect on Aimee. The gravitational tug on Aimee's heart was immense, but she felt intimidated by the sudden intimacy between them and looked down breaking the bond. But Mrs. Morris reached over and took a firm hold of Aimee's hand. Aimee let herself be held and knew it was more than her hand the woman was holding. Then, with an added squeeze, she let Aimee go.

As Aimee left, she felt lighter of heart and somewhat hopeful that this could be a decent environment until Tamara got back on track. As she walked to the subway that would take her to work, another sensation took hold. There was the presence of a person in there with her, a partner in the emotional maze she had been navigating alone. *Perhaps, this isn't all bad. And with the money we save we can hire additional tutors to prep Tamara at home for what lay ahead.*

4

THE CHRISTMAS TROLL

"LADIES AND GENTLEMEN, THE CAPTAIN has turned off the seatbelt sign. We are nearing the trailing edge of this storm, so we may continue to experience turbulence. If you need to move about the cabin, please do so with caution. While you are in your seat, we ask that you keep your seatbelt fastened. Again, we apologize for any discomfort you may be experiencing."

Trailing edge of the storm? If only that were true. Aimee saw staccato flashes of light illumine a series of memories from Friday's storm. She looked at Tamara. *That tempest is still brewing.*

"Do you want anything to eat?" she asked her daughter.

No answer. Tamara slashed at the paper and chafed at the limits set by her pen as she sought to free this phantom from its two-dimensional prison on the page.

It should have more precision. You're too focused on his eyes, and the shading has thrown everything off balance. Including me! Aimee's spirit pulled at Tamara's fitful effort as if she could add her own will to her daughter's and birth this creation more completely into being. But the intensity of what Tamara felt scalded them both. *Come on, honey. Pull out of this. You have so much more to show us. Show us the light we saw so briefly this morning. Give us some color for a change.*

"I wish you could paint that; I'd love to see it in acrylics," she said to Tamara.

"I'd love to see it in flames," said her daughter as she ignited fire around the figure's feet. Aimee became sorry she spoke and turned toward the dark storm mass outside.

Aimee couldn't have imagined a better visual accompaniment for the memories now overtaking her. *Terrance came at me with an axe.* The flashes of fire that rained down on the mountain Friday night had illuminated their inner landscapes and revealed to each of them hidden, vicious truths now ripping away at their relationships. *What chased Tamara out of that well?* The gray banks of clouds pushed Aimee back into herself as a frantic series of memories were cast upon the screen of her mind. *There is nowhere to run from this.* She made the mistake of running back to Tamara's drawing.

The ghastly figure was wading through flames; his eyes were dark with anger. The resolve in his face was fixed on something beyond the frame of the drawing. *Who are you chasing now?* Behind this figure, Tamara carved out an arch which soon became the mouth of a tunnel. With angry slashes of her pen she worked as if she couldn't get the darkness dark enough, attacking any hints of light lingering in the tunnel, digging more deeply into the cavernous expanse, giving the darkness a violent texture, ripping the paper, opening up more white behind it which Tamara filled in on the page beneath it. *Leave her alone!*

Then, roaring out from that darkness came hot searing flashes of memory Aimee wanted nothing to do with. Tamara's pen was proving to her just how entangled their minds had become.

In the winter of Tamara's seventh year, one snow-storm after another banked up mounds of wintry ice in their hearts. As Christmas approached, Aimee fretted over what their families would encounter -- a child who was no longer suiting anyone's description of what a beautiful grand-daughter ought to be.

"Better to celebrate with your family than mine," Terrance reassured Aimee, who sat at the kitchen table with her head resting on her folded arms.

"I just don't want to do it all," she said, knowing it to be a fruitless wish. "At least not with them. Not this year. Can you imagine Christmas dinner with Tamara in the state she's in?" *It's hard enough to be at the same table with my socialist brother these days, and you'll just disappear and watch football with my uncle.*

"You sound angry. To be honest, I think you've been a little hard on her this past week," said Terrance.

Aimee shook her head. *If you'd been around at all you would know why.* "Nothing I have done has made any difference, Terrance," she complained. "I've tried to get her in the Christmas spirit. I took her shopping – she wouldn't set foot into FAO Schwartz. She didn't want to help decorate. Every time I put on Christmas music, she turns it off. You saw her at the Rockefeller Center tree lighting!"

"I know a lot of people who grow grouchier the closer it gets to Christmas," he demurred.

"Not in this family, you don't!" Aimee rose to her feet, daring Terrance to contribute anything more that would further spoil her seasonal aspirations.

Friday evening, the day before Christmas eve, the *au pair* would be packing for a night flight to Germany, and Terrance would be working late. Aimee probably should have taken the day off; she had been distracted since the opening bell. *The bell should have jingled instead of that scroogy old clanging! Wouldn't that be cool!* Despite her worries over Tamara, however, she was feeling more like an elf than a stock broker. As sophisticated and business-like as she was all year long, Christmas turned Aimee into a kid again, and the Christmas child within her resisted growing up. *She's going to brighten up. She has to. It's Christmas!*

So, she exited the subway two stops early and took a meandering stroll through the holiday wonderland her town became at that time of year. *No place on earth dresses for Christmas like New York City.* She reveled in the light dusting of natural snow that whirled amid the lights. The city always sparkled. That night it glistened with brilliance -- a whole block was wrapped like a package under a tree and the store windows took her on one enchanted adventure after another. She had one gift still to buy, a dress for Tamara to wear on their outing tomorrow afternoon, then to dinner at her parents' home on Christmas day. *Less frills this year – either she is growing up too fast, or this mood she's in will torpedo anything too girlish.* But as she walked and pondered her daughter's darkened disposition, Aimee let that errand go for this year. *If she feels better in the morning we can slip out and do it together. It's time she took more interest in selecting her wardrobe, anyway.*

Aimee turned down her street and was disappointed that hers was the only house on the block that was dark. Lights from their tree should fill the bay window just above street level and three stories of candlelit windows should brighten the face they showed their neighbors.

"Tamara wouldn't let me turn them on," explained the *au pair* as she rushed through the house, still gathering her belongings. Aimee glanced at her watch; the taxi would be there in twenty minutes. *Please don't miss your flight. Last thing we need is to suffer the consequences of your scattered brain at Christmas.*

After seeing the nanny into the cab, Aimee went to the kitchen to fix herself a drink and found a package from her mother marked, 'Open right away.' She poured herself half a glass of brandy and added some eggnog.

Whatever was inside was carefully packed in bubble wrap. She gently freed its contents, then sat down on the sofa with an antique porcelain doll cradled in her arms. The delicate little girl wore an intricate scarlet dress in a Victorian style with deep blue satin trim. Handmade lace graced the brim of her floral bonnet. Aimee hugged her old friend. *It's been a long time, Priscilla. A lot has happened since you came to my seventh birthday party.* There was a card in the box from her mother: 'Came across your doll the other day and thought you might like to pass it on to Tamara for Christmas.' *We've got a lot of catching up to do, Miss Prissy. Wait till you meet my daughter. Though, I'm afraid you may not have very much in common.* She laid the doll back in its box and unrolled the new tube of gold Christmas paper. *If nothing else, you'll add some class to that menagerie of misfits she's always having tea with.*

Aimee fastened the bow on the package and set it beneath the tree. *I think I needed that.* She let the lights of the tree wash through her and felt immersed in that seasonal glistening bath that softened her edges and warmed those traditional sensations of holiday gladness. *I just hope I don't have to do it alone this year.*

When Aimee turned around she was jolted to find Tamara curled up in a fetal position on the couch. Her daughter had entered without a sound.

"Hello there," said Aimee.

Tamara stared darkly at the tree.

Fetching her eggnog from the table, Aimee sat down beside her daughter, but Tamara nudged her off with her feet and hid her face.

One more day until Christmas, and then what?

When Terrance was a boy, his parents began a family tradition by necessity. Each Christmas Eve afternoon, they shipped the kids off with either a house-keeper or the odd relative to watch a movie and fill the slowly passing hours. His most memorable Christmas movie event was the year aunt Tamara took them to see *A Christmas Carol*.

"Oh, for heaven's sake!" Aunt Tamara laughed at the first appearance of Scrooge and the surreal similarities between the old miser and her brother, Terrance's grandfather, from whom his father inherited many Dickensian qualities. That night at dinner, she kept taunting her brother with threats of impending visitation if he didn't mend his ways. Terrance was sure his own father was as susceptible to ghostly invasion and kept a night-light on in his room, just in case.

Aimee and Terrance continued the Baxter tradition by taking Tamara to see the latest holiday blockbuster each Christmas Eve since she was three. The morning of that Christmas Eve, however, Tamara rejected the shopping expedition and refused to eat anything for breakfast. Aimee compensated by putting the house in order so it would sparkle when they came home. *Just stay out of Tamara's way and push on toward the three o'clock show. Give her some room, then we'll scoop her up, tote her off, and see if either the city's Christmas spectacle or the movie has any effect on her.*

Aimee was propping herself up with the only childhood faith she really had: a Christmas miracle. All the holiday specials she watched on TV, the surprise gifts and magical moments engineered by her parents to keep the Christmas illusion alive elevated Aimee's aspirations to religious proportions where Tamara was concerned. The little elf running around in Aimee's heart scurried to pull the outing together, but her daughter refused to change out of her pajamas.

As Tamara's resistance collided with Aimee's aspirations, the Christmas elf within Aimee flew into a tantrum. Then, the one adult voice in the room finally spoke. Terrance put his parental foot down, and Aimee's Christmas wonderland closed its gates. Whatever faith she had in whatever this holiday was supposed to mean evaporated.

The afternoon grew worse as she sat beside Tamara who was curled up on the couch. Aimee let the lights of the tree absorb her gaze and take her on a nostalgic tour of the ornaments hanging there. Her eyes bounced from one decoration to another. Aimee's tree was decorated with a collection of family cast-offs her mom no longer wanted but which helped define Christmas for her. Most of the ornaments glowed with some childhood memory; there were a few Tamara had made and one or two had been gifts from Terrance.

Then, there were the heirlooms that held supernal significance for Aimee. One set of those, she had just noticed, was missing. They were glass baubles of a Victorian design that had belonged to her great-grandmother. They had been passed down to Aimee when she and Terrance celebrated their first Christmas together in their new home.

"Honey?" she asked Tamara. "Have you taken any ornaments off the tree?"

No response.

"Tamara? Can you answer me?"

Tamara straightened out her legs, then her upper torso, making herself rigid, pushing Aimee away. Then, she retracted and kicked.

"Hey, young lady! What is that all about? Look at me," she demanded. But Tamara remained unbending in her posture and attitude. Aimee took a deep breath and closed her eyes. Resolved not to let any more erosion take place, she got up and went to the kitchen to begin dinner.

The Baxters traditionally had a fun, snacky type of dinner because they were always coming back from the show and no one wanted to spend time in the kitchen on Christmas Eve. Aimee felt lost. She tried to pull together what should be more of a meal, *something* to mark the night. She had a few steaks in the freezer but didn't have the heart to thaw them out. They were next to the leftover Turkey she set aside from

Thanksgiving, so she thawed that instead and prepared to have sandwiches. They could watch a Christmas DVD and salvage something of the night, she hoped.

They took their plates and went into the den. Everyone settled into their usual places as Terrance started the movie. But as he sat in his recliner there was an unmistakable sound of crunching glass.

"No!" shouted Aimee, as Terrance jumped up and pulled out the cushion. Not a bauble survived. The faded colored glass was in hundreds of shards, and each one stabbed Aimee in the chest as she stared in horrid disbelief. It seemed an act calculated to make Terrance do something that would hurt Aimee and leave them both feeling shattered.

"How could you do this?" screamed Aimee who was no longer trying to maintain control, Christmas be-damned. The rant she launched exceeded description and failed miserably to gain any sort of emotionally satisfying response from Tamara. The girl's emotional withdrawal embittered Aimee's mood with more vitriol which she poured out upon her daughter in ferocious measure. Terrance had to intervene and pull her down.

"You sit right there, young lady," said Terrance. "I'll be back, and you can explain."

Terrance walked Aimee out of the room, sat her down at the kitchen table and poured them both a glass of eggnog with a double shot of brandy and nutmeg. They drank in silence and neither one of them knew how to take a next step, whatever that might be.

Holidays are meant to be a set of dance steps passed down through the generations. That was part of their beauty. Even if they added multiple layers of busyness and family stress, holidays gave meaningful structure to the year. So, for all their trouble, that dance had to be danced. It was in their DNA, and without the yearly cycle of birthdays, anniversaries, Valentines and Fourth of Julys, all the heartless push and tug going on year-round would drive them steadily to despair. These annual feasts allowed them to put a few dislocated pieces of their lives back in place, remember who they belonged to, and what they were supposed to mean to one another.

That Christmas Eve, Aimee and Terrance didn't know the steps, and they were both disoriented. Neither one of them wanted their last sip of eggnog because there was nothing after it except to go to bed.

Well, there's always tomorrow. She was making a heroic effort to rekindle her Christmas faith, smothered as it was. Aimee got up, and Terrance followed. They went to find Tamara who had already moved herself to her bedroom. She stood in the middle of the floor looking lost. Aimee lightly tapped on her door and stepped in the room.

"Honey? Are you ready for bed?" Tamara didn't respond. "Let's crawl into bed and get some sleep so Santa can come." They were tentative steps in the sacred dance, those words every parent says, and though she didn't feel at all sure of them speaking the words restored a little balance.

"Santa's a troll," said Tamara.

"He is not!" said Aimee, still finding her supply of self-control down a quart or two.

"He only gives you gifts to turn you into a troll, too. And the more gifts you get, the more trollish you become."

Before his wife flew into another tirade, Terrance kissed his daughter and then escorted Aimee to their bedroom.

"I can't believe her," said Aimee.

"I was six years old," Terrance said as he unbuttoned his shirt, "when I learned just how true that could be."

"What could be?" asked Aimee.

"Just how trollish someone could be at Christmas. My brother had opened his last gift, a pair of cowboy pistols in their holsters, and as he drew them out he pointed them both at me with an air of triumph. He shouted: 'Ha! I got more than you did!' Technically, it was just one gift, and the brotherly balance of equal bounty was officially maintained. But since he could hold that gift in two separate hands it was twice as much in his eyes. He pulled the triggers and fired off the red paper caps. Then he set off galloping through the house raving, "I got more than Terrance!" (Bang, bang, bang!). The hallway smelled like gun-powder. You know, forever after, whenever I thought of Hell, I always wondered if that's what brimstone smelled like."

The confusion Terrance and Aimee shared as they fell asleep was with them when they awoke, which was much later than usual.

Tamara's part of the Christmas dance included gradually pulling the covers off them as she sang Jingle Bells. She was strictly forbidden to go downstairs without her parents, since Aimee didn't want to miss one sparkle of Christmas magic. But it was 8:42, and they weren't quite sure whether to lie there and wait or go investigate.

Terrance had to use the bathroom, so he slipped out and tip-toed down the hall. He would glance in Tamara's room, and if she were still asleep, they would concoct a new approach to Christmas morning. But she wasn't in her room.

By the time he got back to their room, Aimee was already pulling on her bathrobe and slippers. They started downstairs, but Aimee didn't make it before she gave out. From the landing she had a clear view into the living room. Every present was opened. Their contents had been scattered over the entirety of the first floor. Even Terrance's and her gifts had been opened. At the bottom of the steps lay the headless torso of the porcelain doll her mother had bought for her when she was a girl.

5

Lost in the Tunnel

A BLAST OF BRIGHT LIGHT BROKE through the clouds and blinded Aimee momentarily. She turned toward Tamara's notepad but the corona left in her eyes prevented her from focusing. Tamara shoved the pad into Aimee's hands then unbuckled her seatbelt to go to the bathroom.

As her eyes readjusted, Aimee stared into the darkness Tamara had so firmly etched into the paper. *I think we've been chasing one another through that tunnel for far too long. I thought, this morning, we might have finally emerged.* She looked into the eyes of the phantom beast Tamara had drawn, those angry eyes so intent on whatever it had in its sights. *Where are you leading us now?*

The book in her hands made her tremble. She looked to see if Tamara was coming, then thumbed through its pages. The rest was tame by comparison. That face, wrathful and horrible to look at deepened Aimee's remorse for her daughter. *You caught her, didn't you? She's not running anymore. You got what you came for. Then, why aren't you satisfied?*

Tamara negotiated her way back into her seat and Aimee handed her the pad once she was buckled.

"Why is he so angry?" asked Aimee. As Tamara uncapped her pen then addressed herself to finishing the drawing, Aimee turned away. *Why are YOU so angry with me?*

Then: "Wouldn't you be?" said Tamara. She was sharpening the definition of the long stick in the figure's hand, which might be a walking staff, though it was thrust outward as if the figure were using it to herd sheep. But there were no sheep.

❧

New Year's Eve arrived and Terrance and Aimee decided they needed a night out with some friends, so they hired a sitter. Aimee phoned home twice and was relieved by the report each time. At midnight, she called to say they were leaving the restaurant and was told Tamara was tucked soundly in bed and fast asleep.

As they drove through the city, Aimee confessed she was very frightened.

"I just never know what she'll be like," whispered Aimee.

"You mean, besides grim, angry, moody or sad?" he said, more to himself.

They had avoided such talk over dinner, hoping to keep the evening light and romantic, but the closer they came to home, the more Aimee's tensions mounted. Just going through the front door released fresh demons. She could never be sure what lay lurking in the shadows of her little girl's mind and it was taking its toll on her.

But all was quiet. The sitter assured them it was an uneventful evening. When they looked in on her, Tamara seemed peaceful.

The two allowed themselves to love one another, though every touch was tentative, as if it must do more than convey affection. Their brokenness lay exposed and naked and vulnerable especially in their intimacy, and their release came more through tears than physical satisfaction.

Though Terrance lay beside her, Aimee was deeply affected by the solitude that enfolded them both. She would never tell him, but at one point she was certain her thoughts evolved unconsciously into prayer. God seemed very distant, yet she sensed the velocity of her emotions could cover the chasm that lay between them as she sought to release her fears to someone bigger and more powerful.

Just as her exhaustion began to overcome her anxiety, a shriek from down the hall lifted her straight up in the bed and brought Terrance to his feet.

"What the hell…" he uttered as they both met at the door and pushed through it running toward Tamara's room. Her bed was empty, but the air was charged with terror. Shouts rang out from under the bed, where Tamara thrashed so much the bed jolted and bumped up and down.

Terrance dropped to the floor and tried to extract Tamara who resisted by shrieking and thrashing back at him. Aimee rushed to the foot of the bed and lifted that end off the floor so Terrance could get his arms around her and pull her close to him.

Terrance held her, rocking back and forth. He wiped her forehead and sought to calm her sobs, which eventually subsided into whimpers punctuated by sudden inhalations as though her lungs refused to cooperate until they absolutely needed oxygen. Terrance hadn't seen her leave, but Aimee reappeared with a mug of warm milk. As they tried to get Tamara to drink it, they weren't sure she had awakened.

"Honey," said Aimee, rubbing her hair, matted with sweat. "Can you drink this?" Tamara's eyes flickered but never opened. Aimee touched the mug to her lips and Tamara took a small sip.

"Baby, what happened?" asked Terrance. "Can you tell us?" But Tamara shook her head and clinched her eyes even more tightly.

"Tamara, honey. It might help to tell us," pleaded Aimee. "We're right here, and nothing's going to hurt you." But something excruciating was hurting Tamara, a psychic splinter was lodged in her daughter's mind and Aimee wanted, for all the world, to pull it out and soothe the sting.

"Look at me, baby," said Terrance. He held her firmly by the shoulders, then kissed her forehead. "Can you look at me? It's only us. You can open your eyes."

Instead of opening her eyes, Tamara whispered: "I'm lost in the subway."

"No, honey, you're safe at home," assured Aimee.

"No. I can't leave. I can't find the stairs. It's too dark."

Terrance drew her close and held her tighter.

"Honey, it's a dream," Terrance whispered. "We've got you now."

"No. I'm here forever," insisted Tamara.

"Not forever," said Terrance.

"What do you mean, forever?" interjected Aimee, laying a hand on Terrance's shoulder. "What do you mean, honey?"

"I'm dead."

They both felt the impact of those words, and neither knew what ought to come next.

What do you say to that?

"Tamara," whispered Aimee. "Tamara, you are not dead." But her daughter clinched her eyes all the tighter, and nodded her head.

"The tunnel began to glow," she said at last. "And I tried to stay away from the edge, but I couldn't. I kept walking over to the yellow line. The train got loud. The tunnel became bright. It was so bright I couldn't see the floor in front of me. Then, I fell, and I kept falling."

Aimee was hyperventilating unable to regain control of her emotions. She paced as she crossed her arms across her chest and squeezed her whole upper torso as if she could push something from deep within her up into her mind that might help. Terrance's gentle rocking, with Tamara snuggled close to his chest, restored some rhythm to their breathing. Aimee glanced at the teddy bear clock hanging on Tamara's wall. A new year was well under way.

Tamara refused to return to her bed, and if her parents were to salvage any sleep from this night, it meant coaxing her to join them in theirs.

It took a while for everyone to settle and find their place in the bed. Aimee was the last to drift off and the first to awaken. She had overslept and had to dash to get herself to the subway if she was going to make the opening bell at the stock exchange. As she sipped her coffee and paced on the crowded subway platform, she wondered how she would function on so little sleep.

The subway platform was overly crowded. Aimee looked down the long dark tunnel from which the train would soon emerge. *We have got to hurry this up. It's rush hour, for Christ's sake. It never takes this long between trains.* She looked at her watch and fretted her way through all the things she was going to have to compress if she was going to get everything done before the market opened. Thankfully, the tunnel began to glow, and she could feel the wind the train makes as it pushes air ahead of it like a great plunger. It blew her hair back with more intensity than usual. She was aware of how bright the light of the train was, though her most urgent concern was to find a seat so she could get into her laptop for a few moments.

Aimee's phone rang; it was Tamara. *Damn it all. That girl is going to be the ruin of my career.*

"Honey, what is it?"

"I'm here," said Tamara.

"I'm about to get on the train, honey. Where are you?"

"At the station, looking for you."

For crying out loud! Not now. NOT today!

"Tamara, why in the world ... where are you?" screamed Aimee, now frantically scanning the crowd.

"I'm on the yellow line."

Aimee spun around and stood on tip-toe. Then she saw her, teetering on the edge of the platform, even as the train was emerging from the tunnel. Aimee fought her way through the crowd as it surged forward and closed in around her. She was suffocating as the mass of people constrained her every movement. Her daughter's scream echoed in the cavernous dungeon of the station. Aimee leaped to see over the horde of business men.

Then, she saw Tamara trip and disappear into the chasm.

The train never slowed but roared on through the station. It was empty. Not a soul was on board. One vacant car after another whipped by her until it was sucked into the far tunnel.

Aimee sat up in bed and couldn't catch her breath. She fought for air, disoriented by sensations she couldn't trust. She was wet; her hair was matted to her face, and her eyes refused to focus on her surroundings. Her gaze retracted into her sub-conscious to search for her daughter among the rails beneath the subway platform. She felt for Tamara and her chest convulsed when she found her baby coiled up in the blankets. Aimee pressed her hand firmly on her daughter's back as she heaved up one sob after another.

But Terrance was gone.

Aimee found her husband downstairs on the couch cuddling with a cup of yesterday's coffee staring into the empty fireplace. She sat beside him and held him as hard as she could. She was just about to tell him her dream when he spoke first.

"I dreamt I was on a subway," he began. "Not in the passenger section but up in front where the conductor sits. And I didn't know how to drive it. But it kept moving faster and faster through long dark tunnels. Every turn smashed me against one wall or the other. I kept shouting for help, but there was no one else there. Then, I saw a light up ahead and the automated voice announced the station. But instead of slowing down, we sped up. As we came out of the tunnel, there she was. I watched her fall, just feet in front of me, and she saw me. She looked me in the eyes, and then… it all went dark as we entered the tunnel again."

The new year felt old before breakfast, such as it was. No one had the stomach for food and no one knew what to do with each other when they were in the same room. So, each member of the family drifted to those solitary places where, if there wasn't comfort to be found, there was relief from one another.

Tamara looked lost, but neither Aimee nor Terrance new how to find her. Her eyes were empty with no one looking out through them. Her hair was knotted and needed combing, but when Aimee attempted such a simple motherly task, Tamara brushed her away and walked out of the room.

By nightfall, Tamara was pale and cold. Aimee helped her into her pajamas and tucked her in to bed, but she wouldn't stay put. She would get up and move about her room as if looking for something, though what it was, she refused to say. Twice more Aimee coaxed her to crawl back in, but Tamara grew agitated. Aimee found a story book and opened it, but Tamara pushed it away.

"Let's let her wind down some more," whispered Terrance as he took Aimee's hand and gave it a tug.

"In a minute," she whispered, as he slipped out of the room.

Aimee turned out the lamp on Tamara's dressing table then switched on a small night light by the door. She pulled one of the little tea table chairs over, sat down beside Tamara's bed and placed her hand on her daughter's cheek.

"I love you, baby," she said.

Tamara turned her face to her pillow and left Aimee to melt in her remorse.

Aimee lingered in the shadows cast by the night light. It was shaped like a baby lamb and cast a warm, white glow that kept the room from feeling so grim. It wasn't chasing the grim from Aimee's heart, however, and she was feeling the swell of grief rising within her. Tamara wasn't yet asleep, and Aimee didn't want to break down with her near. She quietly exited and barely made it to her own room before heaving up all of last year's sorrows and flushing them out to make space for what the new year would bring.

The muted street noises, usually so familiar they went unnoticed, were keeping Aimee awake. She had learned long ago not to think too hard about what went on in the streets after hours especially on the cold nights of winter. It was a fringe benefit of the society she now kept. Strong, expensive buffers were securely in place, but she had seen the faces of those turned out by their families, the twisted bodies of those who slept on pavement, the chapped and crusted faces of those too long exposed to the wind, and the cavernous eyes of those evicted by the institutions once established to care for them.

Aimee's mind fixated on a woman she saw relieving herself behind the trash bins just two blocks over as she walked home from the subway. The woman was squatting by the wall, draped by a soiled tan overcoat as the puddle broadened beneath her. She couldn't have been twenty years old, though she looked fifty and as disoriented as an Alzheimer's patient.

Tears streamed over Aimee's cheeks as she solemnly resolved that Tamara would never wander alone like that. As hard as it might be to care for her daughter, Tamara would always have a family to come home to, and parents to love her.

Then, the horror of where Aimee's mind had been taking her caught up with her; she flattened her face in her pillow, and screamed.

A pall hung over their lives for days. Tamara became increasingly despondent; her aspect was dark, and her eyes were like ashes, gray with no apparent moisture or reflection. She walked around for the rest of the holiday week as though something in her had been struck by that train and stolen into the tunnel.

On Monday, Tamara began asking questions about death and what would happen to her stuffed animals when she died. The week that ensued drew a tighter and tighter ring around Aimee's psyche constraining her ability to think freely of anything beyond Tamara's mental state. She returned repeatedly to that crowded subway station ruminating on how far out of reach Tamara was.

At the end of the second week of this, Aimee knew they needed serious help, not just for Tamara, but for herself. And, her marriage.

6

THE SOUND OF SHATTERING GLASS

THE STAFF-WIELDING FIEND WAS ADVANCING on its prey and venturing deeper into Aimee's psyche. Tamara's passion wouldn't release Aimee, who felt shackled to everything going on inside her daughter. *What does that feel like? Are you enjoying this, or is it torturing you as much as it is me?* The violent slashes Tamara made with her pen unearthed Aimee's long buried remorse over giving up her artistic aspirations. *I wish I could channel all these feelings in another direction right now like you can, but I can't imagine drawing all that is going on inside me right now. What would that look like? No idea. But, you spend a lot more time inside yourself than I ever did. All of this looks so familiar to you.* Aimee tried to climb out of the emotional eddy and look on as a critical observer, but she was drowning in Tamara's ordeal. *Is there anything roaring around within me that is so powerful it silences all my words and could only escape through a visual scream – images so hot I would have to evict them before they incinerated me?* Aimee couldn't distance herself sufficiently to critique her daughter's technique, or even imagine how she would render the subject in her own way. *But that's just it, isn't it? It was my lack of artistic craving that allowed my plans to morph so easily into something I thought would be more beneficial in the long run. Or, were my insides incapable of exploding like that?*

Tamara returned to the figure's eyes and sought to intensify his gaze, which added to Aimee's discomfort. As ferocious as they already were, those eyes clearly didn't reflect the power Tamara saw in them. *You are overdoing it.*

The face had lost the intensity Tamara desired, frustrating the artist, who slammed her pen on the tray table, folded her arms, and closed her eyes.

Aimee made a silent vow: *one thing I can do for you is to redouble my efforts to support your artistic pursuits.*

⁂

Tamara was still in her pajamas one Saturday morning when she came in for lunch. No amount of prodding from Aimee, including the offer of a trip to the Central Park Zoo, could persuade Tamara to get dressed. It was a mild day for January, and Aimee felt claustrophobic. Her daughter slathered some peanut butter on a piece of bread and disappeared.

Lying beside the opened jar of peanut butter was a folded piece of paper. Aimee opened it to find a small drawing of a snake devouring itself beginning with the tail. *Where have I seen you before? Some ancient symbol, I believe. Wherever it was, this is a stark improvement. Or, maybe not.* The ferocity of the snake's expression was severe, but it was the caption which jolted Aimee. It read: "Sandralina was eaten by Thorafura."

Aimee walked the note up the stairs to ask Tamara what it meant and found the long, purple stuffed snake tied in a knot lying on the hallway floor. She tapped lightly on Tamara's door and when there was no answer, she let herself in. Tamara's gifts were still where Aimee had placed them the Wednesday after Christmas; not a toy, not a book, not an article of clothing had been touched. Tamara was seated on the floor, her back to the wall, her head between her knees.

"What is it?" whispered Aimee as she started across the room. When Tamara looked up and saw the snake in Aimee's hand she buried her face and wrapped her arms around her head.

"Sorry," said Aimee. She tossed the snake out the door then squatted by her daughter. "Snake's gone," she said.

But Tamara shook her head and from between her knees said, "No. It's not." Tamara contracted her body so tightly it became physically uncomfortable for Aimee to watch her daughter.

If you made yourself any smaller, you would vanish altogether. Her daughter's retreat was becoming more complete all the time, and like an emotional singularity, a black hole in psychological space, she was pulling her mother ever more deeply inside with her. *Is that what it's going to take? God knows I don't know what else to do, honey. It's either let you go on by yourself or lose you to psychiatrists and pharmaceuticals.* Tamara slumped against her mother. *Or, follow you in. Half the time I feel like I'm in there with you chasing you somewhere else. Though, if I ever catch up, I'm not sure I'd know the way back out.*

Unsure of what else she had to offer that Tamara would accept, Aimee kissed her daughter on the head then drifted down the hall toward her bedroom. She looked hard at herself in the mirror, then picked at the debris on her dressing table, hoping to bring some order to one small corner of her life. *She is wearing you out, Aimee Baxter.* She massaged her temples and pulled back her hair. Her eyes looked lifeless and there was little smile left in her lips. *A face-lift won't hide that.*

She heard a door open, and Tamara passed by in the hall. Aimee watched her in the mirror then noted again how weary her own face looked. *You have no idea what's going on inside her, do you? You've been running away from her. Afraid of what you'll find.* She scanned her reflection, then studied the room beyond, wondering where Tamara was headed. *My own little Alice.* She listened until the sound of Tamara's footsteps couldn't be heard. *Lost in Looking-glass House, running through the backwards world of her own home where everything is turned the wrong way out, and the harder you to try to escape, the more trapped you become.*

The imagery jolted Aimee. *She needs you to follow her.* On the far side of the room was the passage-way into an overturned reality: out through a shrinking portal, down a lengthening hall, onwards into… where? *Where doesn't matter. She's already there.*

The mirrored view of her reflection, coupled with the broken fragments of her thoughts, unsheathed a terrible memory of the day her childhood looking-glass fantasies came crashing in on her. Aimee was six years old. She had been sent down the street to stay the afternoon with a snotty kid who never liked her while her mom tended to unexpected business. Aimee wearied of the tedious game the girl was playing with her dolls, so she wandered through the house until she came to a formal parlor with a large gilded mirror on the wall. She stood transfixed before it and explored this delicate Looking-glass house. She was transported to some faraway land filled with ancient artifacts and brightly colored trinkets all of which were powerfully magical. Stepping through the glass, she went in search of hidden halls and portals. And, yes! At the end of the great room the door was open. She tip-toed down a long hallway lined with doors. She was just about to let her imagination flip a coin and choose a gateway into some new world, when the other girl snapped at her: "What are you doing in here!"

Aimee was too enthralled to answer at first, so she continued her gaze until she was pushed.

"Hey!" yelled Aimee. "Why did you do that?"

"We're not allowed to play in here," said the other girl.

"I wasn't playing," shouted Aimee.

"Think you're so pretty, then! Admiring your face?"

"I was not!"

"Yes, you were. You think you're prettier than everyone else."

"No. I was exploring – Looking-glass house," she said in a sheepish voice.

"Looking-glass what?"

"It's just a game. Look. In there. Everything is backward and mysterious, not the way it is here at all, but turned so many other ways around. See?" Aimee hoped to catch the girl's imagination and find something they might both enjoy, but the other girl intended to be obtuse, and laughed at Aimee.

"That's stupid!"

Aimee knew it was, and she felt ashamed, but she didn't want to look at the girl, so she turned her attention back to the mirror. She must have stared one moment too long.

"Play your stupid game. I hope you do fall in there, then I can break the glass, and you'll be stuck in there forever for all I care." She stomped down the hall to tattle to her mom that Aimee was playing in the parlor. Several moments passed before Aimee realized she was suffocating – unable to breath or pry her gaze away from the world that might have become her prison forever. She would be entombed in a strange world filled with another family and their memories, their things, their fantasies. She had never anticipated that danger.

When she was sent up to bed later that night, Aimee refused to look at the mirror in her bedroom. Its power of reflection haunted her and became a backward prison that could slam its door shut and shatter any means of escape. It was her world, her make-believe neighborhood, her view of the universe beyond. Yet, if its exit was shattered there would never be right-side out again. Forward would always be backward and fantasy would be nightm…

Aimee knew that every creature lurking beyond the door and down the hall might look sweet but that was reversed. She brooded over what would happen when her mother discovered the shattered mirror. Would her mom know where she was? Would her mother think to put all the pieces back in place and restore Aimee's means of return? Or, would she just sweep them up, throw them away, and leave her daughter in there forever? Another possibility: If everything was backwards in Looking-glass house, the mirror might remain whole on the outside while shattered and blocked on the inside. Then someone might come in that way but have to search for another exit that could bring them out… but, where?

"Jaunt!" shouted Tamara from down the hall. "You disgust me!"

Aimee flinched and broke free from the inside of the backward-looking room. *What now?* Her body felt heavy and immobile; the weight within her chest made taking the next breath difficult. *Is my life really all about being that girl's mother? Or, is it about staking my claim as a woman of power?* She closed her eyes and massaged her forehead. *I just can't keep chasing back and forth between those two worlds and survive. I've been struggling to realize my place, fully, in both, but each of those separate lives is robbing me of the other. Taken together, each life amounts to a fantasy not coming true; a chasm of death into which Tamara keeps falling. I don't even know what is real around here anymore. And I have no idea who I am. I think she has just about eaten the soul right out of me.*

The backwards hallway, and the mysteries beyond, were pulling Aimee into that dimly lit world through the looking-glass. *But I can't just let her keep falling. I can't let this go on for either one of us.* The way before her held few clues and spoke no assurances. *If I am a woman of power, then it's time to utilize that power in new ways.*

She looked again in the mirror and followed her reflected path down the hall and traveled around the corner. The faintest light crept through the crevice of the partially closed door of her daughter's so very backward bedroom. A shadow interrupted the light but not her vision, for in her looking-glass house, darkness brought clarity, and sanity was tossed on its head. *This is insane. But it's the only thing that makes sense right now.* With that clarifying darkness, came a rush of resolve. She knew it to be looking-glass resolve because on her face she still saw fear. But there, in her looking-glass world, her fear was turning her around and walking her backwards into another field of battle. There, she would see her daughter advance against the Jabberwocky then bring order to a realm in which she was crowned a queen. *I have to try. I can't remain an outsider anymore.* Aimee could see Tamara standing tall and straight with a mother-of-pearl tiara set upon her head, and a scepter made of choral in her hand. And on her face, the radiance of laughter.

Who else would chase Tamara through that world of down-side-up-ness and show her the way home? Yet Aimee knew, before the thoughts coalesced in her mind, that this was going to be a one-way leap through this psychotic portal. Already she was hearing the cracking of glass. She would have to leap soon, or Tamara would be lost inside without her. Aimee was through with simply guarding Tamara's means of escape. Her daughter was too far out ahead and a long way on toward meeting the fiends who would devour her in those tangled forests of her mind. Tamara needed a champion. Who else would follow her in, find her, and search out another exit?

Before she could rethink it, Aimee went to her lap-top and composed the e-mail that would shatter her looking-glass from the inside, trapping her in there, where everything was outside-in, the sun set in the east, and the way home took you through the poppy fields of Oz. Then, from the relative calm of her bedroom, she went through the door and down the passage-way in search of her daughter. She heard the shards of glass hitting the floor behind her.

7

WHAT THOSE EYES CAN SEE

FLASHES OF MEMORY SPARKED THROUGH Aimee's mind and took her back to the mountain. *How could our marriage have deteriorated so thoroughly? He came at me with an axe!* Terrance had closed his eyes and looked peaceful. *I wish I could do that for a few minutes. I need to put this out of my mind for a while.* But closing her eyes invited more visual spectacle from Friday night. Instead, she considered asking her daughter for a piece of paper but worried Tamara would think her silly. She felt the urge to draw again, and grew envious of her daughter's strokes and shading, which Tamara executed with such dispatch and skill. Aimee wasn't sure what she would draw, but her hands craved the feel of the pen moving across the page. *I wish I could find something new inside me that I could bring out into the light like she can, something fresh that could take shape before my eyes. Something reassuring.*

Finally, Tamara had left the figure's eyes alone. Unable to give them greater intensity, she had filled them in and turned them into dark, lightless portals. Aimee rarely considered her daughter's effort to be anything less than brilliant (in her dark and disturbing way), but she assessed this effort to have fallen below Tamara's standard.

Yet, as Aimee scanned the picture, she reconsidered her opinion. No matter where she wanted to look, those eyes provided more gravitation pull than anything else on the page. Aimee could not refuse their summons.

Aimee's last subway ride home from Wall Street took her through some disorienting emotional terrain. Her environment grew fluid as she careened through her memories of the day's events. *No one even really said good-bye.* With each stop, she tunneled more deeply into herself and found only emptiness. She was falling through the subway tunnel toward home and couldn't cope with the idea of stepping over the threshold into a new life so barren of professional purpose. *I need to slow this down and set another pace.* When the train came into the next station, she lept out three stops short of her normal destination. The lingering daylight was too much for her raw eyes as she emerged onto the street. The city had lost its solidity as her tears distorted her sense of place and being.

Don't you mock me, old man. The bobbing head of Paul Baxter flashed through her mind. *I'll be back. This is only temporary. There is always money to be made, and if you think I'm wasting my talents, you're wrong. I'm a mother, dammit, and that is all that matters right now.*

A brilliant afternoon sun set the westward facing facades on fire. Normally, her imagination would have climbed up into their ramparts as she catalogued the enterprises being launched in their corporate suites. This was her city. The capital that had passed through her hands on its way to financing much of what she saw around her was incalculable to her. *I'm not through with you yet.* But she became dizzy and halted her stride. *This is only temporary. Catch your breath and slow down. Just take this a little at a time.*

The front door of her home imposed its own rebuke as she let herself in. She hesitated at the threshold, unsure she was even home. *Someone could have left a light on. And turned up the heat.* Unable to curb her mounting anxieties, she set down her briefcase and scanned her now unfamiliar home. The note from the housekeeper said she had to leave a little early. Tamara, said the note, was sullen but okay. *She'll be in her room sulking. And Terrance won't be home for several hours.* Their nanny, Gretta, had taken an early train to Connecticut to begin life with a new family. A small, wrapped parcel had been left on the kitchen counter: a set of salt and pepper shakers. The card from the nanny said simply, "I will miss you, but I promise to stay in touch." *I'm sure you will, just like all the rest.* She had to assign herself a purpose, and quickly, so she went to the kitchen and stood in the middle of a room that never seemed to fit her.

What is that smell? The casserole warming in the oven was now overcooked. *Not tonight, thank you very much.* Aimee grimaced at the slopping sound it made as she emptied their dinner into the disposal and ground it into mush.

She looked around her kitchen. *I never appreciated just how cold this room was. Certainly not like my mother's kitchen, though that was partly the point when we had it put in. So sterile.* Stainless steel, black counter tops, just the necessary utensils and nothing more. She could see herself in every surface. Her mom's kitchen was a wonderland of culinary craft, the workroom of an artisan who was serious about producing the best food for the best reason: to feed a family. *I should dig out some of the old cookbooks she gave me.* Aimee's kitchen was equipped to thaw out frozen food and serve a catered buffet but not to nourish her daughter. *I'd love to figure out that meatloaf she used to make.*

Her mom always had a glass of sherry on the counter. A small glass. Not a goblet, a jelly jar glass into which she poured a few fingers of cheap sherry, which she nursed as she let the dough rise or kept vigil over the roast in the oven. *Just a small glass.* And she rarely finished it. Once the timer went off, there was too much to do in those few moments to get it all to the table, and nothing would distract her.

Aimee didn't have anything in the house she wanted to cook, but she found a small glass into which she poured some very expensive port. A few of those later, and the doorbell rang. She paid for the calzones she ordered, and called Tamara to dinner.

No one spoke. Tamara poked at her food then refused to eat it. Aimee felt the time was right to make a fresh start, but the silence had seized her words and wouldn't give them back. *We need to talk this out somehow. I need to find some way into that head of yours.*

"You know today was my last day of work, remember?" she said feebly.

Tamara put her fork down and stared at her mother.

"What's on your mind?" asked Aimee. But more intensity from Tamara's dark and unfeeling eyes was all she got in response. *Say something! Don't just fry my insides. Are you mocking me, hating me, or just trying to push me away?*

For the slightest moment, Aimee met her daughter's stare. *I know you're there.* But dull dark silence was all Aimee experienced. *Just speak so we have something to start with.* Had she been eye-to-eye with an associate, Aimee would have mastered this moment. But the longer her daughter stared, the smaller Aimee became. *Please don't do this.* Aimee felt her inner self turned out and dumped onto the floor. *You always do this to me.* She dropped her gaze but sensed her daughter circling her insecurities like so much carrion drying out in the sun. Unconscious memories, long buried anxieties, new regrets, and whole complexes of guilt, most of which she thought she had worked through, had just come unraveled. *I'm not going to let you do this to me.*

"Aren't you hungry?" she asked her daughter. *Is there anything I can do that will make any difference to you?*

A rather slight girl on the outside, Tamara's simple physique masked the complexities within her. The darkness behind her eyes went on forever as if her psyche was riddled with tunnels, an interlocking maze of alley-ways that became a hopeless labyrinth for anyone who got lost in there. Tamara stood, but she refused to free her mother from the intensity of her eyes.

Let me go. Aimee shut her eyes in self-defense. *Just be with me here.*

"I've got dessert," said Aimee.

"Can I go to my room?"

Tamara had opened gaping chasms of darkness in Aimee, flushed out creatures in there she didn't want to face, and now simply wanted to disappear again. *No! Stop running away. And stop looking at me like that!*

"Yes," Aimee whispered, feeling nauseous.

The next morning, after coaxing a non-compliant Tamara onto the bus, Aimee couldn't bring herself to go back inside. She was already out of breath and having a hard time getting the day moving in a positive direction. The house oppressed her. Every inch of it reminded her of what they were enduring as a family and what she faced as a stay-at-home mom. She strolled a few blocks down their street and then turned south onto Park Avenue. The familiarity of her neighborhood bored her, so she started to meander, over one block, up a street, weaving her way, she calculated, toward Times Square. There, she would have a bite to eat then stroll home. She felt that old familiar spark of awe for the city she always loved. *I thought I knew you, but you're always full of surprises. I'm going to have to do this more often.* She was seeing sights in the city that were new to her, and the sensation broadened her mind beyond the claustrophobic little world into which she had fallen.

A beautiful old church, built of stone, caught her eye. Still a few blocks away, its profile against the city was striking. The closer she came, the more hopeful she was that its doors might be open. *I just need a moment of solitude in a place of peace.* As that little inch-worm of an inspiration worked its way through her mind and encircled her soul, she thought what a refreshing sight the church was amid the forest of city structures. She loved the nursery and Sunday School in the church of her childhood, but the chore her parents made of getting them up and out to church made it a burden, then a fight, until they let it fade into a special event, then, none at all. *Just a moment of peace.*

The great latch on the door clicked loudly and she stepped through her portal of peace, but pulsing music and neon lights slammed against her mind and disoriented her. Upscale boutiques selling makeup, clothing, and jewelry were teaming with affluent, trendy young adults. *Yep. That's all it's become – whatever faith I've ever had has been bought and sold on the open market, traded for something a lot more dazzling than a lifetime of Sundays in church. Just another fleeting fashion statement.*

Her heart plummeted, and she turned toward the exit. Then, something rather amazing caught her eye—through the glass cases stared the faces of stained-glass angels, saints, and heroes of the Bible. Looking straight up, the old bones of the church were doing their job holding aloft the vaulted ceiling that called her gaze heavenward. The rafters and arches stood majestically overhead, and they beckoned her to climb up. A balcony, wrapped around the perimeter of the interior edifice, promised a view of the open expanse. With each step up, she saw fresh wonders between the merchandise. There was a small, humorous carving in a stone pillar of an angel watching over a cat. Other symbols of the faith, some of which she still recognized, adorned the walls: keys reminding her that Peter offered access through the doors of Heaven; the Greek letters alpha and omega, the beginning and the end; and a little lamb, looking lost in such a foreign world as this. *Where's the shepherd who's supposed to watch over this little one?*

Her eyes were drawn outward over the open space in the middle of the arcade, but as she made her way to the far end, then through a little archway, she was disoriented by the enormous face looking at her. There, above the market, much of the master window could be seen. Reaching out, enrobed in colors of gold and white and red and purple, stretching his arms out over the whole affair, was the risen Christ. The nail holes in his hands were visible as if to bless every shopper there, and say to them all: "Even for you I was crucified." And the light of his glory declared: "Even over your marketing and merchandising, even over your fast-paced self-centered lives: even over this, I still reign."

Too close to take it all in, Aimee stepped back against the rail, but her perspective was confused and she could only focus on small pieces of it at a time. Her mind shut out all the noise around her and the impact of the image silenced her all the way through. Her curiosity underwent transformation into adoration. *Holy...* The beauty of it was striking.

Jesus' left hand, which blessed her upon her entrance onto the mezzanine, bled freely from the open wound in his palm, but his strength was undiminished and she felt him reaching toward her. The folds of his tunic led her to his strong shoulders, draped with royal red and gold. His long, dark auburn hair looked as natural in glass as it ever had in her imagination, which she knew was a long way from reality, but it marked him a king among men.

His eyes were invading her periphery, but she had taken this extended tour to put off looking in to them. She knew, however, they were looking into her. *I don't even want to know what you see in there – certainly not the woman I hoped to be by the time I come face to face with the Lord!* She girded herself and met his gaze. Large and brown, flecked with gold and white in a sea of pale yellow, the artistic construction of his eyes sparked her wonder. She was sure that from down below the worshipper's eye would have blended the colors into an expression of warmth, but to see him like this was a shock to her senses. The face surrounding the eyes swamped her awareness with awe, and she fell more deeply under his influence. His expression was invitational, the hues of ivory and yellow which mellowed his darker beard warmed her and called her closer.

Then, wonder gave way to fear. The mystery of his holiness pushed her more deeply into the depths of her own anxious being. What she saw in there (and knew without hesitation that *He* saw) was a lengthening shadow, grim and without definition, warning her of worse to come. And, yet. She knew in her soul that where there was shadow, there must light exerting its influence. Though the light was hindered, it was persistent. The effect disoriented her and she grabbed hold of the balcony banister to steady herself. How long she stood there, she couldn't say, but pulling herself away proved more difficult than she felt it ought to be. *Some peace.*

A new sensation took root within her as Aimee ambled home. Not exactly peace, but she knew she did not resent her decision to stay home with Tamara anymore, and that awareness wanted to blossom into something else. *What are those eyes seeing in me that I can't see for myself? I have no idea.* But where peace was lacking, there was a hint of hope. *Perhaps they are not all that different from one another. But, where is such a hope leading me?* At most, it resembled the deep sigh one releases as one stands up to face something inevitable, having come at last to that point of resolve, even if one is not yet able to define precisely what that next move should be.

Later that evening, after Tamara excused herself from the dinner table, Aimee and Terrance found themselves with a few unguarded moments alone.

"Here, let me get the dishes," said Terrance, hastening to his feet and falling into his routine for getting him out the door to the next thing.

"Just leave them. Sit for a moment," said Aimee, grabbing his hand. She meant it to be a tender gesture, but it agitated him. She withdrew her hand and couldn't meet his gaze.

"Please."

He sat down, but stared furtively at the wine goblet across from him.

"I had a good day today," she said.

He let the silence wrap around her words.

"Ever thought about going back to church?" she asked, and the moment she did, she knew it was too extreme, too fast, and the look he gave her set her on the defensive.

"Today," she paused, and swallowed hard. "I began to feel we need to reconnect with something more than ourselves, something that might help pull us out of this slow dying we seem to be doing these days."

She hadn't thought of it that way until this moment, but as the words emerged, they taught her the truth that had been hiding behind the events of her day. *Slow dying.* Their relationships had atrophied, and their emotional asphyxiation was poisoning the blood supply that brought fresh oxygen to their hearts. *Each of us is dying our own death separately, and the family, together.* Her gaze into Jesus' eyes had ignited something new, though she was struggling to shield the flame and keep it safe. *I've got to make more of this than just marking time at home with Tamara, or it will be a meaningless waste of my life. And I can't do it alone.*

"And you think *church* is the way to do that?" As disciplined as he could manage to be in the face of such nonsense, Terrance intensified the inflection in his voice to make it brutally clear that was not a question he was asking.

"I don't know, honey." There was fresh defeat in her voice. "I resigned so I could be with Tamara, but that isn't enough. If we don't add to that somehow, then we'll just continue to stagnate."

"But church?" Terrance would fixate on that until she relinquished, so she did.

"Then what about our families?" she asked. "We've held them at bay for far too long. We haven't let them help because we haven't wanted to let them in, so they are all just living their lives without us. We need to reconnect."

"I agree with that," he said. "But I thought you wanted that separation."

Aimee flushed and turned from him.

"I just mean, you resigned so you could manage the plans you've laid out for Tamara, and I thought it best, since you are going to be with her most of the time, to give you the room you needed. In the past, when those opportunities came along to be with family, you always said it was too tense, or too short notice, or too *something*."

Aimee ended up clearing the dishes as Terrance drifted out of the conversation, then out of the room. Having verbalized her need to reconnect, she knew the first family member she needed a fresh start with was her husband. *Perhaps, re-immersing ourselves in the larger clan might free him up, bring him out of himself, and closer to me. It can't keep getting worse, or it will all be over, anyway.*

8

Everything Will Be Okay

THE AIR IN THIS PLANE is getting stale. Or is it a good stiff drink I need? Aimee was suffocating in her thoughts and decided to break the silence.

"What have you got this week?" she asked Terrance.

"A lot of catch-up to begin with. I had two meetings I pushed off into this week so we could come up here."

He pulled out his phone and began scanning his schedule.

"Oh. And dinner with the family," he said, with an extra lathering of bother in his tone.

"When is that?"

"Saturday. We're expected there for 4:00."

"Thanks for telling me."

"Sorry. I guess I had blocked it, myself."

"Is there an occasion I should get ready for?" grumbled Aimee.

"No. Some of the aunts and uncs wanted to fly in for a show or something so mom wanted to get us all together. Oh. And there's talk of vacationing together in Quebec."

"Quebec?" Aimee couldn't recall when Terrance's parents had ever been to Canada. They tended to ricochet between Florida, Atlantic City, Colorado and occasionally to Europe, but they had always held a simmering antipathy toward Canadians for some reason.

"Well, for dad it's mostly about business. He's negotiating with a Canadian bank so he set up a week's worth of meetings. The bank has corporate shindigs and invited them to make a vacation of it."

As their weekend in New Hampshire had just proved once again, vacations were toxic subjects with Terrance and, after this weekend, Aimee was sure he would never tempt those fates again.

"And they want us to come along?" Aimee asked with sincere surprise.

"Believe it or not, they do."

"You sound tempted," she said with some dismay.

"Well, I'm open to hearing what they have planned," he said.

Aimee's silence allowed Terrance to dip back into his paper. *Another Baxter family fiasco. After Colorado? No, thank you. We almost lost Tamara then as well.*

☙

Every few years Paul and Maureen would dream up an excuse to gather the clan at one of their family compounds and, for their fortieth anniversary, the destination would be Vale.

"I'm not sure this is the best time to be cooped up with your family so far from home," Aimee thought out loud. "Tamara's been on edge lately. She seems so anxious all the time."

"Well, maybe she needs a change of scenery, like the rest of us do," countered Terrance. "Aside from the banquet they have planned on Saturday night, most of them will be skiing. They'll all keep to themselves and mix with the others in the evening. So, we could set our own pace."

"That's a long flight," said Aimee, and it was.

They booked an overnight flight hoping Tamara would sleep, but after everyone had dozed off, she slipped past Aimee, who quickly awoke when she heard Tamara speak in tones too bright and clear for that time of night.

"You are going to die?" she heard her daughter say. Aimee bolted upright and searched out her daughter's location. She was standing behind them in the aisle speaking with a lady wearing a bright dress whose head was tightly bundled in a radiant yellow and red scarf. Before Aimee could act, the woman responded in a beautiful Caribbean accent.

"Yes," she said. "I am going to die."

"Tamara!" whispered Aimee as loud as he could, horrified at what she was watching. "Tamara, come here, right now."

But the woman looked Aimee in the eye and held up her hand with a commanding air that halted her from saying anything further. Then, she bent toward Tamara.

"But everything is going to be okay. No worries," she reassured the young girl.

"When?" asked Tamara.

"Maybe next month, maybe next week. I am going home now to say good-bye to those I love. So, I can say good-bye to you, too."

"Will it hurt?"

"No. I have medicines and my family that will help me."

"Do you want to die?"

"It is time for me to die. That's all."

"Then what?" asked Tamara.

"Then what? Then I will see God, and he will heal everything there that he chooses not to heal here."

"Where will you go for God to heal you?" asked Tamara, but this time it was to Tamara that the woman held up the command to be still.

"I think it's time for you to go sit with your mama and get a little sleep now. And just remember, everything will be okay. Right? Everything. Don't ever forget that."

Small as she was, Tamara made use of every inch of the room allotted to her and squirmed the rest of the trip. Her seatbelt, which Aimee insisted she wear, was the only thing confining her.

"When are you going to die?" she asked her mom.

Good lord. This is not the time. But you'd better answer her, or she won't let you go. "No time soon, I promise you, honey." *Unless the plane goes down. God. Why do I let her do this to me?* "Honey, you need to settle down and get some sleep."

"But the lady knew," Tamara protested.

"The lady may have cancer or some disease that she knows is taking her life," Aimee explained as quietly as she could. "We're all healthy, so don't worry. Now, close your eyes for a little while."

It was too quick and too blunt a conversation to be having at eleven-thirty on a crowded, sleeping plane. But Tamara had her teeth in this one and wasn't letting it go.

"Isn't it better to know?" she asked, but Aimee put her foot down and refused to keep feeding the conversation. Then, Aimee found it impossible to sleep.

When they arrived at the family's lodge, Terrance was the only one who felt refreshed. Aimee was exhausted and preoccupied by the conversation she had with her daughter. Tamara was dragging, complaining about everything, tired as she was. By lunchtime, Tamara had become un-manageable. She was defiant one moment, docile and limp at another, she refused to take a nap, or comply with anything. She was like the fly that kept buzzing around everyone's heads which no one could shoo away, catch, or satisfy.

Later that evening, after Tamara gave in and went to bed, Aimee joined the rest of the family downstairs. The Lodge was constructed around a massive stone fire-place large enough to park a mini-van inside it. There were wooden rockers and plush recliners that arced around the room, all focusing inward. Overhead towered a cathedral ceiling held aloft by massive timbers. Overlooking the great room was a balcony level which contained the guest rooms all of which were accessed by a grand staircase.

They were all dipping into their third or fourth drink when someone shouted and pointed toward the upper level. Tamara was standing atop the balcony railing, her arms spread wide as if she was about to take flight. Aimee screamed as Terrance's father moved under his grand-daughter to break her fall if it came to that.

"Tamara, get down, right this instance," or some version of that was shouted by a chorus of voices as Aimee struggled to piece together a safe way through this.

"Everything will be okay, mommy," Tamara said. "Don't ever forget that!"

Terrance bolted for the stairs, taking them two at a time and didn't slow down until he had his arms around her. He pulled her backwards, and both fell to the floor as Terrance smothered her with the weight of his body. He wouldn't let her up until they were joined by Aimee who managed to coax them to their feet, and then led them in to their room.

Now, there was a new haunt. Their daughter was playing haphazardly with death. The psychological boundaries that barely protected her from a mind full of goblins were now crumbling along more eternal borders. Tamara already struggled to fend off the intrusions that snuck up out of her subconscious and invaded her waking world. Now, they were luring her to higher ledges.

Terrance hadn't let go of Tamara and sat on the edge of the bed with her in his lap. She had grown docile and curled herself into a small fetus-shaped bundle in Terrance's arms. Her muffled sobs were absorbed by Terrance's chest, and he felt every one of them resonate throughout his torso. He stroked her hair and held on to her. He soon became aware that it wasn't just Tamara's sobs he was hearing.

Aimee was out of reach. Across the room she had back herself against the wall and slid down it until she was squatting on the carpet with her arms wrapped around her head heaving and gasping for air.

"Aimee?" he said softly. "Honey, how can I help?"

"Take us home. It was too soon."

"I thought she seemed better these past few weeks."

Aimee shook her head.

"Her teacher called the other day and said she could tell Tamara was sliding again. And I could tell. She hadn't done homework in a week, and she refused to eat all day on Thursday."

"You didn't say anything."

"Yes, I did. You just didn't listen." There was defeat in her voice and she buried her head again.

Terrance managed to lay Tamara on the bed. She was dead weight with no energy and her sobs were ebbing. He sat beside his wife, wrestled his arm around her neck, and pulled her toward him.

"She is always so sad, or so agitated, or so distant and lost," said Aimee. "And now this."

"You sound surprised," said Terrance.

"She's very moody, but I never thought…" Aimee couldn't finish the sentence.

"Really? I'm afraid there are days I can't get it out of my mind. I find myself waiting for that phone call," said Terrance.

"Terrance, she's nine. Nine-year-olds don't think about suicide," she said, hardly audible.

"But how do you not worry about that?"

"I refuse."

"Simple force of will? Then what's the point? You know it's there as well as I do," he persisted.

"But I don't let it become real."

"How do you pull that off?" he asked.

After a long, tortured pause, she said: "I had read, a month or so ago, I don't remember where, that instead of giving in to my fears and becoming immobilized by them, I had to walk away from them, get some distance, and some help, before I could face them head on. The article said I needed allies."

"Makes good sense to me," he interjected.

"But I just tried the walking away part. The article said I should never feed those demons since it just made them angrier. Starve them, it said. Visualize the hole they inhabit and walk away. Don't knock on their door. Don't argue with them. They feed on that. Walk away. Otherwise, they are going to reach out their tentacles and pull me into their lair where they will suck the life force out of me. That struck a chord. I do that all the time – get sucked in and eaten up. So, I began envisioning Tamara's moods as these dark holes in the ground. There were different holes that held different demons: her nightmares, her angers and illusions, her paranoia and anxieties, all those holes into which I fall again and again. So, I started imagining walking away from them. When one opened up, rather than diving in headfirst, I tried to give it distance. But lately, she seems to be preoccupied with death, and that hole just keeps growing in my mind. I can't seem to walk away from it fast enough."

Aimee became silent, closed her eyes to resupply herself, but then started heaving up sobs and had difficulty continuing.

"What is it?" whispered Terrance.

"Last night, on the plane, I was trying to walk away from it, but the faster I moved the faster the hole grew. Now, all I can see is Tamara balancing on the far edge, and that edge is getting farther and farther away as the hole continues to expand. I can't reach her."

9

A Walk to Somewhere New

"LADIES AND GENTLEMEN, IN JUST a few moments, we will be coming through the aisle with our refreshment cart. We also have a list of items from our bar for purchase located in the seat pocket in front of you."

Aimee glanced over to see how Tamara was progressing on her drawing.

Abandon hope, all ye who enter here. Aimee wanted to scratch Dante's words into the stones above the dank tunnel that emanated such despair. The longer she stared at that darkness, the more foreboding it became.

Something else crawled out of that tortured mind of yours while we were in New Hampshire. What? This grotesque fiend? Was he chasing you, or was he fleeing whatever keeps those depths so foul and your soul on fire? As she studied the figure Tamara had sketched, Aimee sensed he must be in charge. *Then what did he leave behind in there, anything?*

Aimee lingered on the doorstep of the cave's opening. *I wish someone could carry some light in there to see just what it is that inhabits those regions of your mind. All the clues might be right there for us to see. But I give up. I can't make sense of it anymore.*

"What is that?" Aimee asked before realizing it. Tamara had just sculpted a new shape that hadn't yet coalesced into recognizable form. Her silent rebuke reminded Aimee she wasn't to comment. Then, the image became all too plain. It was the head of one of her stuffed bears.

A fresh series of memories screamed up through Aimee's mind, forced from those depths and pushed into the light by the figure with the staff. Aimee saw one of Tamara' stuffed animals punished at the end of a hangman's noose. There were those doodles of headless cats, and the black finger-paint Tamara had caked on in the middle of her mirror preventing her reflection. Aimee saw Tamara spread her wings like an angel, coming far too close to eternal flight. Then she visualized blood draining onto the bathroom floor, the large kitchen knife still in Tamara's hand, and the dead menagerie in her daughter's bedroom.

It was incomprehensible that their daughter could want to end her life, but the seed had been planted in that collective imagination they seemed to share. Aimee's fears had been feeding Tamara's anxieties about her life and fertilizing a more intense curiosity about death.

Tamara's thoughts were morbid. Her facial aspect was morose, and the further she withdrew into herself, the more desperate Aimee was to chase her through that looking-glass house in which she dwelt. Stairs that ought to lead her up and out only took her further down, into the drippy mire of Tamara's mind. And deep inside there, Aimee had gotten lost rooting around in the darkened caverns where no light could be found, and no words could live.

This hole, this chasm, became the lair of Aimee's "silent scream," where the shards of her faith went to whither, and the scabs of her hope were being picked to death. The backward alleyways she was navigating on all fours kept reversing her perspective. Everything she heard down there had to be thought through backwards before it felt right again. And if it felt right the first time, she knew to watch for the tentacles of fury that would lash out and constrict her hope in what might have been a point of light, a way out, or a source of solace. But there was no way out. The looking-glass was shattered, and there was no one out there who knew how to put the pieces back in place and rescue them.

Question after question Aimee asked of that darkness, yet her queries only deepened her emptiness. Aimee pursued Tamara into those moods and behaviors. She kept asking questions, but the sound of her voice reverberated aimlessly in the cavernous darkness that haunted them both. If any of those sound waves that carried Aimee's questions had entered Tamara's conscious mind, they lost their way, wandered off, and died. And with every unanswered question, Aimee became more possessive of Tamara.

The emotional environment became funereal as death crept into every crevice of their home. That depressive atmospheric pressure, weighing down on Aimee's gut, kept her nauseous with fear and rancid with guilt. It was pressing in upon her womb, gnawing at the soul of her motherhood, as a still born piece of placenta that had never fully passed. She was holding on to a part of her daughter that never came forth in the birthing, and it was still kicking, turning in her, wanting out, but she was exhausted from pushing. A maternal adrenalin, a psychic hormone, was coursing through her, pushing out tiny bundles of insight. But the insights came forth premature before any hope could come to term. Her demons feigned answers to questions she couldn't stop asking, and then laughed at her naiveté: "This is death," said the demons. "Death. The only answer lurking so closely behind those slithering question marks is, death."

Still, as tortuous as it was, that maternal mystery took her by the hand.

All Aimee could manage were the very basic mechanics of mothering, but that still small voice that finally convinced her she was pregnant nine years earlier kept whispering to her the next truths she had to act upon. The instinct told her to pull her daughter up from the emotional fetal position that had become so normal for Tamara and set her on her feet.

"We're going for a walk," said Aimee, who was feeling as depleted as her daughter, yet it carried the only supply of determination between them.

Tamara was seated at the dining room table. Her head was laid on her folded arms with her schoolwork strewn around her. She had been poking at the same page of math problems for forty-five minutes making no headway.

"Let's go clear our heads and stretch our legs," insisted Aimee. She was gently rocking Tamara trying to dislodge her from her chair.

"You really suck at this." Tamara looked her mother in the eye. There was no emotion in her voice, and there didn't need to be, because

Tamara knew all the emotional force of the words would be borne by her mother. She only had to say it once, and then Aimee's conscience would carry the freight for the rest of their time together.

"Put on your coat. We're going," insisted her mom whose maternal concern had been scalded by daughterly rejection.

Tamara had located that glistening soft spot of her mother's underbelly, but Aimee was never quite sure if Tamara was lashing out in rejection of her, or if, through her pain, she didn't even try to filter her words.

"How do you want to die?" Tamara asked her mother, as she put on her coat.

When such questions were born out of serious emotional darkness, Aimee was learning that verbal answers weren't always what Tamara was looking for. Tamara absorbed her mother's responses like a black hole gathers light. Her daughter's introversion and depression stole from the atmosphere instead of replenishing it with anything. When, from that mass of morbid stillness, a question invited Aimee's engagement, it would have been such a gift were it not so muffled by the death that saturated it.

Where Aimee had to draw the line was when her daughter used death as a weapon against her, which was often. When you have a weapon that disarms your opponent every time you take it out of the holster, you use it whenever you can. So, when Tamara grew furious with her mother's prying and worry, she would stab her right where it hurt the most.

"Which do you think would be less painful?" she taunted. "Drowning or slitting your wrists? I saw online that you are supposed to cut along the vein, not across it. Is that true?"

Somehow, Aimee would need to pursue her daughter into those shadowy forests of death and hunt down the suicidal fiend that had taken residence there. She could make out the fiend's silhouette on the horizon, standing erect against a blood red sky, waving at her, shouting, "Bring it on." She and Tamara would be contending against one another for the life of her daughter for a long time to come. For now, Aimee was going to drag her daughter through the streets on what had become not so affectionately known as a forced march.

On that gray spring day, they set out and headed down the street. The bite in the air pulled Aimee more deeply into her worry. She felt as alien and cold within herself as the day was outside. After several blocks, they had left their neighborhood behind and she barely took notice until she was accosted for loose change. Yanked out of herself, she stared down at a man in a wheel-chair. His legs were missing, and his lap was covered in a tattered POW flag. He wore a faded fatigue jacket and held an old ammo box containing a thin layer of pennies and nickels.

"Oh. I'm, so sorry. I don't carry cash with me, I'm afraid," she said. Aimee stood there, immobilized and unsure of what to do next.

"It's okay, lady. Don't sweat it," the man answered.

But Aimee was frozen in place. Every sensation in her shut down, and her periphery became dark. She tried to dislodge her eyes from the man but her stare was fixed.

"Lady? You okay?" asked the man, inching his chair forward a quarter roll of the wheels. He stuck his hand inside his coat, came out with a rather dingy piece of cloth, and handed it up to her. She hadn't realized she was crying, but a swelling tide of tears lipped over the lower edge of her eyes and washed down her cheek. She reached for the rag but withdrew her hand, shook her head, and apologized.

"Fighting your own battles, I see," said the veteran. "You don't have to tell me what that's like. Good luck to you, ma'am." He snapped his right wheel, did an about face, and rolled down the street.

Then, as if lightning struck the street where she stood, awareness bolted back to her and she knew instantaneously that Tamara was not there. Violent fear closed in around her and she was just as aware she didn't know where she was, either. Her chest tightened. She felt dizzy as she scanned the streets for clues.

"Tamara!" she screamed.

"I'm right here," said Tamara, standing by Aimee's left leg.

"Where did you disappear to?"

"Nowhere. I've been right here."

"Come on. Let's go," said Aimee.

"Where?"

"Home."

"Fine by me. But we just left home."

Aimee glanced at her phone. Only fifteen minutes had passed since they had left the house. She stood in a daze, then made a few calculations against the map in her head and reclaimed some sense of where they were, but she had to fight to pay attention. Her mental exhaustion was nearly complete. *I used to be so sharp. I've got to dial this back somehow. But what can I renegotiate?* She looked down the street and shivered. It was such a gray world. *Do we really want to do this today?* Every face, bent downward and cast in shadow, bore the weight of whatever world each was carrying on those slumped, beaten shoulders. *What can I let go of? Nothing. Is Tamara safe? No! But can I ever fully protect her?* The overcast sky didn't allow much light to filter between the buildings. Their unwashed, grime-coated walls reminded her of the filth and debris she sought to avoid every day as she traded and sold the world's wealth. Now, she carried the city's filth within her. She had walked away from that pristine, ordered world and was wading hip-deep in human misery. *Then, who? Who can help?* The short leash she had on her daughter was working like a noose around her own neck.

Aimee halted at a cross-walk and didn't have the energy to decide their next direction, so she chose whichever signal let them go first which meant going north. Her fear of losing Tamara was feeding the fiend that was killing her daughter. *Is there anything I can let go of without losing her altogether? What could possibly be the point of getting lost with Tamara in these nether-lands of death which is the only place we've been for weeks?*

Tamara kept falling behind. She was losing steam and Aimee was losing patience. The infernal drone of sirens and honking horns and street hawkers and profanity shouted from one pedestrian to another was eating away at Aimee's resolve to pull Tamara through the streets.

Then: "Mom!" shouted Tamara.

"What!"

Tamara pointed. The light had changed and Aimee hadn't noticed. She had attained a cruising altitude in her stride and wasn't paying attention to anything else but the stream of thought coursing through her mind.

Aimee did a quick calibration of their position then made a decided turn westward. She had to get out of this noise – the noise from the streets, and the noise in her head.

I used to bristle with watchfulness. I could resuscitate failed potential all the time on the trading floor. But there, I had a share in the power that made things happen. Fortunes. Retirements. Businesses. Empires. Now, all of that is so ephemeral. Now, I'm as powerless as an orange peel. Was that world real? Or was it just some sort of diversion – illusion? – that I need to survive. But that life is a world away now. Or, that world is a life away. As fast as that world moves, two, three lifetimes have elapsed against the one I have been living since I left. Does it have to be dead? It's pretty dead. Could it be resuscitated? Do I have any power left?

When they made it to 5th Avenue and crossed the street, Aimee headed north until she found an entrance into Central Park. The canopy of trees made a gray day darker still, but the buffer it gave her from the streets of the city helped her take her first deep breath and slow her pace. They walked about a hundred yards, then Aimee found a bench and sat down. The bench looked out over the Jacqueline Onassis Reservoir, an expansive basin ringed with trees and a halo of tall buildings, all of them bustling with purpose. Tamara leaned on the black, wrought iron fence, looking into the water.

"I want to feed the ducks," said Tamara.

The request disarmed Aimee. At first it was another annoyance, a daughter wanting to do something Aimee was unprepared to allow, a simple request she couldn't fulfill, made by a daughter who probably knew that and just wanted to poke another hole in her.

Then, Tamara's words rearranged themselves in Aimee's mind and let in a little light. It was, after all, a perfectly normal request. Normal, as in, that's exactly what a young girl would want to do. Feed ducks. *Of course, she wants to feed the ducks. How long has it been since any of us interacted with the natural world?* As she mused about this, four more ducks soared downward and glided into the water to meet up with those already congregated there. *Had they heard Tamara's request like it was a dinner bell?* Aimee watched her daughter's eyes as the ducks paddled around the marshy bank. *When was the last time I saw any hint of fascination on her face? When at all? Now. Just now.* Her eyes lost focus for the water mounting up in them. Another deep, deep breath, and she felt a few of the tectonic plates shift in her soul. *What could this be? No idea.*

Throughout their slow walk home, Aimee let Tamara lead as she watched her daughter through another new filter. *She is growing up. But she has never been that happy little girl we wanted. Why couldn't she just feed the ducks? Did we rob her of something she has been craving? No, we feed her art. Then, what?* The intimations of maturity Aimee wanted to see in Tamara were effaced by the psychological commotion that kept interfering with any adult behavior Aimee hoped to encourage. Aimee thought of the tea parties Tamara still hosts with her stuffed animals. *Are we preventing her from growing up, still hoping she'll be a normal kid?* She had outgrown the little dining room set in her bedroom, but Aimee couldn't relinquish the thought that there was still a little girl in there. *Tamara doesn't seem to care if it's always set for a tea-party with friends who never come anymore.* The disruption of redoing her bedroom as she matured seemed to be more trouble than Aimee wanted to manage in light of Tamara's moods.

Aimee knew Tamara was trying to find that livable place that lay between the healthy imagination of a young girl and those forays into psychological hell that took her away from them. Every year, as Tamara matured, Aimee saw more signs of what she feared could be life-long damage, both to Tamara, and to their family. She still hoped, with all her heart, to find a little girl with a normal imagination peeking through, one who could regain her focus and begin maturing into the artist Aimee knew her to be. *For now, I'd have traded several shares of Baxter stock for crackers so Tamara could have fed those ducks.*

10

Too Many Fiends at the Party

TERRANCE FINISHED THE ARTICLE HE was reading in the Wall Street Journal and asked Aimee if she would like a glass of wine.

"Love one!" she said with a thankful widening of her eyes.

He caught the steward's attention.

"Could we get two glasses of wine?" he asked.

"White for me," said Aimee.

"And a red," said Terrance.

"I'll have the rose," said Tamara.

"Don't be fresh," said her mother. "What would you like?"

"Ginger ale, then," she said with mock disdain.

"Very good," said the attendant.

Terrance glanced down to see how the drawing was taking shape.

"What kind of fiend is that?" he asked.

Tamara didn't look up; her face was flushed with intense emotion but she showed no sign of responding.

Then she whispered, "That's no fiend." And to prove it, she put her pen to work in another direction. I'll show you fiends, it was saying, as small, intense eyes emerged from the flames surrounded by ghastly faces and angry snarls. These images poured forth in ink with such fluidity. They bore evidence of familiarity, faces she had seen again and again.

Then, two, long, graceful lines emerged from a single point and ran parallel with one another until they formed a grotesque, diamond shaped head with searing eyes and slashing fangs. This monster, more than any of the others, seemed most familiar to the artist. Its details surpassed anything else on the page.

"Your drinks," interrupted the attendant.

"Oh. Thank you," said Terrance, who passed the cups to the two women beside him, though Tamara took no notice. She was going to finish the details of this sketch before doing anything else.

Both parents, enthralled by Tamara's fervor, watched a succession of horrific acts of family pain coalesce on Tamara's sketch pad. Scenes from the mountain and past acts of emotional violence poured out in torrents of fluid, visual anguish. When she lifted her hand, laying by the mouth of the cave was a large kitchen knife, and next to that, an axe.

Tamara's tenth birthday was approaching and Aimee wanted to treat it as a milestone. *A decade. Ten very hard years. If nothing else, just to have them behind us is worth raising a glass to.* Terrance watched from the sidelines as she set her plans in motion.

"This should be as much for us as it is for her," she said one afternoon while compiling a guest list. *Ten years of sleepless nights, distracted days and family chaos.*

"We have made enormous sacrifices," she said, more to herself. *Like my career and state of mind.* "After ten years, it's worth the effort."

"I guess we've managed to hold it together all-right," said Terrance. *Just barely, though, and we have a long way to go.*

"May 27 is on a Saturday this year," said Aimee. "We could start early in the afternoon with a party for the kids and let it evolve into an evening dinner gathering with some friends and associates." *Hopefully, we can reclaim some relationships and make a fresh start of it.*

Spring tended to be a pretty good season for Tamara, and everyone was of a lighter mood. Aimee approached the subject of a party with renewed vigor, and Terrance didn't want to undermine the mood, so he stepped back and let her go. Aimee had some sense of who Tamara knew at school and who, among their adult friends, had kids around her age that could come and blend in. *She needs friends her age, and I need to keep my foot in the door. So, this needs to be something special.* She wanted the party to be a surprise.

"Well, you could, but is that wise?" Terrance responded.

"It could be fun to surprise her with something that might pull her out of the mood she's been in this week."

"Or, it could blow up in our faces."

"Then, what do you suggest?"

"Well. This could be a good opportunity for some collaboration. Plan the party together. You know, a little mother-daughter bonding."

The moment he said the word, it putrefied in her mind. He could see it in her face. She grew pale and dropped her eyes.

"What?" he asked. And waited.

"Terrance. I… I have been 'bonding' with her for so long we are practically fused together. Ten years, Terrance. Every day, for ten years. Ripped apart between work, daughter, YOU. Ten years of an emotional free-for-all I can't win anymore. And for ten years, you have been finding increasingly clever dodges from fatherhood. You took up tennis, for God's sake. You said you hated tennis when we first got married! You are now consulting for two of your father's banks in addition to your own career. Three Board directorships. And usually you are only getting home just in time to kiss Tamara off to bed, if that. Ten years. Ten years ago, the most important thing to you was to be a daddy. Ten years ago, you made an effort. But over these ten years, I've seen you drifting away from both of us.

"You know, Terrance, there will never be a better time for you to engage with Tamara than right now. She will be ten years old. Ten! I think it's long overdue that you took some personal time and devoted more of it to her."

She was using every ounce of her self-control. They were only talking about a birthday party, but it was morphing into something else, a snake that was about to strike at them. And Aimee wasn't of a mind to charm that snake back into its basket. She was growing angrier by the second, and her thoughts weren't keeping up with the intensity of her emotions which were coiling, rearing back, tightening, taking aim at its prey.

"What are you saying?" asked Terrance, frozen in place.

"Ten years," said Aimee as she held her head in her hands, looking down at the table, working extra hard to choose each word. "That's what I'm saying, Terrance. And I am tired. I need more of you, here, with her. Us. She's getting older, and I'm not sure you understand that." Her eyes were simmering.

Terrance was reading all the warning signs of a fight, and he looked for an exit. He never could hold his own against Aimee. She was the decided master of the debate and had a renewable supply of energy that gained its strength from the contest. He was quickly drained by domestic conflict and never had ample ammunition to keep his side in the battle for long. That was usually because he never saw it coming. Aimee brooded for days. She marshaled internal resources, predetermined the course of a conversation, and planned for multiple avenues of attack. Laying up an arsenal of offensive verbal weapons, any of which she could deploy masterfully depending upon the course her adversary took, she was a force. And in this, their marriage, he knew that whenever she took up an adversarial stance with him they had both lost if he went on the counter-offensive. Far better to back off and add space then find a way to come back at their problem as partners.

"What can I do?" he asked.

"Terrance, I need you to plan this party for Tamara. I will plan the get together for the adults. But Tamara's party is up to you. I can't."

"Then scale it back. I don't really understand why it's such a big deal."

They both felt the mistake he just made. Terrance flushed, and waited out the repercussions. He had dodged again, not thirty seconds after acquiescing to her need. He had diminished whatever significance Aimee had attached to the event. He braced for impact, and it came.

The force of the assault lay in all it lacked. Aimee's anger was swallowed up by a deep and horrible silence. She got up from the table, walked to the kitchen and stood in the doorway with her back to the room. He wasn't sure if he should move, so he didn't. He also wasn't sure if he should speak, so he held his tongue. Then, he worried if his silence was making it worse, and it was.

Aimee lingered a few moments, shaking, ready to lash out. But then, she walked away. Each of her movements after that signaled defeat. Yet, even in her defeat, she had demolished Terrance.

He heard the bedroom door shut upstairs and then looked around the empty dining room. The table was littered with scraps of paper: menu suggestions and caterers, gift ideas, possible party themes. He picked up a list of potential guests many of which had been crossed off. Couldn't come? Or, she didn't want to face them? Those firm marks slashed through the names of old acquaintances and business associates spoke volumes to Terrance of his wife's social and professional confusion. He hurt for her and felt paralyzed within himself.

Ten years. The sound of her voice reverberated in his head. Ten years. Brief glimpses of his daughter's life flashed through his memory, not a chronological sequence of images but a kaleidoscopic mirage of psychic bursts, spasms of feeling laced with visual cues that dislodged memories long hidden in his mind. As these cinematic life moments flashed into view, he saw them in his imagination but he felt them in his gut. Ten years with a daughter that had turned his wife into a woman he never would have married. Ten years with a woman devoted to a child none of them understood. Ten years of a rampaging enigma who turned them all into strangers. Ten years of unanswerable queries from family and friends that pushed them into the social hinterlands. Ten years of a lackluster career in banking, a career that could have been so much more if it hadn't been for ten years of inner doubt over the stability of his family and what he would find when he went home at night. Ten years.

There would be no party. Tamara's psychic collapse, probably brought on by the tensions surrounding the event, shattered any hope they could invite others into the vortex of their lives. They had just entered a fight to the death with the demons that were eviscerating her.

A night or so after they broached the subject of the party with her, Tamara appeared at the foot of their bed. Aimee was sound asleep. Terrance lay awake, sorting through several matters he would be facing in the morning, when he heard the bedroom door open. He shifted to see, but the room was too dark.

"Tamara?" he said. "What is it, honey?" No answer. "It's kind of late to be up." Tamara shifted, but stood firm in place. "Head on back to bed, honey." Nothing. "Come on baby," he whispered. "Go on." She didn't budge, so he took a deep breath, rolled out of the bed, and placed his hand between her shoulder blades intending to steer her back down the hall. But she didn't steer easily. She pulled away, and backed up. Terrance laid a hand on her shoulder and pushed her down the hall. She muttered something he couldn't make out but assumed she needed a glass of water, so he steered her toward the bathroom and turned on the light. There, Tamara stood with the large kitchen knife in her hand and blood all over her arms. Terrance had no recollection of yelling, but he must have, for just a moment later Aimee was pushing her way into the bathroom to see what the commotion was all about.

What they saw would alter their relationship with their daughter, again, forever. Blood was puddling up on the floor, and Tamara was disoriented. Terrance dropped to his knees, grabbed Tamara's wrist, and gently loosened the knife from her grip. He searched her arms. It was her hand that was cut, not any vital arteries. She might need stitches, though, and he began a mental list of the next steps that would get them to the emergency room. For the moment, however, Tamara shook with agitation, and all her verbiage was garbled. Whatever she said was captured by Aimee, who disappeared.

"Terrance," she shouted from down the hall. "Terrance!"

But he was right behind her. Stuffing and shredded clothing covered every inch of Tamara's room. Tamara's menagerie of ponies and tigers and owls, and those teddy bears she had cherished all her life, were dead. Very dead. That is exactly what they were. They were clearly meant to be dead.

Aimee initiated a frantic search for help, bumping from one therapist to another, usually starting fresh again the moment medication or hospitalization was discussed. Terrance was now eager to listen to such options, but Aimee remained pathologically resolute. The years had only solidified her prejudice of the mental health field.

"Don't you think I've considered that?" she erupted one afternoon. "There are days, Terrance, when I would have pumped her so full of anti-depressants she would have floated away. And on those days when she's out of her mind with rage, or near psychotic with anxiety, I would have loved to flatten her out. But I can't. I can't do that to her."

She became introspective. "I'm afraid it would blunt the edge of her passion, and poison the well from which her art comes."

She kept insisting that once a diagnosis was cornered, then the experimental phase of searching for a medicinal palliative would begin: six weeks of any one medication before results could be realized, only to have to rebound with another mix of psychotropic drugs to balance, or counter those now obviously failing, while never finding a cure.

"Their aim is not to heal, Terrance. They can't heal her. All they can do is alleviate symptoms, manage distress, or deaden whatever trauma they can subdue into some purring kitten of a mindless life. Meanwhile, there would be the eternal cycling in and out of the hospital."

He had heard her arguments over and over again.

"I have not given up ten years of MY life to MY daughter just to hand her over to some medical machine."

In her more luminous moments, Aimee had confessed her fear that refusing to pursue a psychiatric approach might border on neglect, or even abuse, and be causing as much harm as they were trying to avoid, but she rallied quickly whenever he suggested they pursue other options.

On the other hand, they were at their lowest ebb, and Terrance had given her a deadline, after which she would have to acquiesce to a more traditional course of treatment. As a concession, he had investigated a few therapists that professed to be more "holistic" in their approach. He made a list of names with contact info for Aimee. She could choose among them, but she would have to choose. He was firm.

It was now Wednesday afternoon, and by 4:00 he would call the hospital for a referral. He walked through the dining room as she was making calls.

"I have six more names to try," she said. "Just give me some room."

He went in to the living room and picked up the Wall Street Journal but remained distracted by her progress.

Three dead ends.

"Want some tea?" he asked her, after giving up on the paper.

"No, thanks," said Aimee, who was on hold.

No appointments available for six weeks.

Number five. When the conversation lasted more than a few exchanges, Terrance keyed in. As she walked around then spoke in hushed, casual tones, Terrance intuited she had taken the person on the line into her confidence.

"We have an appointment for tomorrow," she said, almost as if she didn't believe it herself.

"With whom?" asked Terrance.

"A Dr. Stephen Samuelson. Sounds a little 'out there' but I'd like to go meet him just to see."

They found Dr. Samuelson in a little basement office in Greenwich Village. His office window, small and rectangular, was set five feet off the floor and looked out at ground level onto a Bocce field. His walls held woven hangings and pictures of Gandhi, Carl Jung, and Bob Dylan. A statue of St. Francis stood sentry in the corner, and one full wall was lined with books. There was a crucifix on the wall, but its design was unfamiliar to both Terrance and Aimee. Instead of Jesus nailed to it and dead, he was clothed in royal robes with his arms raised in triumph, extending off the cross, as if to embrace the whole room.

"That's called, 'Christus Victor,'" he said, as he noticed Aimee fixated on it. "The Victorious Christ."

"I've never seen--" began Aimee.

"No," he said. "And you won't, unfortunately. Protestants are so concerned with Heaven they removed Jesus from the cross and nail doctrine to it instead. And Catholics are so fixated on the concept of perpetual sacrifice they can't take their eyes off the crucifixion. This, on the other hand, announces his victory over evil, injustice, sin, and death through his crucifixion and resurrection, so supremely, that all of heaven and earth are re-consummated in the light of his glory."

Terrance and Aimee had no response to that, especially Terrance, for whom the office door was the only thing that had any revelatory significance for him. It simply meant, out.

"Now," boomed Dr. Samuelson, "what can I do for you good people. The look on your faces tells me you didn't come for a comparative theology class, but your comments on the phone, Aimee, did let me know you are deeply troubled about your daughter. Please, have a seat."

After a few awkward moments of situating everyone in the small office, Dr. Samuelson looked at each of them, and waited. When they remained silent, he began to ruminate on his therapeutic approach.

"The mind is far more complex than most medical practitioners want to admit anymore," he told them. "Neurosciences are carrying the day, now, and their findings are stunning. I confess, however, the older I get, the more of a mystic I become about all of this. I've always thought that emotional, psychological healing requires extensive contemplative work on everyone's part to search out the depths of an individual. Our unique inner world is comprised of multiple layers of mystery, life-experience and self-reflection which either bear fruit in wisdom, or psychosis. The behavior on display is often a symptom of something we haven't yet seen, a complex of concerns that would need to be unraveled, one strand at a time. Could it be primarily neurological? Possibly. I'm not there yet, I'm afraid. Just laying all my cards on the table, okay?

"Now, I don't ever completely rule out neurological trauma, chemical imbalances or physiological causes that may need to be treated clinically, but that's not my starting point. What is causing the imbalance? That cause, Mr. and Mrs. Baxter, is the creature we will hunt until we find it. I believe the brain to be highly susceptible to pain and pleasure, and each experience produces a new matrix of understanding, resulting in new behaviors. Those pains or pleasures are received, processed and incorporated into the psyche in unique ways. Conversely, the mind is a miasma of impulses and causalities, any of which could lead towards intense pain or pleasure. Depending on how those impulses are received, the mind can prevent you from discovering meaning, redirect you away from what is real and cause you to completely ignore that which is most obvious, all for the sake of satisfying its own version of the truth. And minds are fiends when it comes to persuasion. Truth as objective reality has no place in far too many minds which are, first and last, subjective in the way they take in data and interpret it.

"I'm sad to say, many medical practitioners aren't sufficiently adept at delving creatively beneath the 'presenting issues' to search out a meaningful path forward into true healing. Usually, most health care professionals are in a rush to alleviate pain. And that, I believe, is the great heresy of scientific medicine now shaped by cultural sensitivities. Our culture has demonized suffering and stripped it of its wisdom, its purpose, and its meaning. I don't believe in prolonging suffering, I assure you, but I do intend to learn from it, use it to our advantage, and allow it to strengthen and shape our lives. Your daughter's suffering, and the pain it causes you, to be blunt, is a gift you have yet to unwrap. Of course, these are just generalizations and may not apply to your daughter. She may, in fact, need more neurological intervention than I can give her. I will need to take time to get to know her. But from what you've told me, Aimee, I think we can begin with a few exploratory sessions, at least."

They were both swallowing hard. Aimee could see the cynicism in Terrance's eyes, and she was so completely out of her element, she didn't know what to grab on to.

"To supplement the psychological nature of our work together," he continued, "we will have to look as deeply into her spirit as her mind."

That was a non-starter for Terrance, who was a humanist to the core and had made a studied, albeit biased, decision to reject that sphere of human experience, considering it no true experience at all, but delusional escapism. His was a world that always had to have a bottom line, a solution, whose math could be checked and rechecked and still realize the same result.

Aimee had stopped trying to sort out anything more esoteric than the daily weather report having thrown off the mild-mannered Episcopalian faith of her parents when she was in her teens. Her drift away from the religion of her youth was more of a family systems rebellion than a rejection of the "otherworldly" which she felt complicated life more than it needed to be. She was a member of the mundane majority who saw Sunday as a day to cope. By now, however, her resistance was so low she was ready to give Dr. Samuelson a fighting chance. And Terrance, to his credit, was willing to give his wife a lot of latitude in dealing with Tamara, so long as they had a plan in place.

"How long will this take?" Terrance asked him.

"Forever," Samuelson said. "This is the work of a lifetime. There will be terrors along the way, some of which could be life-threatening if we let down our guard, but if you are determined to avoid other psychiatric routes, this is what we need to expect, and accept. The result could be an extraordinary life with new depths, every bit as beautiful as they are terrifying now."

Samuelson paused to consider his next statement and then looked Aimee in the eye.

"Mind you, however, our first concern must always be for Tamara and not the pursuit of our own ideals. I will insist that her well-being remain our priority, and I reserve the right to take whatever steps necessary to insure her safety. Are we clear on that?"

Aimee looked down, but nodded that she understood.

"Where do we start?" asked Terrance.

"As much as anything else, I hope to equip you to accept suffering as a form of gift, not just Tamara's, but your own, as well. Think of it as an extended pregnancy with long term birth pangs that bring both redemption and new life. Even if you don't subscribe to the Christian faith, you might consider the Christ-event as a useful metaphor to describe the experiences you will invariably move through towards healing. Think of it as a form of death and resurrection going on in your family."

"Christus Victor?" said Aimee.

"You might say that," agreed Samuelson.

Terrance sank back in his chair and took a deep breath, but Samuelson persevered.

"I know that from a psychiatric perspective this may sound like so much quackery, but the human soul is a wonder, and the more I spend inside human souls looking around, the more certain I am of their divine creation. What a work of grandeur! And here's the thing, this divine wonder responds wonderfully well to love. Do you get that?

Love. How many psychiatric remedies call for a daily regimen of selfless, sacrificial love?"

"We would not be here, Dr. Samuelson, if we didn't love our daughter," said Terrance.

"This is going to take more than your love," the doctor responded thoughtfully. "And your love, by the way, will need to be strengthened even beyond what you've been able to give Tamara so far. Now, I'm talking about another order of love altogether. And, I'm sorry, I really don't mean to turn this into a theology class – I'm not trying to make converts and I'm not trying to impose any sort of 'biblical counseling' upon you folks, God forbid! But I do believe there is a spiritual foundation to our humanity, and I do know that I have seen healing beyond what I am capable of accomplishing as a man of medicine and science. So, forgive the intrusion of the religious metaphors, but I do find they soften the approach toward healing. They make it less clinical, certainly a lot less sterile."

"Go on, Dr. Samuelson," said Aimee, who was intrigued by his train of thought, and sorry to have it interrupted by Terrance.

"I think I was going to say something about this being the love of a 'dying and rising God,' who insinuates himself into our suffering, harrows out our hell, and calls us forth from old tombs of death.

"Our lives are virtual graves where we bury our wounded selves now clawing at the casket lids and screaming to rise out of that darkness and into the new light of life. You might think we can affect healing simply by utilizing our best understanding and research, or that the human organism is of such wondrous construction that it holds its own restorative powers. If that were true, you would need only the right stimulus to tickle those hidden curatives into the light. But right now, your little girl has been dealt an unjust blow she didn't deserve, by powers and principalities of the mind we have no way to exorcise except, perhaps, by taking this agonizing journey, searching and hoping for intervention beyond anything we may prescribe or regiment in her life. We are going to experience many deaths before we are through. But there are greater forces here than any of us realize, forces devoted to her survival that will have to be sought from beyond her, not within her. A larger battle for life is going on, and our best recourse is to surrender and trust that our pain will strengthen us, transform us, and ultimately give us back

more life than it robs from us. If your daughter's experience plays out like we hope, those forces will reach down into the very tomb of her hell-infested soul and pull forth the true Tamara, into the light of day. Do you believe this?" He asked them.

"Yes," said Aimee.

11

THE FIVE C'S

TWICE A MONTH, FOR TWO hours at a time, Aimee, Terrance, and Tamara met with Dr. Samuelson. One session would be held in his office, the other in their home. They would do battle with demons, wrestle with angels, and learn again who they were to one another. Samuelson's hardest job was to convince the parents that it wasn't just Tamara that needed all the attention. Terrance thought that once therapy had begun, he could slip back into a normal routine. He was more than bemused by the reality when it set in.

They began by learning how to tell their stories and how to listen to one another.

"I want you to watch for the five C's," Samuelson coached them during their fourth visit. "As normal as your story may sound to your own ear as you tell it, it will evoke a point of conflict in the other. That's the first C, conflict. For instance, each of you was raised by very different kinds of parents who sought to instill different values. Aimee, I've noticed that as you listen to stories about Terrance's parents, you tend to cringe just a little. Well, Terrance is just as conscious of those parental foibles, but that was how he was raised and he, likewise, feels a bit conflicted when you talk about your parents and your upbringing. Those points of conflict are important because that's where your parental partnership feels uncertain. But that conflict can become the arena of real creativity. That's the second C. You learn to use those conflicted feelings like a furnace to forge new approaches that will be all your own, and they must be all your own, or they will not work with Tamara. Right now, Tamara is the one demonstrating creativity where your conflicts are concerned. Have you noticed that? You are handing her all those openings and leaving yourselves at her mercy. She takes those open wounds in your marriage, weasels in, and exploits them for all she's worth."

Aimee felt the surgeon's knife.

"But you have to create something new now, together, and your conflicted feelings and relationships are going to point you in that direction. Now, the third C," continued Samuelson, "is cohesion. There are parts of your stories that are so in sync you could finish one another's sentences and flesh out one another's images of what life should be like. In fact, they sound like the same story, no matter who is telling it. When you are professionals together, you are a true team. You can read each other's thoughts and discern one another's heart. But in those points of cohesion lies the danger of complacency."

"The fourth C," interjected Aimee.

"The fourth C," affirmed Samuelson. "That is where you want to hide. It's your fortress, and it guards what you value most and hope to protect even at your daughter's expense."

"And the fifth C?" asked Terrance, wanting to get this over with.

"The fifth C is the most important," answered Samuelson. "Catalyst. What were those experiences that initiated transformation in your lives, those events that pushed you into a new stage of life, such that you could then say you are now a new person?"

"Like graduation, or getting your driver's license?" asked Aimee.

"Well. No," said Samuelson. His voice became solemn. "If only it were so simple. No, I'm afraid the catalysts I want you to pay attention to are more likely to be events in your lives you've been trying to forget."

"Why would we want to do that?" asked Aimee.

"Because those experiences drew you into crisis and knocked you off your horse hard enough that you didn't want to get back on that same horse ever again. During those catalytic moments, something in you died, so that, by varying degrees, you could become more fully alive. You came to me describing a lot of death now at work in your family. But you've suffered other deaths, traumas through which you've come with new strengths you didn't realize you possessed until, probably through some suffering, you emerged newly formed for the next phase of your life. You want to be cultivating dynamics of vitality, promise, and hope. Those earlier catalysts may teach you something about what you have been going through and how you are going to proceed in the future."

"I don't like the sound of that," whispered Aimee.

"No one does," acknowledged Samuelson. "But it's how I suggest we proceed."

"What do you want us to do?" asked Aimee after a long, thoughtful pause.

"You'll begin by reflecting on some of the stories you've already told me but going in to them deeper by asking each other a series of questions. Those stories were fairly well-rehearsed, I believe. But there's more to them. I want you to make fresh discoveries of one another, so pursue your interest in who the other person is. Don't assume you know the full story. And as familiar as parts of them are, don't take the stories at face value. Pursue each story to your satisfaction. We'll begin with you two, and let Tamara listen for a while."

Terrance became visibly agitated, and as Samuelson watched Terrance's face turn red he said: "We're going to take this very slowly. The important thing, right now, is to proceed at your pace, so who would like to begin?"

Over the course of a year and a half, one at a time, they listened to each other until they could begin hearing their common story together. Samuelson patiently coaxed more of their experiences to the surface. As he allowed the stories to forge a new bond within the family, he watched for trapdoors into those hidden spaces where Tamara' psychological rifts were most acute and had caused so much collateral damage in her parent's marriage. From there, he would begin mapping the various streams and alleyways that ran throughout the collective soul of their family. He would then help them discover new catalysts for transformation.

As Aimee, then Terrance, went through their family life, Tamara listened with indifference. Terrance became disconcerted by Tamara's withdrawal from the sessions. He felt Samuelson was ignoring her and should do more to draw her in.

"Every time she hears part of your story, she is thinking more deeply about her own," Samuelson explained. "It's an impulse no human can resist. She may look bored, but you are her genesis, her origins, and there is nothing mundane about that. She doesn't know how yet, but she intuits that all she is, and everything that exists in her, was created as she emerged from you. Not that she consciously holds you responsible for her condition; don't get me wrong. But as she listens to you, she is unconsciously formulating her own narrative, reaching back to her beginnings, considering key events, and searching for what they might mean. You are opening the way for her to do that by being honest about your lives. And the more honest you are, the freer she will be when it's her turn."

The intimacy disoriented Terrance and vitalized Aimee. Terrance told Aimee he found the introspection distasteful and was a waste of the money this was costing them. Aimee, on the other hand, had feared what they might discover in her, but as her experiences came under scrutiny, she discovered that the oxygen and light now entering those closed off rooms in her soul was fueling fresh vigor. An odd dynamic erupted in their marriage, intimidating one and invigorating the other. Terrance wanted to clam up and hide after the sessions, sneak back into work, or go for a run. She was hungry for more and found the story-telling to be a cathartic cleansing ritual she wanted to pursue. She would corner him with follow-up questions long after the sessions were over for him.

When it was Tamara's turn, however, it wasn't as simple as Dr. Samuelson had hoped. She struggled to think of her life in narrative terms. In her mind, there was no beginning, middle, or end to what she had been through. Her parents would relate stories about her life she couldn't comprehend. Rather, her inner world revealed itself as pulses of light, followed by shattering seasons of dark into which memory fell and died. When memories eluded Tamara, Samuelson mined her for the faintest sensations of awareness, sense memories, tactile traces of anger or hatred, visual cues that evoked horror or remorse. Into those pits, Samuelson kept plunging them, assuring them that what they pursued still lingered in shadow, longing for air. He was driven to let those lost carriers of meaning breathe again. His aim was to reintegrate the various strands of emotional chaos into a new whole that would eventually bring them all some semblance of peace.

Such a peace would come at a great price.

"This is killing her," said Aimee, after one of their sessions left Tamara nearly senseless.

"Yes," said Samuelson. "We should let it."

As the cabin steward collected their empty cups, Tamara set her pen aside and held the picture in both hands. The faint shiver of the airplane gave it movement though the flames and forward stride of this demon-shepherd didn't require additional special effects to evoke a visceral reaction from everyone who gazed at it.

No one spoke.

"When do we see Dr. Samuelson again?" asked Tamara.

"Not until next week," answered her father.

Terrance opened his Wall Street Journal and Aimee closed her eyes.

"Parents live a mystery beyond all reckoning," Samuelson had mused one afternoon, "and children thrive amid the swells of their parent's good ideas and fretful ineptitude. They suffer the throes of parental insecurities, and they get battered back and forth between indecision and vision, faith and fear, mercy and making do. And for all that, they tend to survive rather well."

As Aimee filtered those words through her weary mind, she knew their daughter, and the sum of their experiences with her could never be tallied or explained by anything that Samuelson had done for them thus far. On several occasions, Samuelson had sought to open up the subject of faith to see where it might lead them, but Terrance kept shutting him off. If they had been religious, Aimee and Terrance might have had a template for interpreting the mystery of Tamara's existence and attributing meaning to the seasons of fear and elation through which they were traveling. This journey, with an unknown end, might have seemed more of a pilgrimage toward new depths of being.

The dark tunnel Tamara had dug out of the page that bore through Aimee's heart, the strange figure bearing a staff, and the menagerie of fear that fled before this dark shepherd evoked a mystery that staggered Aimee. Her fear of the unknown didn't speak the language of faith. There was no beauty in this she could convince her eyes to behold. Furthermore, the "gift" their suffering was to have given them eluded her, and had left Aimee bitter for the experience.

The drawing finished, Tamara's eyes were closed – a moment of respite for them both.

She turned from the darkness of Tamara's mind to the brilliant light filtered through the bank of white clouds outside her window. *Why can't I see anything?*

Aimee was incapable of seeing the Divine at work in any of this, but she was not without a measure of awe. She just didn't know how to translate that into wisdom, explain it in terms of grace, gaze upon it in wonder, or accept it as an avenue toward something even more elusive, joy.

Her vocabulary didn't measure up to all she needed to articulate, and this trip to New Hampshire left Aimee feeling like a toddler looking for new words. The one momentary glimpse of light had come through their encounter with an old woman named Barb. For the briefest moment, Barb penetrated Tamara's darkness in ways all others had failed. And to recall the way she accepted Tamara, and received them all into her home, gave Aimee her first sensation of peace since their flight began. *If that is what faith really looks like, then I need to reconsider my life from the bottom up. Next week may be our most important session with Dr. Samuelson ever. But, can we wait?*

PART TWO

12

THE CATALYST

The immediate chain of events that led the Baxter family to New Hampshire began as Tamara went back to school in the fall of her fourteenth year. Ten weeks in to the semester, Tamara was stable, and her work in school was beginning to show promise. Aimee, however, grew restless. As she looked over Tamara's first quarter grade report, she gave herself permission to explore a few private schools that specialized in the fine arts. One school, the Upton Academy for the Arts, ventured they could consider enrolling Tamara in a normal classroom, though she may be behind a grade given all the interruptions to her education. She would need to present a portfolio of her work which Aimee had been assembling.

"We can't rush this," warned Terrance.

Aimee paced. *Rush! You can't be serious.* "Tamara's grades are steadily improving, but her art is stagnating, and if we don't improve her options…"

"Then hire her a tutor," said Terrance, hoping to halt the argument.

"It's the whole environment that worries me," she persisted. "It's not conducive to an artistic temperament. The whole school culture is driven either by sports or math and sciences. You're either a jock or a geek. Art is purely extra-curricular, and the teacher doesn't know how to nurture real talent."

"We should have talked about this first," he insisted.

"It doesn't matter at this point," she said with some defeat in her voice. "They don't have any immediate openings, not until the fall. Even then, she still has to bring her grades up and submit a fresh portfolio at the end of the school year."

"Those are some pretty big ifs," whispered Terrance.

If those had been the sum of Aimee's aspirations, however, they might have avoided this catastrophe, but Thanksgiving had gone well and they were tip-toeing toward Christmas. The air was crisp with the prospects of a bright new year ahead, and Aimee began to imagine a fresh beginning for herself.

One day in mid-December, Aimee ran into a former manager who had moved to another agency and was recently promoted to a vice-presidency. This firm was planning a merger, which should happen mid-February. The casual encounter led to a friendly get re-acquainted lunch, then, to an offer.

Terrance was feeling the whole bottle of champagne they had just finished over a dinner of roast-beef, brazed potatoes, asparagus, and chocolate mousse as they discussed Aimee's prospects. He had taken the first sip cautiously, but by the time she had walked him through her scenario for the next few years, he was refilling their glasses and toasting those sparkling eyes. He wondered how long it had been since he had seen them in that light. But as sparkling a moment as it was, as they clung to each other in this moment of victory, neither realized what their gladness would become.

For fourteen years they had seen their careers stall unable to invest themselves at a pace that would have brought bonuses, advances, and the kind of relationships they needed to sustain the trajectory they had envisioned for themselves. Trusted associates had taken a step back in case their family situation imploded. Others weren't willing to take risks with them sensing their focus was diminished and their priorities had fallen out of corporate balance. They had burned up enormous amounts of energy just being parents. Now, they reasoned, their time had come again. Their hopes for Tamara, who was showing new signs of maturity, were firming up as she seemed to be entering the early phases of her own womanhood.

Instead of putting small pieces back in place one at a time, however, Aimee and Terrance were overly eager to make their new start a bold one. Aimee would begin the first week in March. Her new aspirations had a liberating effect on Terrance who decided to tell his dad he would take that offer to head up their international division. He would manage overseas market funds in hopes of strengthening his family's holdings in other regions of the world. But they skipped a couple of critical steps on their way toward renewed success.

On a cold, but sunny morning in March, Aimee raced through Tamara's room trying not to be late on the first day of her new life.

"Up, up, up," said Aimee, who was brushing her teeth, already dressed in her corporate finest. "Up you go, young lady. You need to get yourself off to school today by yourself. I've got an early meeting, so I need to go now and won't be able to ride the train with you. You'll have to take the bus. Dad's already left for the office, so get some breakfast and please, please, please don't miss the bus." Then, she was gone.

Tamara didn't know what happened. Her mom was always getting her clothes ready, fixing her cereal, making sure she had everything she needed in her backpack. Lately they had been taking the subway together, but her mother didn't want her to walk to the three blocks to the subway stop alone; the city bus would pick her up at the corner. Tamara hated the bus.

"Mom!" she screeched.

"What is it, honey?"

"Mom, where are you going?"

"Honey. I start my new job today. We worked all this out last night, remember? Now come on, let's get up. Here, you can wear this." Then, she bolted from the room.

Wiping more of the sleep out of her eyes, Tamara looked out the window at the streetscape. It was a little earlier than usual -- 6:10. She had over an hour to get ready. The bus that took her to her school usually came around 7:30.

Aimee slammed the front door a bit too hard and Tamara cringed all the way to her toes. She was alone. She was rarely alone and did not know what to do with that. Her room felt different now that it was surrounded by all the other empty rooms in the house. A housekeeper would be there when she came home, and all those rooms would fill up with somebody again. She dug under her pillow for her cell phone, but it had fallen behind the bed, so she crawled on all fours until she found it.

"Honey? Everything okay?" said Aimee as she answered.

"Mom?"

"What is it, baby? I can't talk. Just about to duck into the subway. Need to catch a train as quick as I can. What's up? Can't find something?"

"No."

"Then, what?"

"Nothing. Talk to you later."

"I'll call you when I get a chance after you get home from school. Now please, follow through for me, okay."

"Okay."

They both hung up but something was simmering in Tamara. One of her emotional tunnels was opening up and something was about to creep out of it. She knew the sensation like most folk know the onset of a sneeze.

She swiped at her phone and called up her cellar door mix. Dr. Samuelson called it that. He suggested Tamara find a selection of songs that would slam the door shut on the dark stairs that usually led downward into a sub-conscious full of stuff that didn't remain submerged for long when she was sliding into a crisis. The song mix was just a quick response, an impulse she had been taught that would tide her over until she could calm down. Listening to the music, she would walk herself along an imaginative corridor, perhaps one filled with brightly lit windows that looked out on a meadow, or sea-scape, or whatever Tamara might like to imagine that would restore her equilibrium. It was the closest thing to a spirituality she had been given, a kind of therapeutic hug from her inner self. She took a deep breath as the blanket of sound encased her and looked around her room. She took another deep breath and put on her clothes. Took another deep breath and had breakfast. Then, before anything dreadful happened, she was on the bus, seated by an elderly woman with giant hips and an old furry coat who offered her part of a bagel on her way to school.

As the bus progressed from stop to stop, Tamara grew jittery and dug through her bag, only to realize she had left her phone on the kitchen table. She pulled out the tablet of paper her mother had given her for her last birthday and stared at the scathing white surface. She needed to shut out the glistening, snake-like eyes pursuing her through her fears and the serpentine thoughts now constricting her mind. Her long black hair hung around her face enclosing her field of vision around the flat paper surface before her, an endless depth of white void that pressed her to torture it with the images now hiding in the darkness of her head. Swamp those images with the light radiating from the page, or drown them in that glistening ocean of purity and peace that glittered before her eyes. She found an ink pen and slashed at the paper until the vice squeezing her temples began to loosen and she could concentrate on where she was. She had gone one stop too far.

Their first day at this new life didn't go well, to no one's surprise, and Aimee came home in a panic. She had lost part of a report due to her unfamiliarity with the software she was learning, then she confused the investment aims of one of her new clients and had to rework his portfolio. Worse, she had tried to call Tamara twice that afternoon to no avail.

"Tamara!" shouted Aimee as she threw open the front door.

"What!" Tamara shouted from her room.

"Tamara. Can you come down, honey?"

Her daughter eventually appeared and stood in the doorway.

"Everything go okay getting to school this morning?"

Tamara nodded, but didn't look Aimee in the eyes.

"You sure?"

No answer.

"We'll have dinner in an hour. Dad's got to work late for a while, so it's just you and me for a couple of nights."

As Tamara left the room, Aimee felt disoriented. She had been off balance all day, and now she needed an anchor to keep her from drowning in her thoughts. She tried her own therapeutic technique for resisting the cocktail she craved but uncorked a medicinal bottle of red and poured herself a glass as she set the table and searched the fridge for leftovers.

The meal was dead silent. Aimee didn't score any answers from her daughter about her day and didn't have the energy to keep digging, so she let it go and walked down the cellar stairs of her own mind. *This should be a celebration, a mom and daughter starting out on something new together, catching up on their day, laughing away their frustrations.*

Then, Tamara stuck out her tongue. Not at Aimee, not to be rude, she just extended it as far as she possibly could and struggled to try to see the tip end of it.

"What are you doing?" asked Aimee. But with Tamara's tongue extended there was no answer forthcoming.

"Tamara? What is it honey?"

"I'm going to get it pierced," she answered.

"You most certainly are not!"

"Tomorrow."

Aimee had no words, she just guttered something nonsensical. Then, "What makes you think that?"

"Scandal said he'd do it to me."

"*Do it* to you? Are you out of your mind? Who is Scandal?"

"Guy at my school. He's done it to others."

"Done what?"

"Pierced things. He pierces a lot of things: ears, eye-brows, noses, lips, nipples, belly buttons," and as she was moving her pointer finger down her body, Aimee stopped her right there.

"He will not pierce your tongue."

"Already paid him for it, so he has to."

"You already paid him? In advance? And without permission? Tamara! What are you thinking? You may not, under any circumstances, have any part of your body pierced by some guy at school."

"Yes, I can. Already have."

Aimee rose up out of her chair. Those bright baby blue eyes of hers were red with fire.

"You mean to tell me you have a body piercing already?"

"Mom. It's no big deal."

"Where? Show me."

Tamara untucked her shirt, hiked it up, and revealed a small silver ball in her navel. Aimee took it in, trying to find an appropriate response but was defeated on all accounts. She closed her eyes and sought strength from whatever divine source might be passing by.

"Tamara," she whispered. "How could you? *When* did you do it?"

"Christmas. I gave it to myself as a Christmas present."

"Why?"

Tamara shrugged, and wouldn't say.

"Tamara? Who, or what, is Scandal?" As she heard herself ask, Aimee knew her class consciousness was kicking in to provide emotional cover for the inexplicable chaos going on in her imagination. She could swear she was not racist, but she did have a well refined sense of social place. She had cultivated it, after all, as a necessary piece of equipment for the climb to the top. Status had its hand-holds, or rather, something like the spikes a climber drives between rocks to which the appropriate hardware and rope was fastened to secure one's self in place. You could continue to climb, but if you slipped, they were supposed to keep you from plummeting to the bottom. Everyone in her set slipped from time to time, but recovery was everything.

"Honey. Who is Scandal?" She was trying hard not to betray the wild things lurking in her mind.

"Just a guy in school."

"Honey, guys who are *just* guys in school aren't named Scandal. I'm guessing there's a good reason."

"He wasn't supposed to be born."

"I don't understand."

"He wasn't supposed to be born. His parents didn't want him. His mother was supposed to abort him, but she refused. Her boyfriend beat her up, so she ran away. She couldn't go home – her parents had kicked her out because she was pregnant. She tried to raise him, but couldn't, so he's a foster kid."

"And he calls himself Scandal?"

"He said it's who he is, so he claims it."

"He claims it, huh?" Aimee became introspective. No, she was mystified. *Why would a kid "claim" such a thing? To make sense of his life? Add meaning to it?*

"Tell me more," said Aimee.

"More, what?"

"More about Scandal. No. That can wait. First, I want to know about this piercing."

"Why?"

"Why! Because some kid at school punctured a hole in your navel. You've had this since Christmas, and never told us, that's why! I should think that's enough!"

"Mom."

"Don't *mom* me, young lady. Tell me what I want to know."

But Tamara began to shut down.

Aimee had learned long ago to spot those facial expressions that signaled emotional turbulence brewing in Tamara, but as parents, she and Terrance had never quite learned how to navigate those storms effectively. They were both so accustomed to high intensity conversation at work it was hard to turn it off when they got home. But Tamara effectively shut it off for them on her end.

Tamara's darkening aspect betrayed a storm brewing, so Aimee quickly backed off. She stood up and cleared the table, kissed Tamara on the forehead and slipped into the kitchen to give her daughter some room.

Aimee fretted all the next day over what she might find in her daughter's mouth when she came home. The morning had not gone well and they all left carrying tension to work and school. Terrance didn't rise until noon and must have been in the shower when Aimee called on her lunch break. He heard Aimee's anxiety when he listened to his voice-mail and texted her he would phone in around dinner time.

When Aimee came home she found Tamara in the den poised over her notepad.

"Tamara?" she said gently. "How was school?"

Tamara didn't look up, or register Aimee's presence.

"Honey. Can you speak to me?" Every question brought the same non-responsive wall of rejection. Aimee left the room, ostensibly to re-group, but the moment she was out of Tamara's sight the mother-bear in her began to growl. She did a quick about-face. *If that kid laid one finger on my daughter, then Hell's fury will seem a bed of roses when I'm through with him.*

"Tamara, speak to me right now." She couldn't keep the fear out of her voice but let her concern for her daughter drive up the intensity, and it came out with ferocious power.

"Tamara, open your mouth. Stick out your tongue."

Nothing.

"Don't make me force you, young lady. I want to see your tongue, and I want to see it now." As Aimee launched herself in Tamara's direction, her daughter wheeled around in her chair, stood up and stared down her mother. Her face was contorted, with what? Fear? No, decidedly not fear. Wrath. She was determined to match her mother's power, but Aimee had had too much experience going eye to eye with her adversaries.

"Now!" she screamed, forcing herself deep into Tamara's personal space.

Tamara didn't flinch. She held her ground and all the ammunition. Her weapon was fully loaded. With a 44-magnum glint in her eye, Tamara snapped her jaw toward Aimee and with stunning accuracy she pierced Aimee's heart with the tip end of her tongue. Straight through the end of it was a small silver bar-bell, and all around it the tongue was aflame, swollen near twice its normal size. Tamara held her tongue out just long enough to puncture Aimee's inflated posture. The moment Aimee retracted her gaze, her eyes began to swim with tears. Only then did Tamara draw in her tongue, and only a moment passed when, just as suddenly, she spit a large hock-wad full of blood onto the cream colored carpet.

By the time Aimee reached Terrance, she could have spit blood, herself.

"Where the hell have you been? I've been calling all evening. Didn't you get the message it was an emergency?" she shouted.

"I'm sorry but I've been tied up in meetings. What's going on?"

"Terrance, I'm at Bellevue, in the emergency room with Tamara."

"You're kidding! What's going on?"

"She got her tongue pierced this morning by some Goth ass-hole at school, and it is all infected."

"Is she okay?"

"No! She's not okay. That's not even half of it. When the doctor began examining her he started asking questions. Of course, she couldn't speak, so she just shook her head or nodded."

"What kind of questions?"

"What kind of questions! Terrance, where have you been for the last ten years? He asked THE question."

"Have you ever contemplated…?" Terrance's voice trailed off.

"Way to go, Sherlock."

"And she said yes," he said.

"Bingo! 'And did she have a plan?' Of course, she had a plan. With an imagination like hers, she has dozens of plans. But he doesn't know her, Terrance. He doesn't know how we plowed into all those plans with her, and how hard we've worked to make sure she has back-up plans she resorts to instead." Aimee was sobbing, hardly able to speak clearly.

"Did you explain that?"

"Explain! Are you kidding? Of course – I tried. But the moment they heard that, they locked down her room, escorted me out, set a guard and called in the mental health team. They won't even let me in the room."

"Okay, try to calm down. How did it even get to that point?"

"They obviously got the impression she was being self-destructive."

"People get their tongues pierced all the time. Why would they jump to that…?"

"Terrance. That's not all. They also told me there was evidence she'd been cutting herself."

There was silence on the phone.

"Terrance? Are you there?"

"Yes, I'm here. I just don't know what to say."

"Terrance, you've got to come down. I can't do this by myself."

"Darling… I…"

"What? You can't come?"

"Tokyo's market is going to open soon, and there's been some big shake up in the central bank there – that's what all my meetings have been about—and I've got to be here to keep an eye on it. I've got no one else to call in for this one."

"You son of a—"

"Listen. Hang on. Call Samuelson. See if he can intervene."

"I already did."

"And?"

"He's too tied up. Besides, he said they won't let him interfere at this point. They have strict protocols, and we may have to wait until she's admitted, then he can interface with the doctor on staff."

"Admitted?"

"Of course, admitted. You don't get it, do you? It's out of our hands. They are looking for a bed in a psychiatric hospital as we speak. Until then, she's here under twenty-four-hour watch. They said I could come in after they did a full evaluation, but Terrance, she can't even speak. How can they evaluate her?"

"Okay. One thing at a time. My guess is that they will give their medical priority to treating her tongue. How did she seem? Her mood, I mean?"

"She was withdrawn, almost totally shut down."

"So, visually, she was depressed."

"Well. Yes, of course."

"At least they won't medicate for psychosis and mania or violent behavior."

"But they think she's a danger to herself."

"Look, honey, she's still a minor. They're not going to take any steps without consulting with you. They may not listen, but you'll have a chance to talk with them. They can't do anything without our consent."

"They already have."

"You want me to call our lawyer?"

"No. Not yet. Okay. You're right. Let's wait and see."

"I agree. Look, I know you hate this, but I really need to get back. Things are moving fast here."

Her heart was overwhelmed with rage as he backed out of the conversation.

"You have a very sick little girl," said Rebecca Adams, the psychiatrist on call.

As hard as Aimee tried, she was unable to explain why Tamara's condition had gone untreated in any conventional sense for so long. She and Terrance had managed to fend off that demon, but now Aimee was precisely where she never wanted to be.

Tamara had finally gone to sleep and the nurses didn't want her disturbed. She'd been through too much trauma, and they could tell Aimee would not be very good for her, frantic as she was.

Aimee recalled the sensation she felt one summer as a teen after being talked into riding the Cyclone at Coney Island by a gang of girls, and how frantically powerless she suddenly became the moment she heard the clank, clank, clank as the attendants locked the safety bars. Now, all she could hear Dr. Adams saying was, 'Keep your arms and legs inside the ride at all times.' The loudspeaker in her head was promising a harrowing experience as the roller coaster left the station. She was now on the free-fall side of that first big hill and, just as she did then, she threw up.

Aimee had faced a sort of psychotic delusion every day she walked onto the trading floor of the stock exchange as scores of people pursued wild fantasies with only the most thinly veiled rationale for why they acted the way they did. As secure as their reality was before lunch, it could change with the slightest drop in someone else's confidence and become another reality before the closing bell. In fact, their actions were initiated on faith in the most whimsical sprites and lofty illusions dancing before their eyes. Decisions were driven by a hidden uber-consciousness; the investor's desires were an other-worldly force that drove the traders to speculate someone's life's savings, or risk another's future.

But that psychosis was sanctioned by a powerful group consciousness legitimized by those who could afford it. Over time, it came to be governed by laws, precisely prescribed rules of the game, and an elegant philosophy called economics which explained, and sought to predict, the behaviors of those possessed by this psychosis. Aimee was a trained technician on the emergency room floor, where an air of crisis often prevailed. She and other specialists scrambled to stanch the bleeding one moment, forestall death in the next, only to change gloves and mid-wife a new fortune into being before the afternoon shift went home. To visitors in the gallery above, the trader's actions might appear graceful, like ball-room dancers moving their partners about the floor, then, frenzied, like punkers climbing over one another in a mosh pit. Yet, as chaotic as it appeared to the onlooker, the choreography of the dance was well known to its initiates. And Aimee knew it well. When she was on the floor, she was in command of every single one of her faculties which acted quickly, and in concert, to control the outcome she demanded. And she won, over and over again.

Before her this night, however, opened the fanged maw of a monster, whose eyes were searing her and whose venomous breath displaced all the breathable air in the room. She was cornered, and in the slow motion, rapid fire manic-depressive pace of these last few hours, she had punched her fist through everything that might open up a way out and let in some light. But now, doubled over and numb, she was suffocating. So carefully had she directed their daughter's care. With the help of Dr. Samuelson, she and Terrance had danced around the machinations of a mental health marketplace they wanted no part of, always confident they were making the best calculated decisions for Tamara. She was still certain of that, but she was choking, and all her instincts for fight were being swallowed whole by this beast.

Terrance finally appeared, a little after 3:00 a.m. Aimee was dozing in a chair at the foot of Tamara's bed and had only the energy to stare at him when she realized he was in the room.

"How is she?"

"Sleeping. Hasn't budged since I last spoke with you. How's Tokyo? Did you pull her through?" she asked.

Terrance winced at the edge in her voice.

"Any word on the arrangements?" he asked.

"She's going to Mount Sinai. They'll have a bed by 10:00, so they'll get her bathed, fed, and a transport will come by 9:00."

"And what should we do?"

"Follow them over. We'll need to be there for the intake, but no telling when the doctor will be available for the initial screening. Dr. Samuelson is trying to schedule it when he can be there. He's already had her files faxed over. So... that's where we are."

"And what about her tongue?"

"Oh, God," said Aimee betraying every ounce of exhaustion she was suffering. "That's a whole other world. Enflamed, infected. They've got her on pain medication which is why she's so dead asleep. By the time they finished getting the thing out of her tongue – she fought them every step of the way – got it cleaned and stitched up – her tongue wasn't just pierced, it was torn. She was just a basket-case of nerves and pain."

"And you said she had been cutting herself?"

Aimee's emotions were cascading. All she could manage was to clinch every facial muscle she possessed and nod her head.

"My God," said Terrance. He moved closer, intending to embrace her, but she got up and walked to the other side of the room. Her face collapsed into grief and she ducked through the curtain surrounding the bed and disappeared down the hallway.

When he was in his early twenties, Terrance visited his aunt Tamara in a room much like this. He felt as small and frightened as he did then. The family wealth only bought her a little more time than she might have had, but it was one of his first lessons in the vagaries of power. He came from a long line of Titans and the gallery of portraits in the corporate board room showed them all to be bulwarks of fortune. But every single one of his esteemed ancestors was impotent against the mortality that would conquer every last one of them. His aunt was, in his mind, the mightiest of them all, yet there she lay, exhausted of her vitality, diminished in every way he once knew her to be so extraordinary.

Terrance was the tail end of that line, and he was no Titan. He inherited little of his aunt's spiritual legacy, and there was no portrait of him hanging among the sires of his clan. Standing there in this room, among the two Tamaras now haunting him, he couldn't imagine staring up at an oil painting of himself looking back on a room full of admirers knowing what lay behind those eyes of his. If ever he suffered a family curse, it was to watch himself in moments like this, in times of crisis, when it all came down to him. As a young, aspiring capitalist, he knew the pose he wanted captured and lofted up among those towering monarchs of his pride. Before the mirror in his bedroom, he had practiced the stance he would execute and the expression he would use to project power: a brow that conveyed wisdom, eyes gazing deeply into the problem, his lips on the verge of speaking the Answer. But since the birth of his daughter, he saw that portrait fade. Unless the artist could capture the look of bewilderment, the portrait would be a lie. There, in the emergency room, the only pose he had at his disposal was that of a man who had left his post. He was limp on the inside, and he didn't have the fortitude to stand tall on the outside. An hour ago, he fancied himself a rock, reading the transactions as they were reported, calling out trends as he saw them, phoning their most vital clients when he had to. An hour ago, he could have imagined the portrait hanging in the corporate board room. An hour ago, he knew who he was. An hour ago, he had power.

He was horrified at how quickly that power evaporated the minute he walked into this little cubicle where all the monitors betrayed his incompetence in those areas of life that are truly human: heart, respiration, pulse, blood pressure. He tried to make some sense out of them but couldn't escape what they represented, a life that was his daughter, a life over which he had no power. He was twenty-two years old again and needed the wisdom his aunt could have given him. As he had waited by his aunt's bedside then, and watched her vital signs slowly fail, he knew that the only one capable of helping him through the experience was dying before his eyes. He was now surrounded by the latest in medical technology, but not a single monitor in the room could tell him what was going on inside his daughter's mind.

Of all people, Dr. Samuelson had come the closest to seeing inside, but he often resurfaced as breathless as everyone else. He had sought to lend them that emotional helping hand and, over time, gained Aimee's and Terrance's confidence that they could manage what she was going through with a minimum of medication. Wherever that confidence had come from, however, he couldn't locate it now.

Aimee came back in, her eyes dry but still red and puffy.

"Okay," she said. "We see what the new day brings."

13

THE CROW

The day was a miasma of waiting, rushing into meetings, filling out forms, answering the same questions six or eight times to different hospital personnel, getting Tamara admitted and, finally, catching a brief chat with a fresh doctor who was willing to help them synthesize the reality they faced. Tamara's chart was already thick, and the psychiatrist had enough data to hint at a diagnosis. While the psychiatrist seemed disposed to listening, she wasn't inclined to be persuaded by a distraught mother who was bent on stalling and obstructing the hospital team at every turn.

"Mrs. Baxter," she said impatiently, "your daughter is suffering from an array of psychiatric disorders that have been compounded by neglect for far too long."

Right through her soul, again, went that word. Aimee recoiled and closed her eyes to hide any signs that her own melt-down was only a few heart-beats away.

"We are not neglecting our daughter," Aimee countered with rising agitation in her voice. "Dr. Samuelson has been showing us those emotional currents in her that are so fused to sub-conscious issues at work in us. Tamara's episodes have that effect as if they were tunneling into our own souls. Dr. Samuelson has coached us to delve beneath the surface tensions and walk through those hidden alleyways in order to learn more about ourselves. He said that should ease Tamara's episodes and help us find meaning in what she is dealing with."

The psychiatrist took a deep breath. "And?" she asked impatiently.

"And, what?" said Aimee.

"Have you eased her episodes and found the meaning you were searching for?"

"Not yet," said Aimee. She refused to release the doctor from her stare, but she couldn't prevent her tears from undermining her effort to reclaim the ground she had lost.

"Okay. I can see you are trying very hard to work through this," said the doctor. "I'll think about what you've said. Dr. Samuelson is coming in tomorrow, so I'll discuss this with him." She paused and became introspective before she spoke one last time.

"Mrs. Baxter, your daughter is in trouble, and she needs help. She is in the right place to get what she needs. We have the finest staff in the city, and we know a lot about treating what ails your daughter. But we need your help, too."

You've been doing a fine job without me, so far. How much more of my acquiescence do you really need?

"Now, we don't work any magic here," continued the doctor, "but I do think we can alleviate some of her suffering. Beyond that, who knows?" Her voice trailed off and she looked away.

You just don't get it, do you? Aimee stood and confronted the doctor. "I'm asking you not to take any steps until we have Dr. Samuelson present," insisted Aimee.

"Mr. Baxter, is there anything you wish to add?" asked the doctor.

"No."

The psychiatrist stood, shook her head, and left the room.

୨

When they got home, Aimee and Terrance had difficulty going in the house, so they took a long walk through their neighborhood. As they rounded the corner, and their front door came into view again, Aimee halted and spoke of a sensation she remembered from her romps with Alice through the looking-glass.

"There was a beautiful garden, and Alice desperately wanted to see it from the top of a hill. She could see the hill, and even make out several paths that went in that direction, but no matter which path she took it always brought her right back to where she started. I thought I saw that garden, Terrance, but I guess all our paths keep bringing us right back here, instead."

"But Alice did make it to the top of the hill, right?" asked Terrance.

"Yes. That's true. She did."

"And?"

"She saw the land laid out like a giant chess board. But to move through it – it was all madness from there on."

"But in the end…?"

"She was crowned a queen."

A flat red tray held Tamara's meal. The other patients said nothing as they ate, so her first lunch in the hospital was all about acclimating to the bland food set before her. There was a lone crayon on the counter beside her table. Dark blue. The crayon felt alive in her fingers. Its pungent waxiness needed to be smeared across anything that might absorb the anxieties mounting within her. She unfolded her napkin but found it wasn't up to receiving the punishment she needed to give it, so her head held on to the fright and fear she was feeling. She walked her crayon around the lounge looking for paper, but it was too orderly, and she wasn't about to trouble the harried-looking attendant on duty for some.

Opening the drawer in the nightstand by her bed to stow her crayon, she saw the smooth flat surface she needed. On the bottom of the drawer, she drew a long straight line then made it heavier still. A hand clutched the line near the top turning it into a walking stick. Then, like the symbol she saw everywhere in the hospital, she wrapped a snake around the pole. The serpent climbed steadily up the stick with its mouth opened, and its sharp fangs were ready to strike the hand that held it.

As early as was permissible the next morning, Aimee and Terrance were waiting outside the large double doors of the unit eager to get in and see someone. Dr. Samuelson emerged and called them into a windowless conference room where he introduced them to the clinical social worker and one of the staff doctors. They quickly fell into conflict over the nature of Tamara's care. They fought over medications then discussed electroconvulsive therapy and transcranial magnetic stimulation, all of which Aimee rejected out of hand. At the very least, the medical staff insisted that Tamara remain under observation for another day or two, then, if that went well, they could consent to releasing Tamara to a partial day program. They were very careful to make sure Aimee understood that if Tamara did anything that indicated she was a danger to herself they were within their legal rights to detain her. Samuelson tried to get Tamara out of the day program, but the staff refused to budge. They would not release her without some plan they were not still part of. So, all agreed, except for Tamara.

As the week went on, Tamara became increasingly hostile toward everyone she encountered. The staff requested another consultation with Aimee, Terrance, and Samuelson. They wanted her back in program on Monday, though that was not part of the original plan.

Friday afternoon, when the housekeeper arrived to pick her up, she refused to believe it was Tamara she was looking at and resisted signing her out.

Tamara had caked her face in gray. Her eyes were starkly highlighted in black, as were her lips, but the tip ends of her dark black hair had been dipped in red. She leaned against the wall with her arms folded and looked a lot like a crow. She refused to speak and offered no explanation. Neither did the intern at the desk, except to say that their job was not to inhibit personal freedom of expression if it was safe. Tamara allowed herself to be coaxed into the passenger seat of the car, but she stared out the window all the way home.

Aimee got a full report before she came home, so she had moved beyond shock and was simmering just below the boiling point when she climbed the steps and burst into Tamara's room. When she came face to face with her daughter, she realized her imagination had not run wild enough. Aimee's rage was incendiary. The only thing that held it in check was a morbid fear. Aimee locked the entire cage of her body in an offensive posture but every neuron in her soul was sounding retreat.

"What the hell…" But that was as far as she got, for Tamara struck the decisive blow. Slowly, without a word, she looked up into those deadly eyes of her mother and nearly dropped her mother to the floor. Over Tamara's right eye, Aimee's sorority pin was lanced through her brow. The stylized pair of Greek letters was ringed round with fresh blood, shining like neon as it dripped down her gray-caked cheek.

There was no dimension of time at work in that room. Whether moments or hours elapsed, Aimee could not have comprehended. What she felt within her was one of those "deaths" Samuelson told her to expect. It would take her months to be able to verbalize it, but in that moment, she knew it to be true. She had no language or experience that would describe this as demonic possession, nonetheless, the veil between this and some other world had been parted, though she couldn't fathom what that other world could be. It didn't belong in the sphere of this one. There was no hope of shoe-horning the meaning of all this into the world she inhabited.

Aimee slowly backed out of the room and with each step ticked off a few possible next steps: call Terrance, call Dr. Samuelson, call Rescue, call a priest, call the hospital. But then, just as she was about to close the door, a fresh option became available: invade. *Buy, don't sell. She wants to push you out, counter sue, and push back in.* So, Aimee threw the door open and charged back into her daughter's room then into her face.

"Take it out," she demanded. "Give me that pin. It is mine, and you have no right to it." She held out her hand. Not a quaver or a shake. She was in a bullish mood and had no other intention but to charge.

Tamara was stunned by the sudden change in tactics. She backed off and looked frightened, but only for a second. Her words were garbled. It still pained her to speak, but she spit choice words at her mother.

"Don't touch me, or daddy will beat you."

The mere suggestion of it felt like a blow to the side of her head and Aimee dropped her guard for a moment.

"That's ridiculous," she said.

"No. I know he wants to," insisted Tamara.

"You can't be serious. Your father loves me."

"But he also hates you. Why do you think he's never around? Always working late."

"Why would you say such a thing?" asked Aimee.

"He doesn't want to be around you. Or, me."

"Tamara, that's nonsense. Of course he does. How could you...?"

"He knows you don't love *him*," screamed Tamara.

"Tamara! How dare you. I love your father. And he does love me. And you!"

"Then where is he when we need him most?"

"Young lady --" But she halted, recalling the night Tamara was in the hospital, feeling abandoned by her husband. A regiment of words were lining up and taking aim. Aimee wanted to unload all she had, but she froze, and refocused her gaze upon Tamara.

"I want that pin, and I want it now." But she didn't wait for it. She ripped herself from Tamara's gaze and slammed the door behind her.

Aimee's face was hot and she had a hard time catching her breath, so she grabbed a small glass from the cupboard and looked for the bottle of port. When that search came up dry, she grabbed the bourbon instead. She wanted to collapse in her easy chair, but there were firecrackers popping off at the end of every nerve in her body. Terrance wouldn't be home for another six hours, and she was beyond her capacity to remain there, alone, with her daughter.

Twice she started back up the steps determined to take back the territory she lost but kept allowing the voice of Dr. Samuelson inside her head talk her out of another frontal assault: "You can't win. And as exasperating as that is, trying to win will only increase the magnitude of your defeat."

Aimee sunk into herself. Her mind became a mental search engine ripping through her meager therapeutic resources for a response. She needed to capture the images flashing through her and hold them still so she could look at them. All she had were tiny bits of data that wouldn't coalesce.

Most of Tamara's earlier episodes were like wild rides through the imagination. The tunnels that mazed their way through Tamara's mind produced some pretty extraordinary stuff, some of which leapt out into the light of day, but much of it simply crawled around inside her looking for mischief. When her psychic intruders seemed to be friendly visitors, Dr. Samuelson taught Aimee and Terrance to humor them and that would diffuse their energy. To fight them was to empower them, and it only heightened Tamara's anxiety or fear. If the images were menacing, then he taught them calming behaviors and meditational techniques that would lower the temperature in Tamara's mind and ease her away from the crisis.

Aimee's mind refused to focus, but she managed to commence one of the deep breathing exercises as she sat there. After several false starts, her mind loosened up and she imagined she was walking along a wooded path, meandering gradually downward, toward a river deep below her in the valley. She could hear the stream but couldn't see it. With each step, her mood lightened. As her imaginary stream became more clearly pronounced in her mind, she let some of her stress be carried away by it.

When she came to the bottom of her descent, she stood for a while admiring the beauty of the river. She crossed delicately to the middle and balanced on several large rocks in the midst of the stream. The current was torrential. Its roar signaled a mighty force of nature and had a cleansing effect. She leaped to another rock, then another, and followed the trail downstream, until the river broadened and the cataracts calmed.

The river-bed deepened into a great, wide lake. Broad and pristine was the expanse of the water, and she scanned its far horizon where the shimmer of the water met the glistening light still lingering in the sky. She invited the stillness of the lake to becalm her mood and as she looked out into the open cosmos, she let go of one pain after another. Sorrow after sorrow, and long sobs of wet grief poured torrentially out of her. The river behind her continued to deliver its masses of water which blended and melded into the calm opening before her and in her.

For how long she stood there in her mind she couldn't say, but soon all had become deathly still and quiet. She turned around and the river was now a dry bed. All its contents had emptied into the lake, taking her turmoil and submerging it in those watery depths. The long, deep breath she took flooded her with relief, and she felt depleted.

She lingered by the lake. Its stillness was soothing, but it didn't last. A subtle movement in the water turned into a rapid flow as the lake receded before her. She was captivated by the sound it made on the rocks and pebbles as the edge of the water pulled away from her. Her eyes followed the ebb of the tide toward the distant shore of the lake. She squinted, not yet sure of what she was seeing, but she saw the horizon begin to stir, then lift. The mounting water carried her eyes upward toward a night sky brilliant with stars.

The horizon, however, was not just lifting, but approaching. An undertow, caused by the receding water, evoked a sucking sensation in her gut. The pull of the currents seized her and pulled her in to the deeps that were growing darker before her. On the horizon, the lake's edge grew up mountainous before her. White foam gathered on the upper edge and a breaker formed. When her mind finally gave her the word for what she was seeing, the whole of her subconscious became visible in the translucent mountain now marching monstrously toward her. Everything in her past she ever sought to suppress was now towering over her about to be hurled upon the shore. Cresting, arching, the tsunami in her mind was set to bring the weight of the ocean down upon her. Her failures as a wife and mother darted out of the deep green depths like ravenous sharks. Their dorsal fins cut the water. Teeth and tails slashed to and fro and countless unclosing eyes flashed by her, each one piercing her with accusation.

Aimee convulsed in her chair and knocked over her glass. Enclosing her head in her hands, she pressed in against the emotional pain but found no relief. Then, as she rocked and sobbed in the ache of profound remorse, Aimee became aware of her daughter. She opened her eyes but didn't look up.

Just a few steps from her mother, watching with no expression, Tamara stood defiant with her fists clinched by her side. Aimee looked at Tamara as if she were another shark-like illusion washing toward her.

Her eyes wouldn't focus; her daughter was the fluid sum of everything that had just washed over her.

Tamara held out her hand and opened it. The sorority pin lay on her palm. Aimee reached toward her to take it, but Tamara turned her palm over and let the pin fall to the floor.

14

An Unexpected Diagnosis

AT THEIR NEXT SESSION, DR. SAMUELSON helped the family regroup emotionally and reminded them that relapses could be expected throughout Tamara's life if they staid this course.

"As far as things stand," he told them, "the unexpected medical intervention was a valuable learning experience. It provides us an independent clinical baseline for this moment in our progress, which is never a bad thing. However, Tamara's most recent behavior indicates something we have not considered before."

He shifted uncomfortably in his seat as he perused Tamara's chart then closed it and stared gravely at the parents.

"From now on, there may never be a time when you can fully let down your guard," he warned them. "Especially now."

"What do you mean?" asked Terrance.

"Well," the doctor hesitated, looking for the right words. "Seems to me some new complications are setting in." His words were measured, deeply thoughtful, almost tragic.

A funereal hush came over them as Samuelson looked them each deeply in the eyes. He stared longest at Aimee as, clearly, he was struggling to put this in the right words.

"Dr. Samuelson," said Aimee, tears forming in her eyes. "Frankly, I don't know how much more we can take, and we've been talking. We've avoided medication up to this point, but to tell you the truth…"

Dr. Samuelson put up his hand to stop her right there.

"I'm sorry, Aimee," he said shaking his head. "But to be blunt, this is something that psychiatric science is still mystified about. We've had

An Unexpected Diagnosis

all our best minds working on this for years, and every generation or so it morphs into something far more frightening. There isn't anything I can prescribe for this that will help."

"Then, what?" demanded Terrance. "What in the world are we supposed to do?"

"You do," said Dr. Samuelson, "what any parent does in this situation. You hunker down, and pray!" At that point, the expression on the doctor's face began to crack and a little light glistened in his eyes.

Both Aimee and Terrance were wearing identical expressions that made Dr. Samuelson laugh out loud.

"I'm sorry," he said. "I couldn't resist. That's a bad joke I get to play on parents who think their civilization is crumbling and their home has been besieged from within. Truth is, however, it is some good news we can give parents at times like this."

"And that would be?" demanded Aimee.

"That some of this may be fairly normal behavior for a girl Tamara's age. It isn't all in her mind. Some of it is hormones which sets off a form of perceived psychosis in the whole family unit. I mean, nothing will seem normal during the teen years even for the most well-balanced families. Granted, you do have other things in your family chemistry and hormones may, in fact, escalate behaviors that would seem milder in other teens. But as hard as it will be, consider there will be times when discipline, not Ritalin, will be the answer.

"On some level, you still need to raise her as any parent would raise their teen, otherwise she will miss out on some very important developmental work. As Tamara tries to differentiate herself from you, which any kid will do, she may take some very unpleasant trips down that rabbit hole and pull you along with her. I suggest that for a few sessions we focus on some normal teen parenting skills, tweaking them to account for your circumstances.

"For now, my suggestion is that you find a way to try to re-connect as a family. Get to know her as an emerging young adult. At the same time, learn to assert parental authority in another way, not as therapists or as friends, but as the two people who can offer her the guidance and security she can trust through the frightening years ahead. Because, let me tell you this, in no uncertain terms: your daughter is scared. She is frightened for her existence and learned long ago she cannot trust herself. What she finds inside her has led her down some frightening corridors. Outside the family, her external sources of authority have all been medical or educational professionals whose job-one is to keep her safe and on task, not help her develop as a young woman. Who does she have for that? She has you two."

"What do you suggest?" asked Aimee.

"What do I suggest? Well, when's the last time you were away together as a family?"

The question jolted Aimee and Terrance as they remembered the harrowing trip to Vale that left them with a form of post-traumatic stress disorder.

Dr. Samuelson noticed the conflict within each one of them.

"What's the matter?" he asked. No one would answer. He suspected one was waiting for the other to confess.

"I'm not sure I want to be away from here with everything off balance like this," stammered Terrance. "What if there was some sort of crisis?"

"What sort of crisis?" asked Dr. Samuelson.

Terrance wasn't prepared with an answer, so he just looked exasperated hoping someone else would speak. But the doctor only studied his expression, waiting. Terrance shrugged and said, "I don't know. Any kind of crisis. We just got her out of the hospital, for Christ's sake!"

"Ah," said the doctor. "Any kind of crisis. Terrance, all a crisis is, is a set of circumstances you aren't prepared to deal with. But you and Aimee have built up quite a repertoire of responses to Tamara's condition. Really, all you are doing at this stage is managing it, with a little adolescence now thrown into the mix. Maybe what you need is time with one another to build confidence."

A deep sadness crept through Aimee. When she thought of leaving the little support system they had she realized just how alienated she had become from everyone around her. Their marriage had fractured along numerous fault lines, many of which were her doing, but the end result was the same. She couldn't see herself and Terrance away from home with Tamara and imagine it would help any of them. In fact, she could easily see those fault lines rupture into catastrophe.

"I don't know," said Terrance. "I'm not sure we're ready for that."

"Well, it was just a thought," said Dr. Samuelson. "But I know a precious little place up in the White Mountains if you change your mind."

"New Hampshire?" said Terrance, almost incredulous.

"New Hampshire," affirmed the doctor. "Great place."

"You're thinking: us and birds, fresh air, little New England village," he said, smirking.

"Yes, I am."

"How quaint," said Terrance getting up and walking out of the room.

"What?" asked Dr. Samuelson, looking querulously at Aimee.

"Terrance doesn't do quaint," she said.

15

TOO MANY GHOSTS IN THE ROOM

TAMARA CONTINUED TO DISAPPEAR INTO the white surfaces she kept spread before her. Reams of nightmares and page upon page of her daily anxieties were bound up in the sketchpad she kept with her all the time. A slow burning fuse had been lit by her hospitalization that would ignite a series of clashes between her and her parents. Her father had once called those emotional uproars cluster bombs because one explosion wouldn't settle anything by itself. One eruption would unearth stuff that would eat at them until it erupted again, and again, until something else in them died sufficiently to end the war in another draw. No one ever won. They all lost, and when they did, Tamara's only solace was found in the expanses of white she lay between her and the oblivion she craved instead.

If we don't begin making some decisions soon, there won't be any left to make. Aimee's internal thrashing was crushing her. The separation her husband and daughter now kept from her was a chronic source of distress. She was carrying the family bitterness in the gut of her conscience. Something had to be done. And while she had little confidence anything would come of it, she reconsidered Dr. Samuelson's proposal.

We have suffered every horror I can imagine and have survived thus far. The distance we are keeping from one another is simply playing it safe and offers no guarantee we are going to survive this anyway. But if this family, which is nearly extinct already, is destined to disintegrate, then let's make sure it goes down in flames. I want to be certain we have searched down every avenue for every answer and used every weapon in our arsenal to fend off the fiends that have brought us to this point. Something is either going to die or be reborn. Or, both.

The next morning, she put in a call to Samuelson.

୨ର

As Dr. Samuelson settled into their living room, he said to Aimee and Terrance, "I want to tell you a story. The Rusty Axe Lodge is owned by the White Mountain Adventuring Club, to which I have belonged for almost twenty years. The cabin was so named because of a rather large axe embedded in the frame of the front door, a striking symbol of a once rugged existence that helped carve out a niche for settlers in the region.

"The cabin which preceded the present lodge had been built by a local farm-hand for his new wife. They were married on a hot day in late autumn by a justice of the peace since the local Baptist preacher had reservations about doing the service. It had been a "shot-gun" wedding, you might say. They were already expecting a child. Her father demanded they get married, which they were determined to do anyway, but he couldn't rest until he had found every means possible to humiliate the younger man and turn the wedding into a display of his own disgust.

"Shortly after the wedding, her father paid a visit bearing enough essentials to keep his daughter warm through the winter, convinced her husband was incapable of supplying her needs like a man should. After that, he said, he was done with them.

"The tirade nearly broke the spirit of this young man. In a fit of rage, he snatched the axe from the wood pile and walked in the direction of his father-in-law. He hefted the axe and hurled it, end over end, right in the man's direction, but that was not his aim. The axe sailed past him, and buried itself into the door frame of the cottage.

"'There, you old buzzard,' he said to his father-in-law. 'That is my pledge to you, to God, and most of all, to Sally Anne, that I will provide for her with the strength of my back, protect her with the strength of my resolve, and offer her all her days the one thing you have never been able to supply.'

"'And what is that, boy?'

"'Love.'"

Samuelson paused, but didn't seem finished.

"And?" asked Terrance, who sensed there was more.

"Well," Dr. Samuelson hesitated, unsure if he should continue. "The tale doesn't quite end there." Samuelson grew grim and looked at the floor.

"The old man bought the farm with the axe after all?"

"Close, but not quite. It was the young couple who disappeared without a trace." He seemed to be remembering something he'd rather forget. Then, he sought to lighten the mood with a ghost story: "Now, there's a legend someone made up, that on a certain night of the year, if the moon is in the same phase (and all that razzmatazz) it is said that the axe drips with blood, and that blood runs down the door frame of the cabin."

"Cute. But that's not the original house, right?"

"Right. When the old one was torn down, the piece of wood with the axe embedded in it was salvaged and mounted by the front door as something of a tribute. That's all. If I were you, I wouldn't pay any attention to the legends."

"Why are you telling us all this?" asked Terrance with deep suspicion.

"Because I think that's where you folks ought to spend this weekend," the doctor answered, "and I felt you should know something of its history."

"Wait. *This* weekend?" asked Terrance.

"This weekend."

"It can't be this weekend; I have a charity tennis match the office has staked me in."

"I cleared your schedule and replaced you in the match," said Aimee. "And, I made a substantial donation to the cause on your behalf."

"So, you're all set," said Samuelson.

Terrance slashed Aimee in the face with his eyes and she felt her face bleed under the skin, but she was resolved. Whether this was love or hate she couldn't quite sort it out, but she relished the moment of his discomfort. However, she would have to gain him as an ally rather fast so they could tell Tamara and present a solid front together. As unbalanced as Terrance was, she saw an opening. If she could help him find some solid ground to stand on, and if that ground could be with her and not against her, then she would have some indication of whether any of this would work.

Dr. Samuelson watched it all with a widening grin. "I'll leave you to it then," he said. "When you decide to go, call my secretary and she will confirm your reservations. They have a deposit and will hold the cabin until Wednesday. There is a waiting list, and I was able to get you bumped to the top, but it won't last. Understand?"

"Understood," said Aimee, with all the confidence of a Wall Street trader. The fortune was at her fingertips, now she had to work the deal.

Her two adversaries were a long way from becoming allies in this venture, but Aimee would set to work that afternoon making her case. Whatever ensued in those next few moments would reveal much of what the terrain would be like up ahead.

When the door latched behind Dr. Samuelson, his exit stirred a ghost in the room. Terrance wanted to speak but was held still. His will to move or say anything was draining out onto the floor. In that moment, he could have marked the end of their lives together. In Dr. Samuelson's place, he saw a lawyer with a negotiated settlement between them, awaiting their signatures. He saw Aimee leaving to join an old friend for dinner and begin her new life. He saw their daughter in a barren, sterile facility with crayon drawings taped to the walls, and large two-way mirrors strategically placed around the common areas. And, he saw himself loading bullets into a gun, unsure of who he would be aiming it at, but certain someone was going to feel it.

Aimee watched Terrance drown in his indecision. She wondered only for a moment whether the vapid expression on his face was chiseled out of anger or self-doubt. Before she allowed him any options for backing out she swiped at her phone.

"Muriel? Yes, this is Aimee, I hope you're well. Good. Say, we're going to take that cabin so you can confirm it for us, right? And you'll bill us, or how will that work?"

During the slight pause created by Aimee jotting down a few notes, Terrance slapped himself out of his ruminations and was on the verge of slapping the phone out of Aimee's hand.

"Okay. That's great." She paused again, and then nodded. "Well, they're not all on board yet, but we just got one step closer. And, I'll tell you what: I'll go whether they go or not, so we won't have to worry about a refund, now will we?"

Like a Viking lord committing his troops to battle with no means of retreat, she was burning her boats on the beach.

There are some trades that you know in your bones ought to wait, and this is one of them. Take a deep breath. The price is not where it needs to be, and the yield will suffer if we act prematurely. She had lost on these hunches but the gains always outpaced the losses, and her bones were telling her to walk away, let the moment simmer. *The price is still too high, but it's about to come down.* She knew some of her clients better than they realized, and all the leading indicators told her their marriage was about to take a dive. *Ride it down, hold your breath. Don't jump just yet. Ride it down, wait it out.*

She opened her laptop, searched for Dr. Samuelson's outing club, and from there linked to a description of the cabin. There was a picture with the axe mounted by the door, and the story to set the mood. *Damn quaint. He's gonna love this.* After taking a virtual tour of the rooms and amenities (*quaint and simple*) she clicked on a slideshow called "Vista Views." *Oh, my God.*

"That is gorgeous." The words leaked out of the stony silence she intended to keep for at least ten minutes. "Honey," she said without taking her eyes off the screen.

"Hmm," grunted Terrance.

"Look at that." She showed him a view from the front porch of a meadow extending for fifty yards out and downward toward the valley. The landscape opened out upon an unobstructed view of the White Mountains, range upon range of peaks and valleys, bathed in a morning light. The foreground looked impressionistic, brightly painted with spring wildflowers. Beyond, extending unto eternity, the very definition of majesty.

Terrance stared longer than she expected he would. *That's it. Take it in.* She saw the difficulty he was having. Conflicted passions dueled within him, but to say anything or push in either direction would be catastrophic. *Ride it down. Don't get scared. You're almost there.* Then, a glint in his eye. *Look at me. Give me just a moment in there. Look at me.*

Terrance couldn't risk drowning in those blue eyes of hers, or he would be lost. There would be nothing left of him to fight this out. But he couldn't avoid her, either, for inside those eyes existed the only life-line he had left.

He remembered the first time she caught him staring at her over fourteen years ago. He wanted to deposit a piece of his heart somewhere in the shimmering depths of her deep blue eyes. For the first hour they talked, she never focused on him. She kept darting from one side of his face to another never allowing him the intimacy of her eyes. It became an obsession to him, the hunt for the perfect prey, yet she would not be the one slain. She would have to do the slaying. She was a woman of power. She would have to become the pursuer, and all was lost unless the hunted became the huntress. Those powerful eyes were all the more devastating because they would not focus on him. They were the only thing he desired. Until he could soak in those glistening eyes of hers, he had no presence within her, no piece of his being could join any part of hers.

Now, so aware of the prowess of her eyes, his inner spirit spurned her and warned him not to look. But he was incapable of resistance.

His glance in her direction shattered him. Her eyes were wide and wet and as deeply beautiful as a New England meadow set against the purpling sky. But whatever Terrance wanted to see in there had vanished. All he could see was blood.

Terrance rose from the couch and strode toward the door.

"Where are you going?" asked Aimee, sensing her plan, and possibly her world, imploding.

"I need a walk. I won't be long."

Terrance walked briskly for several blocks trying to shake away the face he saw staring back at him across the end of that gun he imagined loading. He was angry for not securing that dark side of his relationship with his family as successfully as he thought he had. His career was in a tailspin. His family didn't trust him to keep his professional commitments because of the interruptions at home. And his marriage was over. He had to find a way out of this.

By the time he decided it was time to get drunk, he had figured out three separate scenarios for easing his dilemma and freeing him of his family. He slammed a hundred in front of the bar-keep in an old Irish bar and told her to keep them coming as long as that lasted. But after his third, he let her have the balance for a tip and waved off the re-fill.

Perched on the barstool, he remembered a night about two years ago. He was furious at Aimee for interrupting an important meeting because of a meltdown Tamara was having. The interruption cost his bank the contract he was negotiating. When he ended that call he put in a call to their lawyer to set up divorce proceedings. His father had issued an ultimatum.

He was still furious, ready to have it out with Aimee when he got home later that night. But the house was quiet. Everyone had gone to bed early. He opened Tamara's door and leaned against the door jamb. Whatever had so demonized her earlier in the day had been sufficiently exorcised to let her sleep. On closer inspection, however, he saw she was tangled in her sheets, and her quilt had been thrown off onto the floor. She was balled up and looked cold. Terrance retrieved her blanket and covered her again. As he did, an old promise was growing inside him, one he knew was way beyond his ability to keep successfully. Nevertheless, he could not step back from it.

As he stood in the shadows cast by Tamara's night light, Terrance remembered something his great aunt had told him during a troubling episode in their family. He told her that he had overheard their parents arguing and he was sure they were going to get divorced.

"They most certainly are not," countered aunt Tamara. "Listen to me, young man, because this is one of the most important lessons you will ever learn about this family." Her expression, so unlike her, was stern. "Baxters keep their promises. Your father is a man of his word. And the thing about promises and vows, such as one makes at the outset of marriage, is that the promise is meant to carry you when your own internal resources ebb."

Though he had failed many times, Terrance had struggled to keep faith, if nothing else, to his promise he made that day to his aunt. If he made a promise, he was to keep the promise. It never seemed to be enough, but he intended to continue following through with these two women to which he had bound himself. Both were asleep, under his protection and care. In that quiet hour just after midnight two years ago, Terrance renewed those vows and went to sleep trusting that whatever became of his standing in the family enterprises, his standing with this little family of his would remain secure.

As Terrance now stood on the curb across the street from his house, all the uncertainties he had before were still trembling inside him. Aimee was waiting for his answer about the weekend, and Tamara was still waiting for him to be a father to her. As he allowed those earlier ruminations to play themselves out, and as he renewed for a second time those commitments he had made before, he opened the chamber of the gun inside his head, dumped those imaginary bullets onto the ground, took a deep breath, crossed the street, and strode toward their front door. He found Aimee seated on the couch talking on the phone. When she saw him, she quickly ended the call.

"Let's go talk to Tamara," he said softly.

"It's going to storm," said Tamara when everything was explained to her.

"I don't think so," answered Aimee, "the local weather report shows clear skies and cool weather, great for hiking or just sitting in the sun and taking it easy. And that's all we plan to do, just take it easy."

"No. We won't," their daughter answered.

"Why not?" asked Terrance.

"You're not capable of pulling it off," she said, dismissing them and returning to her smart phone which remained the only focus of her attention until they finally bowed out of her room. To retreat in that moment was more of an admission than either of them would acknowledge out loud, but internally they had each been slapped red-faced with an unimpeachable truth. This may well be the stormiest week-end of their lives. Aimee felt the swell in her gut push right up into her eyes which, when they met Terrance's search for assurance, nearly drowned him in panic.

PART THREE

16

Nanna's General

THE SKY WAS OVERCAST AS the small commuter plane broke through the clouds and the Baxters left their city beneath them. A brilliant sun blasted through the windows and the intense white landscape that lay beneath them burned Aimee's eyes. Terrance poked at something on his phone, then stashed it. Tamara's eyes were closed and her arms were folded tightly across her chest. *So far, so good.* Aimee could see forever across fields of clouds that radiated light and filled an already blue sky with a quality she could feel deep in her soul. *Nothing ever looks this clear on the ground. If this trip could lead to emotional clarity it will all be worth it.*

Aimee put her head back and closed her eyes. She awoke to sensations of descent. As the plane nosed downward the rural landscape came into view. Aimee felt the green of the countryside seep into her pores. *This could be good. Very good.*

Their rental car, a rather beefy SUV with four-wheel drive, gave them ample room to spread out. Dr. Samuelson told them they would need it to make the climb to their cabin. It was quite a leap from their Porsche, but Terrance secretly enjoyed the rugged power it represented and couldn't wait to climb the trail. It was early afternoon when they left the airport and made their way up to the village of Blossom's Rest, home of the White Mountain Adventuring Club.

The GPS delivered them to the doorstep of Nanna's General, a rustic store evidently famous for fresh baked bread and locally produced cheese. As Terrance rifled through the papers to locate the right address and recalculate, Aimee spotted a sign in the lower right-hand corner of the front window: 'White Mountain Adventuring Club. For information Inquire at Desk'. The sign included a coat of arms comprised of an ice axe crossed with a canoe paddle, flanked by a karabiner and a hiking shoe in opposing quadrants.

"Isn't this…"

"You know," interrupted Terrance, "If you say the Q word one more time I'm going to throw you to the wolves."

"Stop it!" It was their first playful moment since they began their excursion and each felt their anticipation relax a little.

They paused on the wooden porch which was shaded by a tin roof and cluttered with every defunct and obsolete farming implement they could imagine never needing. Aimee smiled and recalled her grandfather's shed. *There would be none of that rust or dents or broken handles. He would cringe to see this! All the same, he would love it.* Her sense of place was shifting inside her, and her soul expanded.

"Smell that air," she said, inhaling deeply.

"I smell farm," said Terrance, "and bears."

Nanna's General was the mainstay for everyone who didn't want to drive into North Conway, about thirty minutes to the south-east. The only other business on the road was Tip's Diner, evidently frequented by local road crews by the looks of the vehicles parked out front.

A little bell tinkled and signaled their arrival as they all walked through the portal into a world that was as foreign to them as Blake's of Fifth Avenue would have been to anyone who sipped their coffee at the diner next door.

"Morning," grunted a charcoalish female voice.

"Hello," said Aimee. "We're looking for the White Mountain Adventuring Club."

"Speaking," said the woman.

"Oh. So, this really is the office?" said Aimee, a bit unsure of what to do next.

"Well, technically, the Club doesn't have a formal office. I just get their local mail here and keep the keys to the lodges. They do most of their work on-line and hold annual gatherings up at Lupine Lodge each Spring. Just missed it – last week, in fact."

"We're not actually part of the club," explained Terrance. "We have a reservation for the Rusty Axe Lodge."

The woman went behind the counter and opened up a lap-top, swirled the mouse around the countertop, clicked a few times then grunted again.

"Name?"

"Baxter. Terrance Baxter."

"Hmm," she said, looking a bit unsure. "Don't see a Baxter. But if you're not a member I wouldn't have your name anyway. I see Dr. Samuelson listed for the weekend. Are you his guests?"

"Yes," said Aimee. "He booked it for us."

A few more swipes of the mouse and a printer came to life producing the contract. Terrance looked it over, signed it, and as he did a set of keys landed by his right hand. The woman produced a small folded pamphlet, which she opened up and spread on the counter to show them a map of the area.

"You're here." She drew a blue circle in the middle of Main Street. Turn right out of the parking lot and drive about a quarter of a mile. You'll pass a few houses. Then, just after where Trevor's garage used to be, you'll take a left through a galvanized gate."

"Wait. What?"

"A long horse gate. It's made of metal. It may be closed, either way you can tie it open once you're through."

"No. I mean, where what *used* to be?"

"Sorry. Local habit. Trevor's garage, a large Quonset hut with a bunch of old wrecks rusting out front. Just beyond that. If you come to a horse farm you've gone too far.

"Now. Once you're inside the gate you'll drive through a meadow," Cindy continued. "You'll go about a hundred yards before you enter the trees, then cross a small stream. Great place for a picnic, by the way. Now, you really start to climb and wind your way up the mountain. Don't worry, the road is pretty good most of the way up, and there shouldn't be anyone coming back down this time of day. You'll cross a hiking trail – it's pretty well marked. A few yards beyond that will be a turn-off. Should be a small wooden sign that says Rusty Axe Lodge on it. Twenty yards after that, you're home. Any questions?"

"Just two," said Aimee. "We were going to do some grocery shopping, is there a market nearby?"

"You're looking at it. Most folk go on in to North Conway for major shopping, but for staples and basic household items, we've got at least one of most anything you might need. There's canned ham and baked beans – that's pretty traditional around here on Friday nights. Got fresh local eggs in the case, and cheese. In fact, I've got some real special locally made cheeses. You'd love that on a little home-made sourdough bread."

"So, you carry fresh baked bread?" asked Aimee.

"Right out of the oven. Scones and marble rye, also. Oh. And homemade donuts for the kids." She winked in Tamara's direction. She leaned in close and whispered, "I can dip them in chocolate if you like."

Aimee was ready to settle in so she scanned the shelves and filled a small basket with what she felt she could make under crude circumstances when the woman called out to her.

"Scuse me, but was that all your questions? I believe you said you had another one."

"Oh. Thank you, yes. Is there cell phone reception up there?"

"Not usually, no. But there is a land line, and so long as you have power you can call out. If you need anything in an emergency you can dial me and I'll pick up here. The number's on the brochure I just gave you."

"So long as we have power?" asked Terrance, seeing red flags all of a sudden.

"Oh, don't worry. That's more a problem in the winter with ice or heavy winds. You're in for a gorgeous weekend. One of the loveliest we've had. Just wait until you see where you're going to be staying. It will take your breath away."

"It already has," said Terrance.

Meanwhile, Tamara had been drifting among the shelves, studying the wares as if she were in a museum where she could at last touch the artifacts. She picked up a wrought-iron hook and with it snagged a stuffed poodle by the collar and let it dangle there. She flew the doggy around the aisle then brought it in for a landing in a large colander as if placing it in a nest. She dropped the hook back in its box and found some vintage candy: horehound drops, licorice whips, hand-pulled taffy. She looked at Terrance and scooped up a handful of jelly beans.

"Use the scoop," he whispered to her, "and fill a bag with enough for the both of us." She quickly obeyed.

God, that felt good, thought Terrance. He stood there, his soul ringing like a bell. Such a simple thing.

Tamara held up the bulging bag.

"Take it to mom so she can pay for it with the other things. Do you want anything else? Go pick out a toy, or a comic, something that you might enjoy while we're here." She vanished, and the moment gave him sufficient pause to wonder if it was something to build upon over the weekend. For the first time since they left that morning, he began to see some sense in all this.

Aimee heaped her wares on the counter, along with the bag of jelly beans and a Dark Knight comic Tamara flopped down on the pile.

"I hope you have a wonderful weekend," said the clerk. "If you're around Sunday afternoon there'll be a bazaar just down the street. It will probably feature a lot of stuff folk made over winter, maybe a quilt or two, plus some early spring crops. Kind of like a farmer's market, only with games for the kids, and a pig roast for supper."

"Sounds great. Our plane is at 3:00, so we'll have to leave in time for that."

"I suppose so," said the woman. "Well, I hope you have a good time. Know you will."

"We appreciate your time," said Aimee. "By the way. Are you Nanna?" The question had been eating at her since she first saw the woman, and felt sure by now she would have introduced herself. Yankee sensibilities ruled the conversation, however; only essential information had been exchanged, and enough pleasantries to be nice without revealing anything personal whatsoever.

"No. Cindy's my name. Cindy Briggs."

"I'm Aimee," she said extending her hand. "It's nice to meet you. Maybe we'll see you again over the weekend."

Cindy nodded that they might.

"Then who is Nanna?" asked Terrance.

"Original owner. Anna Marie was her name but no one called her that. She lived on a farm not far from here. She ran a small vegetable stand out in their front yard until her husband built a little shed. When they outgrew that, they moved it all down the street here and built this." She waved her arm toward the back half of the store. They stocked a few sewing things, canned goods, crops they put up in the fall, and then farming supplies. After the depression, they almost gave it up but a few neighbors pitched it and helped salvage it. Her husband painted her a large sign with red letters that said Nanna's General, and the name stuck. No one's ever wanted to change it."

"Did they ever find their daughter?" asked Tamara, who had crept up to listen in on the fringes of the conversation.

"What do you mean by that, honey?" asked Aimee, shocked and not a little embarrassed.

"She must have heard some of our local legends," said Cindy, who looked suddenly pale, but kept her stalwart demeanor in check.

Tamara pointed up to the wall behind the counter. Aimee hadn't noticed until then, but there hung an enormous quilt, pieced together in what must have been rather vibrant blues, maroons, and whites, now all graying and looking somewhat frail.

"Yes. That's the last quilt Nanna ever made. Gave it to her daughter, Sally Anne, as a housewarming gift. And now you've probably connected all the dots."

"The Rusty Axe Lodge?" ventured Aimee.

"The Rusty Axe Lodge. Old legends die hard and you ought pay no attention to them. Just enjoy your stay."

The woman closed her laptop and walked to the back of the store, where she resumed stocking her shelves.

"She never answered Tamara's question, did she?" said Terrance as he sat in the front seat, about to start the car.

"You noticed that too, huh?" murmured Aimee. *New Englanders.* She worked with a few from Boston and she was always a bit cagey about them. *No one is as closed up as a Bostoner. So hard to read.* She liked transparency in people, and secrecy where it wasn't needed always heightened her apprehensions. *Lighten up. You're on vacation. Well, sort of.*

Aimee was too much a rationalist to be worried about ghosts, but she had enough mysteries afloat in her world and she didn't need the "mystique" of an old legend hanging out there in the air. *No, they never found her. Or, yes, she's buried in the church yard just out of town.* Either answer would have sufficed. *And how did Tamara know any of this? Was she in the room when Dr. Samuelson told them the legend?* She couldn't remember.

17

THE RUSTY AXE LODGE

TERRANCE HEADED UP MAIN STREET to find this gate just beyond Trevor's garage which, unfortunately, was not as hard to find as it should have been. *What an eyesore. What does that say about a community that would leave such heaps of refuse?* But Aimee didn't have long to ponder the sight before she realized just what a climb this was going to be. The road was rutted and potholed as it ran through a brambled meadow that must have been a farm at one point. That quickly gave way to trees as the road disappeared into the woods beyond the meadow's edge.

"This is beautiful, isn't it?" Aimee asked Tamara, more for the sake of her own nerves than for her daughter's. But she was answered by silence from a daughter who met the scene with apparent indifference.

When they reached the stream, even Terrace was surprised by how scenic it was (another word Terrance grimaced at: scenic. You can add the S word to the Q word and the sum total is a lot of expense for more than you really need for a good time.) But it was beautiful and just beyond, he stopped.

"Let's have a look," he said, and got out of the car.

"That is simply gorgeous," whispered Aimee. She slipped out of the car to go stand beside him. The span of the stream looked to be about fifteen feet and the banks were joined by a heavy timber bridge.

"Want to have a look?" she asked her daughter, but there was no response. Tamara sat tight and closed her eyes to the view outside her window.

Terrance and Aimee eased their way onto the bridge and looked down into the water. No one spoke and they let the cascading sound of water fill the air around them. The stream was swift as it flowed over a rocky bed. The gurgles and glugs were hypnotic to listen to. There was a breeze from the west, and the upper canopy was as alive as the stream bed. A narrow foot-trail crossed the road and hugged the north bank.

"We should come back down and do some hiking tomorrow," said Terrance.

Aimee realized she didn't have shoes for such a venture but decided she would risk whatever it took to keep them moving forward this weekend.

From there on, there was no way to go but up. The road was too narrow to turn around even if they wanted to, and Terrance quickly appreciated Cindy's assurance that no one should be coming back down this time of day. But what about other times of the day? Terrance strained at the wheel. He grew tense with the ascent but was relieved to find the hiking trail that signaled they were getting close. The road widened and the trees grew sparse so they could see through the woods. That added light to the road and all of them felt their spirits lift. When they turned up the drive to complete the last leg of their climb, the trees gave way to splendor.

As they stepped out of the car, Terrance slammed his door and began to stride toward the cabin but slowed to a stop as the widening periphery to his left pulled his gaze toward the horizon. The vista before him proceeded to swallow him up and rendered his consciousness small and vulnerable.

Aimee hesitated to step forward at all. She had the virtual sensation of taking flight and felt that if the world tipped just a degree or two, they would slide off the edge and tumble through endless valleys. Just beyond their small yard, the rapid downward slope of the meadow magnified the landscape and multiplied her periphery which extended not just side to side but added a lot of up and down, so much so it disoriented her.

"My God," said Terrance underneath his breath.

A steady breeze out of the west gusted up the hillside and they leaned into it. Aimee moved over and stood just behind Terrance, where he shielded her from the wind but didn't obscure the view.

"Look down there!" she said pointing out a formation of Canada geese flying across the valley below them. "I guess they're coming back home."

She squeezed Terrance's arm and stared silently as the geese flew northward.

Tamara kept her emotional distance. She locked her gaze on the far horizon and let the geese fly by unnoticed. Then, in as grim a tone as she could muster, she spoke: "I told you."

"What?" asked Aimee, not quite ready to engage with a malcontent daughter.

"It's going to storm." She pointed north-west. On the far rim of the mountain range the sky was as black as the skillets hanging on the wall at Nanna's General. And the wind was coming from that direction.

Neither Aimee nor Terrance would concede that the darkening sky could translate into anything more than an overcast evening. But Tamara's mood had broken their reverie, so Aimee and Terrance refocused and loaded their gear into the cabin.

The interior of the lodge was sparse but well appointed. The web-site didn't adequately capture how confining the space was, but Terrance took solace in realizing it was designed for people like him. While this was called an Adventuring Club it was, clearly, the plaything of a rather well-healed group of professionals, men of moderation who liked a rugged afternoon walk before martinis, then steaks on the grill. The décor was ordered lock, stock, and barrel from L. L. Bean.

Tamara refused to step through the door. She grew agitated as she peered in and scanned the interior.

Now acutely aware of the mood taking hold of Tamara, Aimee gave her room to roam around and find her point of contact with the place. Tamara circumnavigated the house several times taking larger orbits until she was poking around at the edge of the forest behind the cabin. Aimee watched her through the kitchen window and worried she might disappear into the trees.

On the edge of the lawn behind the kitchen, Tamara halted and stared into the forest. As Aimee watched her, Tamara placed her hands on either side of her head and gripped her skull, bowed her head and appeared to be squeezing and digging her fingers into her scalp. *What is it, honey?* Tamara dropped to her knees and appeared to lose her balance but righted herself then became attentive once again. She never took her eyes off the trees. *Come on. Get up. Hang in there. What do you need from us to make this work?* But before Aimee could do anything, Tamara climbed back onto her feet, gravitated toward the house, then stalled again at the front door.

Terrance was the first to act out of empathy. The last thing he wanted as a kid was to be holed up with his family on vacation. He was yearning for the expansive environs of the family compounds in which the whole clan could dissipate the moment they arrived, avoid each other until dinner time, and never leave the house. He had been looking for that little corner of the cabin he could call his own but it didn't exist here. So, he strolled to the door and stepped out onto the front porch.

The axe was affixed to a vertical two-by-six that was anchored to the front of the cabin. The head was indeed rusty, and the handle was weather worn, but it didn't show any signs of ever being used for anything other than decoration (certainly not heavy farm work). On closer inspection, the butt of the handle was imprinted with a single word: Craftsman. "Why does this world have to be so artificial?" he asked himself, disappointed that the very thing meant to give the place its ambiance was as fake as a bank note drawn with crayon. But why should he be disappointed, or even care? They didn't come for the ambiance but to re-connect with one another. Then, the other shoe dropped as the week's events revealed as much about himself. What *did* it mean to be genuine anymore? He didn't know.

Reaching for the handle, Terrance gave it a yank, but the axe held firm. As he relaxed his grip, there was a brilliance that washed over the porch, a fleeting flash of light that bathed the side of the cabin in a faint, bluish flame. Tamara wheeled around and looked to the horizon. There was a rush of panic in her eyes that caught Terrance's attention, but nothing that developed into outright fear. Another moment passed, and she relaxed her face.

Terrance followed her stare toward the horizon: just swallows dancing over the meadow and the purple mountain's majesty.

Tamara was still holding her breath with her eyes fixed on the distant clouds. That electrical atmospheric aura which an impending storm creates was acute all at once. Even Terrance, who still refused to budge off his meteorological hopes, had to acknowledge the bath he was taking in ions felt refreshing. He always loved that feeling; it relaxed him. He enjoyed a good storm and, truth be told, thought it might be exciting to watch one from this vantage point.

Then, Tamara uttered a deep, guttural groan. She had closed her eyes so tight Terrance thought she might do damage to them.

Terrance placed a hand on her shoulder and she recoiled at his touch. As she reacted, there was another flash of light. The entire cosmos paused and then a deep, low roar rolled up the hill. The rumble had little energy, yet it climbed steadily upward toward the summit. When it passed, Tamara relaxed.

"Was that thunder?" asked Terrance.

"It follows the lightning, dad."

"Well. Yes. Of course, it does," he conceded. "It's just not supposed to be happening at all."

"I think there's a lot more where that came from," she said.

Terrance watched Tamara's grim face for signs of emerging trauma. As he did, he recalled a dog he had as a kid that could sense an impending thunderstorm long before anyone else. The dog would shake and pant, and his mouth pulled back into a smile that made it look reptilian, but it was sheer terror that convulsed the mutt. The dog would pace and drool and whine, but nothing would calm it until the last peal of thunder finally faded.

Where Tamara was concerned, she was more of an emotional weather vane. Her face was a predictor of psychic storms. When her internal fits began to brew, there was a distinct darkening around her eyes as if the light shining on her was filtered of its brighter hues before it entered her consciousness. A disturbing quiet would fall over her and pull the attention of others subtly in her direction as if her concentration had gravitational mass. Terrance had watched these storms brew again and again, and he had suffered their onslaught.

Terrance glanced from Tamara's eyes to the far horizon and couldn't decide which storm would overtake them first, but he knew which one to fear.

18

They're in the Lightning

Tamara could sense the tensions in those around her before the stresses erupted in outward behavior. She could read what lay at the heart of the disturbance and, with a few well-chosen words, she could unlock emotional vaults of security in others, draw back the protective layers shielding their vulnerability, then strike mercilessly where it hurt most. Lately, Terrance's relationship with Aimee had drawn Tamara in where she wasn't welcome. Tamara's intuitive forays into their marriage had thrown him wildly off balance.

As Terrance left Tamara standing on the porch and turned toward the door, a flash of resentment crashed through him. Through the window, he saw Aimee trying to make sense of the kitchen, a setting where she was always out of place, and he thought she looked pathetic amid such fake rustic surroundings. In that quick glimpse of his wife being someone she wasn't, his throat became tight with rage. When he saw his reflection in the window, wearing a khaki coat over a flannel shirt he had to go buy for this trip because his wardrobe was lacking "adventure" attire, his anger turned into an insatiable urge to look back at the axe.

Tamara still stood guard not far from it. Her demeanor was more relaxed, but she kept a steady gaze out over the valley.

As he eased into the cabin, Aimee was unpacking their groceries. She had set two wine glasses on the counter by the bottle of red they brought. A homey cabin perched in the White Mountains, surrounded by a host of heavenly artisans turning out creational masterpieces, ought to be the perfect setting for just that bottle, those two glasses, and a woman with eyes that could still turn him into romantic mush, if she would look at him. Now, for the sake of deadening the anxieties stoking his anger, he would rather have a scotch instead of the wine and be done with it in a swallow or two. He went over to investigate the fireplace and noticed the first fire already laid up for them.

"Did you lay the fire?" he asked Aimee.

"No. There's an instruction guide for use of the cabin. It says if you use the fireplace to shovel out the ashes and lay a fresh fire for the next visitors. So, viola! Want to start it?"

"Now?" asked Terrance.

"Well. It is getting close to 6:00 and I thought it might be nice to enjoy a fire with dinner."

Terrance took the box of matches off the mantle, pulled back the mesh screen and struck a match to the paper wadded up under the kindling. It quickly went out, and he struck another match. This time, the whole room lit up with an arc of light enough to turn Aimee around to see what happened.

"What was that?" she asked.

"Believe it or not," he said, "I think that's lightning."

"Lightning?" she challenged.

"Yes, lightning. Third time it's happened." And to prove him right, the rumble tumbled through the cabin, though any drama it created lay in its unexpected arrival, not its intensity.

"They weren't calling for storms this weekend," she said, more to the stratosphere to warn it to behave rather than tell anyone something they didn't already know.

"I'm sure it's just summer heat lightning. We used to watch it like a light show as a kid."

"Where's Tamara?" asked Aimee.

"She was out on the porch a moment ago."

Aimee went to the large bay window over the couch and saw her standing in the middle of the meadow, tall and proud, gazing out over the valley. Her hair was lifted off her shoulders by a steady wind. Aimee was in awe of that image of her daughter, set against the evening sky, so beautiful in her immaturity, while showing many signs of what she will look like as an adult. Aimee felt powerfully humbled to be her mother in that moment. Slowly, the awe turned into ache as the simplicity of Tamara's external beauty faded, and the intricacies of her internal world were just as visible. There was a darkness to her aspect that cast her every feature in shadow. Where other teenage girls might brim over with attitude, Tamara couldn't reach out, emotionally, beyond the shroud that blanketed her. As she stood on the mountainside, she looked more like a monument in a graveyard than a living soul. Aimee's ache was increasing. But instead of analyzing her fears, she acted on them and walked down the slope to stand beside her daughter.

"What do you think?" asked Aimee.

Tamara blinked and swallowed, but whatever she was about to say never emerged. She pursed her lips and kept her eyes fixed on the far horizon.

Aimee put an arm around her daughter, but when Tamara went rigid and didn't reciprocate in any way, she let her arm drop back to her side.

"You've been exploring?"

"A little," Tamara shrugged.

"Find anything interesting?"

Tamara shrugged again, trying to imagine what in the world could interest her parents about this place. This was so anti-them.

"Not many signs that this was ever much of a farm," said Aimee, glancing around. "Besides, how could anyone grow anything on this slope?"

"It's more level out back," said Tamara. "Old well, just inside the trees."

"Really? Show me," said Aimee, trying to milk anything out of this moment she possibly could.

Tamara's shoulders slumped, but it seemed to be the movement required to shift her balance off dead center and lurch her forward in her lanky teen-ager sort of way. They shuffled through the shin-high grass to the back of the cabin. Tamara indicated a slight opening in the forest that led them out past the edge of the yard. About twenty feet in, there was a small circular structure made of stone, though the mouth of the well was now capped, much to Aimee's relief. Aimee moved toward it, but Tamara wouldn't budge from where she stood.

Aimee scanned the underbrush and tried to push her vision through the trees, but dusk was setting in and the shadows darkened her view. What she could see, however, were trees planted in orderly rows over a level swath of land that sloped gently upward for about a hundred and fifty yards. There, the mountain took a rapid rise upward where the trees were of greater variety and age.

Then, the shadows cloaking the trees danced rapidly and turned color, from a murky gray, almost black, to an incandescent blue-white that cast the trees in a ghostly hue and made them look alive. Aimee's periphery filled with light. Its unexpected appearance made her duck, as if she were suddenly caught in the headlights of an on-rushing car.

Tamara shielded her eyes and tried to bury her whole face in her arms. A loud sigh, followed by a deep moan, emerged deep from Tamara's chest. As Aimee watched her daughter and tried to understand her fear of the lightning, the thud of the sound wave overtook them. It was louder than before, but clearly it emerged from a long way off. As it passed, Tamara relaxed, took a deep, cleansing breath, and uncovered her face. But before Aimee could say anything, her daughter turned and launched herself back toward the front of the house.

After several false starts, the fire was going. Terrance poured Aimee a glass of wine and was about to make a toast when another burst of lightning lit up the darkening room of the cabin. Tamara snapped her eyes closed and bowed her head, ducking for cover.

"Hey," said Aimee in a comforting tone. "It's only lightning." She set her hand on her daughter's shoulder, which Tamara jerked away.

But as the thunder arrived, Tamara relaxed. She slipped out of her chair and stood in front of the couch, looking out the window. Her mom was about to invite her back to the table when several bolts, in rapid succession, slashed the horizon on the other side of the valley. The lightning was much brighter now that the sun had dropped fully beneath the far horizon, and the glare cast over the meadow was harsh to the eye. As Aimee pulled her attention away from the pyrotechnics outside and looked at Tamara, her daughter was shaking. This time, however, her eyes were fixed, unblinking, until the brunt of the thunder slammed their cabin and rattled the windows.

Both parents held their gaze and waited for Tamara to move. When nothing happened, Aimee let her guard down and spooned helpings of beans onto each of their plates.

"I've had it," whispered Terrance.

Aimee glanced at her husband. A bolt of rage flash through his eyes, which so surprised Aimee she dropped the spoon.

"What?" demanded Aimee as Terrance clinched his right fist, bit his lower lip, then turned toward the plate in front of him. His face was flush. The glint in his eyes betrayed his awareness that Aimee was staring intently at him, though he wouldn't return the look. He just stared at his plate and simmered.

"Honey," said Aimee, placing her hand on his, which he yanked away. He stood, and searched for something to help him decide whether to remain at the table or leave the room.

"Can I get you something?" she asked him.

"A fifth of anything stronger than that, for starters," he said, pointing to the bottle of red. He left the table, turned toward the fire-place, and reached for the poker. He stabbed at the fire, again and again, sending sparks up the flue.

Aimee was rising from her seat when another barrage of lighting quickly followed by the slamming roar of thunder shook the cabin. Terrance threw the poker to the hearth then turned about looking for the quickest way out of the room.

In the midst of that sudden squall of emotions, Tamara made her own move and dashed out the door of the cabin. Aimee reacted instantly. She bolted through the door after Tamara but almost ran into her back. Tamara stood rigid on the edge of the porch; her body braced itself against further onslaught. And it came. The horizon exploded with light as torrents of fire spilled out of the heavens. This time, Tamara watched with firm resolve taking in the full spectrum of the storm. Her eyes were fixed, not on the horizon, but on the meadow in front of her.

"They're in the lightning," she said.

"What did you say?" asked Aimee, but she knew her daughter didn't repeat herself. *They're in the lightning?* Aimee repeated it to herself a couple of times then verbalized it out loud in hopes of clarifying Tamara's statement.

"Nanna. And some others."

"Nanna? Honey -- That can't be." But Tamara was resolute.

"How is Nanna in the lightning?"

"When it flashes, I see them," said Tamara, as though she was trying to believe it herself.

"How do you know it's Nanna?"

"From her picture in the store."

"I missed that."

"It was on the back wall. She was standing in front of that big quilt hanging there."

Aimee rejoiced for a moment to put that mystery to bed. However, in the midst of her current bewilderment, the relief was fleeting. She scanned the front yard which was dark now and hoped to make sense of this new puzzle. She looked for signs that anyone else might have hiked through or wandered onto the property by mistake. They were surrounded by land owned by a wilderness club, and they may not be alone here on the mountain.

Aimee stepped off the porch to walk down the lawn so she could see when lightning struck again, but Tamara grabbed Aimee by the arm. Aimee scanned the terrain during the brightest moments of the arc made by the lightning which lit the yard as though the moon was full. The lightning distorted everything she fixed her gaze upon like a strobe light at a high school dance. But it did highlight every physical feature within sight, and there were no hikers, no wanderers of any sort that she could see. Then, frighteningly quick, came the explosion of thunder (which she forgot would be on its way) and with the smack of the sound waves another simultaneous burst of light.

There were a few moments of respite during which Aimee wondered if the storm had halted. She took a deep breath and turned back toward the door when a fresh salvo of lightning washed over the landscape and the thunder hammered it. Her whole body seized up with the awareness that someone was reaching for the axe hanging by the door. The axe remained, but she had seen a hand grab it and give it a determined jerk.

The sky erupted once again in brilliant flame and Tamara wailed out from the cellar of her soul: "NO!" The cry was long and loud enough to over-shout the thunder now pummeling the cabin. Then, she crumpled and fell motionless to the deck.

"Terrance!" screamed Aimee. Then again, "Terrance! Get out here."

"What do you want?" he shouted back at her, throwing the door wide enough to slam its back side against the wall of the cabin. It took him several moments to realize Aimee was kneeling beside Tamara trying to revive her, and when he did, he acted more out of anger than concern.

"What happened here?" he asked. "What did you do?"

"Nothing! I did nothing. We were just standing here talking about the lightning, and she buckled. For God's sake, help me get her inside," thundered Aimee, and it seemed to melt the spell Terrance was under.

They placed her on the couch. As soon as they had wrapped her up, Terrance snatched for his phone, scrolled through his index, and punched Dr. Samuelson's number.

"Damn. I forgot."

"Who are you trying to call?"

"The Doc."

Aimee nodded as she wiped a cool cloth on Tamara's forehead. Her daughter's breathing had calmed, but she was agitated and her face seemed frozen in fear.

Meanwhile, Terrance had walked to the wall phone in the kitchen and picked up the receiver. "Do you think we ought to call a doctor?" he asked, ready to dial if she said yes.

"I don't know," she said. "No. Let's wait a little while and see how she does."

The receiver shook in Terrance's hand. He decided to call down to get the number of a local doctor just in case, but as he read the number for Nanna's off the card posted above the phone, he realized there was no dial tone. No power. Aimee was coming to the same disheartening conclusion as she searched for the lamp and tried to turn it on.

The storm center had overtaken them now. The lightning and thunder interacted so quickly they were no longer paired as cause and effect but resembled the barrage of canon fire coupled with the simultaneous bursting of shells, firestorms erupting wherever the ordinance chose to detonate. In their panic over Tamara, the thunder stopped registering, but now the salvos were beating their nerves into submission.

Terrance slammed the phone back on the receiver. It was just one more thing in a growing string of screw-ups Aimee had been piling up ever since she forced this fiasco upon them so determined to haul them up here to the top of nowhere. And, for what? To heal? Great day in the morning, he thought. If this is what healing looked like, he'd rather keep slogging through the illness. He stormed over to the fireplace, snatched up the poker, and thrust it into the heart of the fire, restoring the blaze to a full roar, casting another spectrum of light across the cabin. The fire's orange hue should have added warmth to their surroundings, but the dancing flames gave the room another source of menacing shadows to play tricks on their fragile minds.

As he winced from another shock of lightning, Terrance thought he saw movement in the hall; two figures were walking toward the bedroom. As the thunder rattled the windows, he charged down the hall to rummage through one of the closets where he thought he saw a flashlight earlier. Emerging from the hall to another barrage he cursed the heavens, cursed his family, and cursed himself for letting down his guard and getting himself trapped in this disaster. His frustration toward Aimee increased with each course of lightning until he was incandescent with rage. He was done. He stared at her for only a moment then made a sharp turn toward the hall.

"Where are you going?" asked Aimee.

"To pack. We're out of here. Let's go. We can pick up the pieces of this back home."

"Honey," started Aimee, but the lightning barely beat the thunder to the punch, jolting the house to the foundations. Or was that Terrance slamming the bedroom door?

As Terrance entered the room a spasm of light revealed someone sitting on the bed. But his mind no longer absorbed external data. He slapped it down as one more irrational seismic event in a long chain of psychological melt-downs. He threw all his weight into the door, not caring if it was infantile behavior. He had to shut something out.

Aimee had found some matches and lit one of the oil lamps hanging on the wall. Out of the corner of her eye, in the corona of light filling the window, Aimee saw her husband lunging toward her with the axe raised above his head. Terrance's eyes were on fire. Every muscle in his chest and shoulders focused the blow aimed at her. She was sure that if the lightning flash had lingered she would have seen him swing it with all his strength through the window. Though her mind understood it to be an illusion cast by the lightning, she couldn't stop her impulsive scream.

Aimee's scream roused Tamara, who wrestled herself off the couch, looked at her mom for only a moment, then hurled herself out the door into the storm. But as Aimee tried to follow, her path was cut off by Terrance who refused to let her out of the cabin. He grabbed her tight by the arm and spun her around so he could look her in the eyes, which were now made of coal, black and stony, and caked with fear. It was as a mother, however, not as a wife that she acted. She pushed by him and ran from the cabin to chase down her daughter.

As Aimee stepped on to the porch, Tamara was rounding the side of the cabin and vanished out of sight. Aimee pursued her but wasn't fast enough to see where Tamara went. She circumnavigated the cabin with no sign of her daughter. As she turned the corner, the yard lit up, casting Terrance in sharp relief coming in her direction wildly swinging the axe. Aimee froze. Determined to stand down the mirage, she waited for the image to recede, but when the darkness resumed, the image was not some ephemeral phantom but her husband, fully armed to do her harm.

"Terrance!" Aimee turned to run back around the house, but as she did another fireball lit the night ablaze. Just a few yards ahead of her, Aimee could see her daughter emerging from the old well, pulling herself up and out. Tamara was struggling to slam shut the cover, but was fighting something else trying to follow her out. The darkness flashed back as the light vanished, but it had scorched Aimee's eyes with demonic intensity, scoring an image on the backs of her retinas she could still see in vivid detail.

At the next splash of light, Aimee glanced over her shoulders hoping to clarify the spectral image illuminated near the mouth of the well, but Terrance was still right behind her. Aimee passed through the back yard and was about to turn again toward the front of the cabin when she thought she saw Tamara, but had no trust in what her eyes were telling her. Yet, as Terrance was about to pass her, Tamara grabbed a log from the pile by the porch.

Terrance never saw her, but the force of the log across his shoulder blades sent him lunging forward, launching the axe from his hands, just as the sky lit up every detail of what happened next. As Terrance lifted his head, the lightning showed Aimee sprawled on the lawn just a few feet away from him, the head of the axe firmly lodged in her skull.

"Aimee!" he shouted as the realization of what he had done was eclipsed by the lightning which illuminated new horror within him.

"What!" shouted Aimee, who stood over him with the axe. But Terrance had dug his face deep into the sod and wrapped his arms over the back of his head to shield him from whatever reality awaited him.

Tamara stood at the corner of the yard. Her eyes were fixed on the sloping meadow that stretched before the cabin, waiting for the next round of lightning. Aimee walked over and stepped up on to the porch, axe still in hand.

"Honey," Aimee said to Tamara, "come on back inside. We're leaving."

"We can't," answered Tamara.

"We have to, honey."

Still cradling the axe, Aimee walked toward the door. As she opened it, she turned slowly toward her daughter. "Honey, come on now, let's go."

But Tamara remained still. Her eyes were fixed on the yard in front of her. Aimee paused, and for a moment both breathed in the only stillness they had known all evening. The slightest flicker of lingering light dusted the landscape with a sprinkle of glow but revealed nothing. They both held their breath and let the low droning rumble of thunder, now coming from the other side of the mountain, pass through them and disappear in the valley far below.

Aimee glanced over and saw Terrance seated on the ground. His head was buried beneath his knees. He rocked to and fro, deeply agitated. She turned back to Tamara.

"What do you mean, we can't?" she asked.

"The storm's not over."

Aimee stepped off the porch. There were now a few stars emerging on the distant horizon, and the air felt pure. She stood almost an equal distance between her daughter and husband, and as the quiet of the night deepened, a surging awareness that her daughter was right clawed at her. The storm was not over. Though the meteorological phenomenon they just experienced had passed them by, Aimee felt her consciousness had become an old silent picture house as a series of staccato silvery images jerked back and forth before her eyes, too fast for the reality they intended to portray. Yet, the pictures in her mind were as vivid as the digital display on her computer. She couldn't piece them back together, and the harder she tried, the more rapidly they faded, as do most dreams. Yet, amongst the swirl of images the one that stood out was the vision of Tamara emerging from the well. During that second backward glance, the well-cap lay on the ground. *Had Tamara failed to subdue her pursuer? Whatever it was, where is it now?* The images of the well held a symbolic value she wanted to wrap her fist around and shake in hopes of loosening up its meaning.

The old symbols and metaphors they had constructed to explain their lives had lost their elasticity and couldn't stretch enough to contain the experiences of this night. Their family had been running along psychic alleyways that had become hopelessly mazed and knotted back upon themselves. She and her daughter had long been lost behind a shattered looking glass with no way to get back home. Those images were navigable because they emerged from Aimee's childhood fantasy, but Aimee knew another threshold had been passed, another realm entered. She had no time to process it, however.

Her conscious mind didn't kick into gear before instinct acted first. Her palm landed on the butt of the axe handle and gripped hold of it in the same instance she caught Terrance's approach out of the corner of her eye. She had it hefted and cradled in both hands before Terrance realized she wasn't acting in self-defense but had taken a determined step in his direction, landing herself between him and Tamara.

"Wait!" He threw up his arms in surrender, and froze. "Look. I… don't know what that was all about. It was insane. I know that. But I have no idea what just happened."

"You came at me with an axe! No. Don't you take another step," she screamed, halting any additional advance on his part. He quickly obeyed, though neither could imagine what a next step might look like for either one of them. Aimee was just as glad to let the stalemate linger.

"Aimee," said Terrance, and they both let her name hang out there in the air between them. He was paralyzed in a no-man's land that lay between hostile forces, but he couldn't fathom which side he belonged to. Behind him was a fiend that wielded an axe at the only person he had ever known for certain that he loved. In front of him was a wife having second thoughts about remaining a wife, holding an axe, ready to sever every bond between them. Beyond her stood a daughter who had been backing away from him for years. What sort of fiend were they now staring at? He could no longer see himself in their lives. The lightning had clarified what they had been hiding from one another, and now it was all too clear.

Yet these two people had laid claim to him, heart and soul, and in them lay the missing link, submerged deep beneath the psychic shell of their collective lives, a maze of interlacing synapses that fired back and forth across this matrix called, family. The relief he felt seeing Aimee standing there and not sprawled on the lawn, albeit with an axe cocked and ready to fire, was having a cascading effect on his entire emotional framework which was quickly beginning to buckle. His earlier flashes of murderous anger were answered by the thunderous good news that he had not killed her as he knew he had every intention of doing.

Aimee couldn't see his face. The moon now casting its warmth helped her make out his basic shape but it wasn't light enough for her to make eye contact or gauge Terrance's state of mind. As she wrestled through a bout of indecision, she was unaware of Tamara walking toward her. Tamara came alongside her mother and laid a hand on the axe handle.

Aimee clinched it tighter, purely on impulse, but Tamara gave it a jerk and told her to let go. Inexplicably, she did.

Aimee paled with terror as Tamara walked the axe over to her father. Tamara thrust it at Terrance; she didn't give him a choice. She pushed it on him such that he either grabbed it, or it would land on his feet.

Holding the axe at arm's length as if it might explode in his hands, Terrance's immediate impulse was to turn and hurl it with all his might into the brush at the edge of the yard. But then he saw the log Tamara had cold-cocked him with. He hefted the axe and retrieved the wood, then he walked to the porch, aligned the edge of the axe head in the notch from which it came, and drove it home.

As Terrance drifted into the cabin, Tamara lingered on the porch watching the yard as intently as before. She was still on her guard, still awaiting each new moment for what it might hurl at them. Aimee waited but didn't intercede, watched, but didn't want to interrupt. This was different from the emotional episodes that had previously overtaken her daughter. There was now a quality of wakefulness that Aimee had never seen before. On other occasions, Tamara would act as if the world around her had taken a different shape, or as if she existed in another dimension of time and place. But now she resembled an Irish Setter on point with a heightened awareness of her surroundings. Every sense was absorbing information.

"What did you see?" Aimee asked, now taking her daughter's experience very seriously. She had to wait out the answer, but the moments that passed between mother and daughter would begin to cast their relationship in a different mold.

"Nanna's daughter."

"Nanna's daughter?"

"She was cuddling a baby, over there."

"Go on," Aimee encouraged him after a long pause.

"And an old man. He walked over to her and shoved her."

Aimee wondered whether the extended breaks in the narrative represented the gaps between the lightning.

"Then he grabbed her, by the shoulder. He was shaking her, as if he was trying to get her to drop the baby."

From behind, Aimee lightly rested her hands upon Tamara's shoulders, and when the touch wasn't rejected, she tightened her hold on her daughter.

"Go on."

"During another flash, he was shaking her so hard the baby was slipping out of her arms. And then, then he raised his fist."

After several moments, Aimee asked, "Was that all?"

"I guess that's when I fell."

Aimee was finishing the scene in her own mind, watching the old man bringing his fist down violently upon the woman. *No. This storm is not over.*

19

An Unexpected Meeting

Terrance spent their first night in the cabin on the couch fighting for sleep, but the morning light through the big bay window persuaded him to let it go. He arose to the residue of heinous dreams which kept stabbing at him, multiplying the ravenous shame he felt as his mind flashed back to the night's events. Fleeting pictures ricocheted through his mind. The person he saw moving toward the bedroom with Aimee now had a face and a name. Vivid scenes of Aimee's infidelity were choking him, and as he watched them spark in his mind again and again he felt the bile rising in him. The taste of all that anger throbbed in his head like a terrific hangover. The cabin was cold, so he went over to the kitchen to put on some coffee, but there was still no power. He went to the door and found it ajar. Had they been that disoriented?

Terrance stepped out on to the porch and found the morning air brisk. The valley beneath him appeared impressionistic, every edge was softened by wisps of clouds trying to wake up and climb into their appointed heights. The grass glistened under its moistened blanket of dew, and the world around him dripped wet with new birth. The sun's influence was still only suggestive. It would have a ways to rise before cresting the mountain behind them, but even the soft gray of the dawn was a relief compared with the violent bursts of light from the night before. The axe, though hanging at a slightly different angle now, kept its vigil by the door.

He decided to walk for a while. By the time he got back, they would drive down the mountain for breakfast and see about having the power restored. He followed the road back to the hiking trail then paused to consider his direction, but the breeze through the canopy lifted his eyes and dropped him back into himself. He was trying not to think since that only led to more guilt and a burgeoning fear of having to look Aimee in the eyes by the light of day. He was not conditioned to see the wilderness as a peaceful place. Being a child of the city, he found solace in places crowded with people of purpose, like the financial district, or even Times Square, where the lights and converging streets brought humanity crashing together. There, he felt shoulder to shoulder with the Mystery of Life, that shadow side of the human race that grew more inexplicable with each passing year.

Yet here, in the woods, Terrance couldn't climb out of himself, and he became agitated as the sounds of the wind and awakening birds pressed in upon him. He set a measured, cautious pace on the trail that sloped gently downward and rounded slightly leftward. There weren't many sights that caught his eye. The vigor of the walk was what he needed most, and he was glad that the terrain wasn't too challenging. He wanted to break into a jog but was too unsure of the trail. Perhaps on the way back up.

As the trail leveled off, he met the stream, and with the help of a small footbridge, the trail took him to the other side. To his left ran a barbed wire fence around a pasture that had become overgrown. The stream was widening out on his right and growing deeper. As he strode by the pasture, he almost ran into a gentleman climbing up from the bank. After apologizing for startling Terrance, the man introduced himself as Tobias Fletcher. *Reverend* Tobias Fletcher.

"And you might be Mr. Baxter?" said the reverend, startling Terrance, who still had difficulty acclimating to the stifling atmosphere of a small town and its ways.

"My neighbor runs the General," said Tobias, as if that was the only piece of the puzzle Terrance needed to explain his sudden notoriety in town.

"Ah," said Terrance, faking understanding as best he could.

"Enjoying your stay?"

"Ah. Well, we're still getting settled. Last night's storm…"

"Quite a boomer, wasn't she! Man, alive. Rattled our cages here in the valley. Can't imagine what it might have been like up on the mountain. Everything okay?"

"Power's out."

"Oh. Yeah. Well, it may take a little while to get that back." The man looked embarrassed for the family's inconvenience and turned away. "Say," he continued, lifting his tone and hoping to salvage the mood. "We're having a baptism at the ten o'clock service this morning. We sure would love to welcome you and your family to join us."

Another bolt of lightning. Years of animus toward organized religion just flashed through the darker parts of Terrance's soul. Again, he was completely out of his element.

"A baptism?" was all he could think to say.

"Right here in the creek," said reverend Fletcher. "Come look." The man beckoned Terrance to follow him a few feet back up the trail to a small clearing in the undergrowth on the bank. There was a granite stairway that led down to a pool fashioned in the stream.

"We'll start the service down at the church, on Main Street-- it's just about a hundred yards through there," he said pointing down the path in the direction Terrance had been walking. "Then we'll come and gather here. Four young disciples starting their walk with the Lord this morning!" The man was proud, like a new poppa, and grew expansive as he anticipated the day before him.

"Wait," said Terrance. "It's Saturday. You have your baptisms on a Saturday?"

"Course we do," said the preacher, now growing teacherly in his demeanor. "We're Seventh Day Baptists. The Baptist part I'm sure you know all about," he said, more to himself, "but Saturday is the true Sabbath, not Sunday. The Seventh day of the week, not the first. So, we do it more like the Bible says we ought to. We rest in the Lord today so we can rise up and serve him in the morning."

This conversation had swelled way beyond Terrance's ability to navigate it, so he availed himself of a useful tool that usually worked around the office. He said nothing. The meeting was over, and he wasn't going to lay any more fuel on the fire, just let it burn out. But the man was a preacher, after all, so it took him a while longer than Terrance's busy associates, who were usually just as glad to let a meeting burn out as he was. Then, at last came the pause Terrance felt he could exploit to ease his way back up the path. But, here in the woods of rural New Hampshire, his timing was way out of sync.

"You look troubled, son."

Terrance stiffened internally, and he could feel his face go flush. He met the other man's eyes and looked away too fast not to betray himself. The preacher took a pastoral step into Terrance's personal space, and though every impulse screamed retreat, Terrance resisted backing away. Executives don't back away, or down. Normally, he would push back with a cold hard stare, but he felt the minister's eyes reaching for his own. He wanted Terrance to look him in the eyes, and Terrance feared the intimacy would be too revelatory to them both. Terrance didn't want the reverend to look inside him, and he didn't want to face what the preacher might see in there. So, they allowed the stalemate to erode any chance of further conversation and become unwinnable for either.

"I see," said the preacher, who then looked back toward the water. "Well, I do hope you folks enjoy your stay."

"Thanks," said Terrance, relieved the man let go his hold on him. But the man hadn't let go.

"I'll pray for you, and your family."

Terrance caught himself before saying, 'No thanks; I can manage well enough on my own.' He wasn't in Times Square, and this man wasn't a street-corner fundamentalist fire-thrower. In fact, what caught him off guard was just how sincere the man seemed to be in offering his services in that way. So, he nodded, hoping to convey some appreciation, conflicted as he was, without re-engaging the man in any further conversation.

"There is a savior for you, too, Mr. Baxter. And it doesn't always have to be yourself. Well. God bless you, now." The man bent over to pick up an old pair of pruning shears and took the path back into the village.

Terrance pivoted in the other direction then halted and looked back down the bank, now freshly cleared of underbrush. Inexplicably, the pool fascinated him, along with the whole notion of baptism and religious washing. What simplistic beings these people must be, he thought, to gather in this spot just a few hours from now and do something they held to be so holy.

What can wash away my sins? Nothing but the blood of Jesus: Terrance heard again the words of a hymn from a youth revival he was forced to attend as a child. He had spent two weeks with his grandparents on his mother's side in upstate New York while his parents vacationed on Martha's Vineyard. They had seized this as their opportunity to "do right" by the boy and get him saved. A young, white-suited evangelist, not much older than he was at the time, spoke much too intimately of hell for Terrance to believe the preacher could have anything real to say about life. So, when the call to come forward to accept Jesus finally arrived, Terrance felt nothing but revulsion. "Be baptized or be burned!" shouted the young man, behind whom was a large pool in a little alcove at the front of the church. A white curtain had been pulled back to reveal the water and a large mural of a desert scene with a few palm trees. "Wash yourselves now, or wish you had later!" The words hit the congregation like a jack-hammer. The choir hummed the tune of the hymn in the back-ground until the chorus rolled around again then they punctuated the preacher's proclamation with: "Nothing but the blood of Jesus."

It was a harsh and uninviting mystery to him. He felt cruelly taunted by the scene he imagined would unfold later on: twenty or thirty hymn-singing fools, thinking something sacred has taken hold of the four who will be immersed in the bitter cold waters of this mountain stream. What "Vulcan Mind Meld" will the old preacher have worked on them to think they could rise from the waters with their souls washed clean of all their mistakes and all their guilt? They must live pretty simple lives to begin with if their sins are as easily dealt with as that. Must not have all that much to forgive. He could almost envy them their relief, if relief is what they would be feeling. But what kind of lies would he have to tell himself to pull off such a spiritual charade as that?

As he watched the stream, a bull-frog belched then plunged in sending circular ripples to the banks. He followed its trajectory to see where the frog would emerge, but it never did. He imagined a long, muscular black snake watching a few feet away, patient for his prey, silently streaming its liquid body down the bank and pouring itself into the water without ripple or sound molding its body to flow of the creek. Unlike the frog, thrashing against the water with efficient but self-defeating webbed feet, the snake would glide along, as one with the current, a slender wraith whose mind and body were set to strike like lightni---

There is a savior for you, too. The words of the old man flashed through his mind. He had had enough illusion in a twelve-hour period to last him a life-time. It was time he climbed back up the mountain of reality to face what was waiting for him at the top.

As he emerged from the trail, Terrance found Aimee gently rocking in the porch swing looking out over the valley which still lay in a mist. She was wrapped in the down comforter from her bed. He had hoped to work out a strategy for re-entry by the time he reached the cabin, but the trail wasn't quite long enough for that. He figured they would still be asleep, but Aimee had already staked out a defensive position. She owned the field now, so Terrance would have to negotiate with her for every step forward he was about to take.

He waited for her to speak. Then, he found himself simply waiting for her to look at him. But if he had entered her field of consciousness, then she didn't betray any awareness of him. Having spent a life playing power games, he had never met anyone who possessed such mastery of the sport as Aimee. Those eyes could knock the legs from under giants, stoke heroic strength in the timid, or simply deny one existence as she emptied a person of purpose in a conversation. Not for a moment did Terrance interpret her silence as defeat, or weakness, or even avoidance. He was completely disarmed.

The breeze picked up, and as it was rising from a still sleepy valley it had a bite to it. The warmth of Terrance's exertion had cooled, so he crossed his arms and pulled himself in tight against the chill.

"Here," said Aimee, opening the comforter and making room on the swing.

Terrance wasn't sure if he was ready to be so close to her, but he considered the gesture a much greater leap forward than he imagined he would have been able to accomplish. He was aware of her warmth once the wrap was pulled back tightly around them, and this slight measure of grace stung at his heart. He had no right to be so close to her, and no reason to suppose she would reach out to him. The swelling in his chest was making it hard for him to take anything but short, staccato breaths, and the more he anticipated whatever she might say, the closer to panic he came.

Terrance had never, not since he was a teen, openly cried, and he didn't think he had that in him. But he was deeply in need of some sort of catharsis to vent his soul at a controlled rate, or he knew he would explode. Involuntarily, his upper torso began to rock like a Rabbi at prayer. He would have to stand up and walk away if someone didn't say something soon, and all he had in that moment was motion, not words. His chest heaved, and he started to stand. Aimee clamped a hand on his thigh and held him there, though without any change in her gaze or facial expression.

"I saw something last night that frightened me," she said.

"Like me, running at you with an axe?"

"That was frightening. And in a moment, you are going to tell me why." The statement was not an expression of intuition, but a promise she was going to keep on his behalf.

"Whenever the lightning flashed--" As soon as she said that Terrance startled and looked intently at her, stopping her in mid-sentence.

"Go on," he said.

"Whenever the lightning flashed, I saw glimpses of terrible violence."

A spark of recollection seized Terrance. As a child, he was fascinated by the negatives he found in the pockets of envelopes containing the photographs his parents took of family getaways or holiday occasions. Those haunting hues, reversed from their reality, made one look spectral, or even dead. The moment Aimee reminded him of the lightning, his mind raced with rapid shots of film negatives animated by explosive flashes, like those that burned his eyes just after someone told him to say, "cheeeese." Only, these were images of searing reality that evoked intense swelling in his chest. He began to rock again.

"I saw you with the axe before you actually ran after me with it," Aimee continued. "I saw an anger in you I have never witnessed, or ever knew could come from you – until it did, just a few moments later." She paused and they both wrestled with Aimee's observations in silence, but Terrance was nowhere near ready to offer anything verbal yet.

"Terrance. I don't believe in ghosts or demonic possession. And rest assured, I don't even believe that you *are* capable of such violent rage. But we weren't alone last night. Every time there was lightning, Tamara became drawn into scenes of violence, as well. Did you notice that? I believe she was watching something that neither of us could see. She said she saw Nanna and her family, and Nanna's husband was beating another woman. She thinks it was their daughter. And there was a baby.

"There was something else I noticed. Every time the lightning lit up the yard, Tamara became so filled with fear she couldn't move, and that fear lingered until the thunder passed and seemed to clear the air. I felt that fear. It was so strong from her. I've been trying to put my finger on a way to describe it, but I can't. Doesn't matter. It soaked the air around us. Only the thunder knocked it out of the atmosphere. But soon, the lightning was followed by thunder in such rapid succession the sensations of violence escalated. It became more intense, and there was no longer any relief."

Terrance began to say something, but was cut off by Aimee.

"Wait. There's more. As I was running around the house during one of the flashes, I saw Tamara climbing out of the old well in the back yard. I knew, just a few moments later, that it was all illusion because that's when she clubbed you with the log. But as she was climbing out, something else followed her up, and now I can't get that image out of my mind.

"What was it?"

"No idea. There was a lot happening, but it was evil and she was attempting to shut it back inside with the cover to the well. But the more I think about it, the more I'm certain she didn't succeed."

"You saw it get out?"

"No. The light passed too quickly. But everything about last night just keeps reinforcing this sense I can't shake. Terrance, we came up here to try and heal, but I think we've only unleashed fresh demons. If anything, that image reminds me that we are not capable of slamming the lid on any of this. It just keeps roaring back to life. And our baby is only a few steps ahead of it at any time."

Terrance had ceased hyperventilating because he had stopped breathing altogether.

Aimee mistook his puzzled look for disbelief and began to own up to how her own less-than-normal psychological profile must look, but Terrance paused her so he could think.

Terrance retraced the sparks of memory that disturbed him that morning, but he resisted giving voice to them for fear of the reality they represented. Dreams had always presented that sort of challenge to him. Mostly, they evaporated with the buzz of the alarm. Others left an aura, or "stain" on his mood for a while, but that usually subsided long before he got to work. Again, the thing he loved about the city was that it overwhelmed most everything going on inside him the moment he left the house. But on those rare occasions when his dreams remained vivid he struggled, and usually failed, to sort out any meaning they might have.

The contemplative surroundings he found himself in allowed the images of the night overtake his consciousness. What had he seen? Premonitions? A warning from the gods? His own guilt throttling the life out of him?

"I thought it was a dream when I woke up this morning, but as you spoke of seeing things in the lighting…" His mind was racing too far out ahead of him for language.

"You too?" she asked, really hoping that all three of them had not been sharing in some communal delusion.

"I have no idea what I know anymore, to tell you the God's honest truth. But whether I saw it in the lightning, or dreamt it, I can't tell you now."

"But you saw something that set you off," she said, with no inflection or hint of accusation.

"What I saw," he said, and then halted as he decided whether he wanted to verbalize it.

"Tell me," she said, leaving him no other option.

"Simon Martinello. I saw him follow you into the bedroom and shut the door," he began. He let that settle in to the atmosphere around them. He waited, but she didn't contradict the words, brush them off, or offer anything like: Oh, that's just silly.

"Go on," was all she said.

"While you and Tamara were outside, I made the decision we were going to leave, go to a motel and book a flight in the morning. I was done here. In fact, I was done with you. And, her. I couldn't face this anymore, Aimee. Tamara has been telling us, in one way or another, that our marriage is dead. There came a moment last night that I knew she had killed it. Not intentionally, but for all we've been through I just had nothing else to give.

"My mind raced back to something Tamara said the other day," continued Terrance. "She was trying to bait me, and it suddenly made perfect sense that you would start looking for stronger emotional support than I can give you. I saw his face. I saw you sharing that wine with him, and then I saw you follow him down the hall. I saw you back there in bed. So, I started throwing things in the suitcase, not even thinking anymore. The more the lightning flashed, and the thunder rattled my head, the more I was ready to break something. I was in the same room with the two of you, and then – the axe came to mind. I had no idea who or what I was going to hit with it. I just wanted to swing it at something that would shatter into a thousand pieces. Then, when you ran past me, all my rage shifted gears. I didn't think twice about it."

"Until Tamara whacked you," she said. She threw off the comforter, turned his back toward her and pulled up his sweatshirt. "She whacked you pretty good!"

The bruise looked a little like the state of Florida, and the skin was broken in several places. He reared up in pain as she laid her hand on it.

"We ought to put something on that. Though I'm not sure what," she said, under her breath. She told him to hang on and went into the bathroom. She returned with some basic first aid supplies.

"How did you sleep with that?" she asked.

"Not well."

20

God's Under-shepherd

TAMARA SAID NOTHING WHEN SHE was rousted out of bed by her mom and coaxed into the car for the ride down the mountain. She slunk down in her seat and went back to sleep. The drive down the battered mountain road seemed slower than the trip up, but it gave them time to orient themselves outward toward the world once again. To meet traffic and see people about the village doing normal things was a little disorienting to Aimee, who remembered there weren't any places in town to eat except for Tip's Diner. *I'm certainly not in the mood for a large helping of Small Town with my bagel and cream cheese. We need a buffer from this, somewhere out of this village.* She was delighted to see her phone brimming with connectivity, so she did a quick search of local eateries.

"Let's go right and head west," Aimee suggested. "Lincoln's just a few miles in that direction, and it looks like it might have some size to it."

"What about the power?" asked Terrance. "We ought to check in at Nanna's and see about getting it serviced."

"It's after 10:00 as it is," she responded, "and none of us ate much last night."

Terrance's hearty appetite agreed with her, so he turned right on Main. He didn't get very far, however. Just as they were approaching the church, a middle-aged man came bouncing down the front steps and planted himself in the middle of the road stopping traffic in both directions. Following him was a choir, all wearing scarlet robes, processing through the doors and lining the walkway singing.

Come, every soul by sin oppressed, there's mercy with the Lord;
and he will surely give you rest by trusting in his word.
Only trust him, only trust him, only trust him now.
He will save you, he will save you, he will save you now.

Members of the congregation emerged next, following a large white banner bearing a fiery, golden sun, overlaid with a descending dove about to plunge into blue ripples beneath it. The words bordering the sides said: "He Shall Baptize You with the Holy Spirit and with Fire." They were carrying song sheets and singing with the choir.

For Jesus shed his precious blood rich blessing to bestow;
plunge now into the crimson flood that washes white as snow.
Only trust him, only trust him, only trust him now.
He will save you, he will save you, he will save you now.

"That's interesting," said Aimee. "Though they certainly aren't the Mormon Tabernacle Choir!" Terrance slouched in his seat, put his face in his hands, and groaned into his palms.

Yes, Jesus is the Truth, the Way, that leads you into rest:
believe in him without delay, and you are fully blest.
Only trust him, only trust him, only trust him now.
He will save you, he will save you, he will save you now.

There was a large gap in the procession and Terrance started to proceed, but four young women, all wearing white robes, filed out one at a time, each accompanied by an elderly member of the church. As they paraded across the road, the choir took up the rear of the procession.

Come, then, and join his holy band, and on to glory go,
to dwell in that celestial land, where joys immortal flow.
Only trust him, only trust him, only trust him now.
He will save you, he will save you, he will save you now.

Tamara had slowly emerged from slumber and watched speechless from the back seat. When the four white-clad pilgrims had passed, she asked her parents what they were watching.

"I'm not sure," said Aimee.

"A baptism," said Terrance.

They had both spoken simultaneously, so Tamara didn't catch what they said. But before they had time to sort it out, the pastor came out the church door and shut it behind him. As he scurried to catch up with the rest of the congregation, he recognized Terrance in the driver's seat and hurried over to the car. Terrance rolled down the window cursing under his breath for the unwelcomed interruption.

"Knew you'd come," said the elder. "Turn in over there and park. Plenty of time to catch up." And as the preacher dashed off, he fired back one last, "So glad you came!" As he did so, he spoke to the man directing traffic evidently thinking the family needed an escort. The man waved good naturedly then ushered them into the driveway by the church.

Terrance felt his face go crimson red as Aimee's eyes turned on every gigawatt of power they possessed melting him under her stare of disbelief and curiosity. He found himself under the influence of two irresistible personalities and wasn't sure which impulse had to be answered first, to park the car in obedience to the pastor, or explain all that to Aimee, whose face was insisting on answers.

Tamara broke the spell, and the stalemate.

"Where are we going?" she asked.

"Ah…" groped Terrance for something to say.

"Looks like we're going to church," said Aimee, casting Terrance a cynical glare.

Terrance, still suffering from a blend of denial and resistance, just sat there.

"Well, go ahead. Pull on over," Aimee said, still staring at Terrance in dismay.

He could read each look from Aimee like they were semaphore flags: What have you done? Where are we going? How in the world did you get us into this? Funny thing happened on the way to breakfast in a quaint little New England village from hell.

Flashes of lightning slashed through Aimee's memory reminding her of the truth they still had to confront. *This is just too unreal – how in the world are we on our way to a baptism, of all things?*

"If we can just get a moment, I can explain," Terrance fought back, but the man kept shouting pleasantries at them assuring the family of how welcomed they were.

Good luck with that. I can't wait hear how you got us into this one, but we've got more to deal with than just stumbling into a church service. We may be in for real trouble here.

As soon as he pulled into the last remaining spot (designated, of course: Visitor), their personal usher was at the car door welcoming them to Blossom's Rest Seventh Day Baptist Church. His name was Terry, and he couldn't get over the fact that the pastor told him their guest's name was Terrance, which of course was really his own name, but people around here just called him Terry, and wasn't that a nice coincidence, like Terrance was already part of the family.

Terry took Terrance by the arm and led him across the street then on up the path. *That'll teach him something, though what I can hardly imagine.* She was left with a larger worry on her hands. Tamara's bewilderment was shifting gears into low grade anger again. She glanced over at Tamara for a visual progress report and her own emotional temperature continued to rise. Then, she looked angrily at her husband moving further out ahead of them. *Hoisted on your own petard, bucko. And frankly, you're on your own from here on out. Daughter and I will be fine, thank you very much. Last thing these people need is for Tamara's mood to interfere with what is clearly an important day for this church.* Aimee put her arm around Tamara's shoulders and encouraged her to cross the street. When they reached the path and came under the canopy of the trees, Tamara put on the brakes.

"Come on," said Aimee and coaxed her forward.

"Mom," Tamara protested. "Do we really have to do this? I'm hungry." She tried to dislodge herself, but Aimee held on tighter, trying to keep her daughter moving forward.

"What is this, anyway?" asked Tamara.

"Well. It's a baptism."

"I got that much. What is it?"

"It's a little hard to explain."

"You mean, you don't know."

"No. I've seen baptisms before."

"Okay. So, what will we *see*?"

"Honestly, I don't know. Most of the baptisms I've been to have been for babies. But they were in a church." *And most people went so they could go to the party afterward.*

"What did they do?" persisted Tamara.

"They were baptized. Uh. The priest held them in his arms and sprinkled water over their heads. That was also when the baby was officially named. It's very beautiful. Very religious." Aimee struggled to impress Tamara with its significance, but she wasn't able to put much conviction behind it.

"Well, I seriously doubt this priest is going to hold them in his arms and sprinkle water on them. And I'll bet they're already named. So, what is this?"

"Honey, I think we'll have to wait and see."

"You don't know."

Aimee was flattened. *No, I don't have a clue. Is that so wrong? Any other day of the week that would be superfluous knowledge.* Walking with her daughter it felt like another piece of the parenting puzzle she couldn't put together for her. *But, so what? I can't explain nuclear physics to her, either! But it's not the same, is it? Faith, God, one's sense of eternity. The meaning of life. Frankly, it's always been a relief to be able to set those mysteries aside on the train ride in to work. Who cares about that sort of thing on the trading floor? What does it matter in the throes of negotiating a deal or configuring a client's portfolio? THAT'S what power is all about. Those are the forces that have brought my life all the meaning I've ever sought. There is the source of my glory.*

Glory – that source of exaltation. She held it in herself, she always knew, that divine spark of majesty. It thrilled her every time she saw it rise from within as she triumphed over all she has mastered. But this was a moment distinct for its lack of majesty, and she let her moment of retreat linger too long.

"Was I baptized?" asked Tamara.

Aimee took two more steps and couldn't go any further. The question impaled her. The long discussions they had with their parents came rushing back. The resistance they put up against those pressures gave way to the religious 'no-man's land' Terrance insisted they keep in place. She heard again all the accusations from their parents: 'How could you be so irresponsible and faithless? Don't you love her enough to raise her in the faith, save her from hell, cleanse her of her sins?' *So insignificant then. Now, how can I say, 'No, we didn't have you baptized?' Was she not important enough? What harm, really, would it have done? And then, I could say, 'Yes, and we named you Tamara in the sight of God.'* Her lips were quivering, wanting words to give some purpose to the decisions they had made, but she only felt her face contorting in irrepressible, inarticulate sorrow for her daughter.

Tamara didn't know what else to do but stand there and look down at her mother's feet, because she couldn't look her in the face.

Then, her daughter surprised her.

"Come on, mom. Let's go." She pointed down the path. Terry had his arm on Terrance's shoulder by this point, and they were just about to disappear into the trees. Tamara took Aimee by the arm, gave her a gentle tug, then nudged her along until Aimee resumed her own stride.

As Tamara and Aimee arrived, the congregation was still. Their heads were bowed, their eyes were closed. Aimee turned toward her daughter with her finger on her lips.

"They're praying now," she whispered.

"I know, mom." Tamara bowed her head but squinted her eyes so she could see what else they were doing. By the water's edge stood those robed and ready to be baptized. The choir flanked them on the near bank huddled up to her left. Standing in the water were two elderly men. One looked wise, the other simply looked nice, ready to be of help, if needed.

The wise one, the minister who spoke to them earlier, held up his hands. He raised them toward the crowd as if he was warning them not to step any closer lest they all plunge into the water. His eyes were closed, but his face was lifted toward the treetops. The river was pulling against his sense of balance, but he held fast. Despite the tug of war he was having with the river, his words were triumphant, pronounced with a sing-song quality Tamara found captivating.

"...and hear them as they call upon you, Lord," prayed the pastor. "Forsake them not, but answer them in the day of trouble. Lead them along the narrow way, and teach them thy truth. As they lay their lives in your hands, here in these baptismal waters, we pray you lift them up and keep them from everlasting harm. As they die this day with Jesus, let his cross do its work of redemption for them. Save them from their sins. Cast out the devil from their lives and deliver them from all evil. Wash them, O Lord, and they shall be cleansed. Wash them in the blood of thy precious lamb, O God, and they shall be whiter than snow..."

Tamara didn't know how to make any sense of this, but the more she watched, the more she realized she didn't need words to define it. The phrases themselves were meaningless to her, but there was a weight to them she could feel pressing down upon her. As she looked from face to face, she saw that their eyes were closed, their bodies were swaying, and their lips whispered explosive phrases: yes, Jesus; praise you, Jesus; holy, holy, holy, Lord; hallelujah Jesus. There were a few at the edge whose eyes were wide open yet whose lips were sealed tight. Their dignity of expression drove home to Tamara the deep meaning this must have for them. She, on the other hand, had no point of contact, no reference point out here in the woods by a river with strange people seemingly in love with a God she didn't know and couldn't comprehend.

Aimee's view of the proceedings was equally as blurred. Her tears flowed uncontrollably. An older woman pulled alongside her and placed her left palm on Aimee's shoulder and raised her right hand, like the preacher, yet never looked at her. Aimee's first impulse was to pull away, but there was a gentleness and warmth in the touch which felt matronly, protective, loving. Before long, she wanted to roll right over and bury her face in the woman's shoulder but held still for fear of losing what she had. The sensations of intimacy brought heaves from her gut. The woman pressed a little more firmly on Aimee's back, gently rubbed her, then whispered: "Hold on to her, Lord Jesus; hold on to her, don't let her go, Jesus. Send your Holy Spirit. Fill her, Lord, and comfort her."

The preacher finished his prayer before Aimee knew it. When she opened her eyes and they were cleared enough from tears to focus, the first young woman was already in the water.

"Cassandra Elizabeth Connor, do you renounce Satan and all his ways?"

"Yes, Lord, I do."

"Do you confess Jesus Christ to be your only Lord and Savior?"

"Yes, Lord, I do."

"Do you believe that he died on the cross to save you from your sins?"

"Yes, Lord, I do."

"Do you believe that he rose again from the dead and that you, too, shall join him in new and everlasting life?"

"Yes, Lord, I do."

"And by the power and guidance of God's Holy Word and Spirit, are you ready to become a communing member of the Body of Christ, the Church?"

"Yes, Lord, I certainly am!" she said with conviction in her voice and a great big grin on her face.

"Then, my sister, Cassie, upon your profession of faith, I baptize you in the name of the Father, the Son, and the Holy Spirit."

Tamara held her breath and stared in disbelief as this young woman was thrust backward into the river. This was no "sprinkling." The violence of it left Tamara trembling. She felt the plunge in her own soul, a suffocating, sinking feeling that made her grab the tree she stood beside.

As the woman was hefted back on to her feet, she wiped the water from her eyes then lifted her arms as high as she could in triumph. The bank-side erupted with Amens, Hallelujahs, and Praise be to God! The preacher then laid his hands on her head and prayed over her again, begging the Holy Spirit to fill her, guide her, and equip her for a life of ministry in Christ's name.

Tamara would watch this again, three more times, before there was more singing, praying, and then the victorious march back to the church grounds for lunch. But as the crowd dispersed, she sank down to a squatting position and leaned against the tree.

Terrance was as eager to leave as anyone could be, but he had to wait for Aimee to conclude an intimate conversation with an old woman who had sidled over to her during the prayer. Terrance paced in place glancing back and forth between the stream and his wife. Her face was turned downward, partly to look the other woman in the eyes but mostly, thought Terrance, because she had emptied herself weeping and had no resistance to this intrusion, which is all he could have imagined it to be for Aimee.

Truth was, however, it was the best medicine Aimee had had in weeks, maybe years, as she welcomed the expressions of concern from this perfect stranger who listened intently then spoke directly to Aimee's heart.

The woman was rubbing Aimee gently on the back as they spoke. It was the kind of touch Aimee would have expected only from someone very close. The personality traits she had crafted for herself over the years easily attracted, cultivated, even enslaved associates to suit her professional needs. The accompanying walls necessary to project and exercise power through those relationships, however, didn't allow her the luxury of inviting others in to her personal "soul space," as she called it. She didn't mind nose-to-nose face offs. She would often invade another person's circumference of safety, and she would not flinch if anyone presumed to intrude on hers. But she kept a close guard on her soul, those inner regions where, under all that psychological body armor, she felt very insecure. Terrance, and Terrance alone, had found his way inside her long enough to gain her trust, keep it, and leave a piece of his own soul in there alongside hers. He was the only one she allowed to occupy that inner world until Tamara came along. And then, it became very crowded in there, very fast.

Terrance didn't notice pastor Fletcher walk up beside him.

"Ma always did work pretty fast," he said to Terrance.

"Your mother?" asked Terrance, thinking the apple hadn't fallen far from that tree. These people have an uncanny way of getting under one's skin, he went on thinking, wishing he could make it back to their car without any further complications. It was not to be, however, and deep down, he knew it.

"She is the Lord's under-shepherd if ever there was one."

"I thought that was your job," Terrance said, hoping it sounded good-natured, but heard his own note of sarcasm which was too well rehearsed not to bleed through.

"Professionally, that may well be true. But ma's got a rare gift. When Jesus asked the crowd, 'How many of you, if you'd lost one of your sheep, wouldn't leave the ninety-nine and go look for the one who strayed away?' I sometimes think my mother was the only one in the crowd that really heard him. If there was a troubled soul in Fenway Park, my mom would root 'em out and see to it they found their way back to Jesus before the next inning."

Terrance had to choke back the sarcasm rising within him as he wondered what she would do with the gaggle of bums that led him to give up his season tickets at Yankee Stadium, belligerent drunks who got more socially unacceptable each time the beer guy came around, and twice as bad if the Yankees were losing. But, he supposed the man was trying to be hospitable in the only way he knew, so Terrance just let the verbiage slide by without taking any of it very seriously.

At last, the woman was releasing his wife from her grip and Aimee was beginning to make her way toward him. Now, he just had to collect Tamara wherever she was. His relief collapsed again, however, when he saw the preacher's mother squatting by his daughter, then settling in very comfortably, down on the ground beside her. It was going to be a long day.

"We've been invited to lunch," Aimee said to Terrance, almost daring him to react as she knew he wanted to.

"Well... I thought we were going over--

"Over to Lincoln for BREAKFAST. But since we're way beyond that, we may as well have lunch, don't you think?"

The reverend excused himself diplomatically saying that he had to get back since no one would start before he had the blessing.

Terrance was relieved to have a moment to his wife alone, but she swept right past him.

"Pastor Fletcher," she said imploringly. He paused without turning around, letting her catch up to him.

"Your mother..."

"Yes?"

"Your mother said there was a picture I should see in the church."

"A picture?"

"Yes. She called it the 'Prodigal Daughter.'"

"Ah," grunted the reverend in a slightly professorial way.

The other parishioners were still setting the tables and arranging the various dishes everyone brought, so Pastor Toby thought he had enough time to show Aimee and Terrance around the church.

The sanctuary was sparse but intimate and warm. The banner they had carried to the river now lay against a simple pulpit which was slightly elevated from the main floor. There were sixteen pews, eight on each side of a center aisle. The windows were tall and made of clear glass. They walked down the aisle to a door by the right of the platform then into to a short hall with several small meeting rooms off it. At the end of the hall was a large gathering room where a lot of activity was going on in preparation for the meal. Pastor Toby ushered them into a cluttered sitting room.

There was a circle of mis-matched living room chairs around a small coffee table upon which rested an open Bible. A set of book shelves against the far wall was packed with old hymnals, worn out Bibles, student books, commentaries, atlases, picture books of Holy Land sites, and other religious artifacts. There was a tea set on one shelf and six cups beside it. The walls were covered with paintings, photographs, charts, even a couple of orthodox icons, one of which depicted Mary holding baby Jesus on her lap and another of Jesus' transfiguration.

"This is my mother's classroom."

Terrance felt claustrophobic, oppressed not so much by the size of the room, but by its overwhelming religiosity. The artifacts and images were a blur to him, and his mind rebelled against the presence of a faith from which he wanted to be delivered.

Aimee ignored her husband and was drawn in to the heart of the room. She looked around with unexpected amazement, immersed in what she sensed was a lifelong work of love that radiated the joy of one person's devotion, both to God (which was supremely evident), and to her students. *Those old ladies love being in this room together. I wish I had all day to take more of this in.* A small icon of the crucifixion drew her in as the light inflamed the gold background and set Jesus' suffering on another plane. *Amazing. As flat as that surface is, as two dimensional and stylized as this little painting was meant to be, one's eye doesn't stop there on the surface, does it?* As she tilted the icon, the light illumined her awareness and drew her further into the act of sacrifice depicted there. *Glorious. This really is where it is found, isn't it?* She set down the icon and scanned the walls for the picture she sought, but it was more of a hunt than she expected. *What an interesting hodge-podge of art! A lot of these pictures aren't very religious at all. At least they're not like anything that adorned the walls of my Sunday School. If they had been, I might have stuck with it.*

Pastor Toby watched Aimee with some fascination as she reacted to the room and mistook her facial expressions for confusion.

"You might want to excuse my mother's taste in religion. She is the sincerest person I know but, to my mind, a bit unorthodox. She does love the Lord, and those old ladies sure love her. They have a pretty good time in here, you might say."

"So, which one of these is the Prodigal Daughter?" asked Aimee.

"Well, let's see if I can remember," said Pastor Toby, putting on his glasses and squinting at the collection.

"Here. This one." He showed her an old photograph of a teen-age girl. *Good Lord. White trash, if you asked me. And she can't be any older than Tamara.* The girl wore a dingy smock and her feet were bare. Her long dirty blond hair partly covered her face which was deformed by an expression Aimee couldn't read. She was in flight, or trying to be, thrashing against the grip of an old man (*Is that her father?*) whose own expression looked both firm and sad. *Why in the world would Barb want to show me this?* Aimee had a hard time looking at the young girl's face but couldn't take her eyes off it, either. Like those portraits in which the eyes follow you around the room, or whose smile can suggest a variety of moods, the facial expression of this young woman wouldn't sit still. *Is that wrath? It would be if it were me. Or, self-loathing? God. How sad. She's either fighting mad or whipped by defeat. Or, both at the same time.*

"So, this is called Prodigal Daughter?" Aimee asked.

"I think that's what my mother titled it, partly, I think, because she sees herself in it. You'll remember, the prodigal son demanded his inheritance and rejected his father. And his father let him go. My mother says that would never have happened with a daughter except through marriage or death. She wouldn't have made it on her own without property or a husband except as a prostitute. So, she leaves in the only way she knows how, by rejecting the father, hating him, hating herself, hating the world, and making herself so miserable to live with that either the father will kill her, or she will eventually kill herself."

"Oh, my God," Aimee said as she studied the picture even more closely.

"The irony is," continued the pastor, "that her redemption comes from the very hand she rejects. Look at the grip the old man has on her. He ain't letting her go. And while she hates it at first, it is finally what saves her."

"Saves her?" asked Terrance. "From what?" He sounded incredulous, having concluded that the father must be abusive, perhaps sexually, given his socio-economic background. Terrance interpreted his facial expression as one of ownership, not paternal concern.

"Well," Pastor Fletcher began, not sure how much he wanted to get into this story before lunch. "You see, my mother had a very hard man for a father. He beat his wife, and though his two daughters were what he prized most on this earth they didn't fare much better. Mom hated him, and he anguished over that, I believe, in ways that were destroying him, if not the whole family.

"When mom's sister, Sally Anne, got pregnant before she got married, he went on a rampage that frightened the whole village. If Sally Anne's fiancé hadn't left town for a while, I do believe her father would have killed him. I really do. Everything that old man did drove a wedge between himself and my mother. And if my mother had not found her faith when she did, I believe none of us would be standing here now, because I would not have been born.

"Mom was on the verge of leaving him in the only way she knew she could get away with it once and for all. I do believe it was that close. But he kept a grip on her. He loved her and kept a keen eye on her because he knew what she was capable of, and it scared him as nothing else ever could. He refused to keep even a bird gun in the house, and a farmer without a shot-gun around here is a bit of a curiosity. But the tighter he held on, the more disturbed she became.

"One night, he remembered something he had to do out in the barn, so he pulled on his boots and went out. When he flicked on a light, there stood my mother on a milking stool with a length of rope tied off to a rafter. She was just fitting the noose end over her head. In a rage, he flew at her, kicked the stool out from under her, and as she crumpled to the ground he just lost it. He fell down on his face, crawled over to where she was and pulled her into those huge arms of his, weeping like a baby. But mom would have put a knife through him if one was in reach. She kicked and squirmed until she got away and ran out of the barn, across the field, and disappeared in to the woods over by the river, not far from where we were this morning.

"When he finally recovered, her father got up and stumbled down here. He let himself into the church, knelt down by the communion table, and he gave her up to God. He told God she was out of his hands. He had done his best, and his best was far from good enough. He pleaded with God to take over as her father. Adopt her as his own. Just keep her safe was all he asked.

"Mom wasn't seen or heard from for almost two days. Everyone knew the worst, and her father slumped into despair. Refused to see anyone. But she came back. And when she did, no one would say she was a new person. Not yet. She was still mean as a blue jay, but there was a new quality no one could quite put their finger on except to say that she had finally come home in a way that she had never been home before. She became her father's daughter, for instance, and her sister's sister. In fact, the two girls became so close people who didn't know couldn't believe mom once thought Sally Anne was the devil's seed."

There was a gentle knock on the door by someone asking if Pastor Fletcher could come say grace now.

"Be right there," said the pastor. "A few months later, she walked the aisle here in church and gave herself to the Lord. She still had many,

many struggles, and she never became a perfect daughter by any means. But many years later, she confessed that if it had not been for her father's grip on her, and his refusal to let her go until he was sure God had hold of her, she'd be eternally lost to us by now."

Compared to that, lunch was a rather superficial affair for which Terrance was just as glad. He didn't mind being neighborly over baked beans and ham so long as no one reminded him his soul was in mortal jeopardy of an eternity in Hell.

Aimee was just thankful for some well-cooked food, and at 12:35 with no breakfast in her, her head was hurting. She thought about how Tamara must be doing with Pastor Fletcher's mother, thankful for the woman's gracious invitation to care for her so they didn't have to pull her through a social gathering that would only have made everyone there very uncomfortable.

Aimee thought how much she resented this aspect of her daughter's troubles. She was tired of second-guessing what might be appropriate for her and hated with all her heart having to raise the debate in her mind at all. Why Tamara couldn't just be "normal" was one of the questions she stopped beating herself up with years ago. She had managed some acceptance that her daughter was who she was – beautiful in a way other young women were not. Her regret was that her daughter may never enjoy the simplicity of a tea party among friends or the elegance of a soirée with people of true distinction. And that was not a class thing, she kept telling herself. No. She had come to know some amazing people of distinction who enhanced her appreciation of the world, and she grieved that her daughter might forever be excluded from such encounters.

But as it turned out, Tamara was doing just fine, getting to know one of the most influential people she would ever meet.

21

A Rest by the River

As the worshipers had departed from the river's edge, Tamara slumped down on the bank and leaned against a tree. She closed her eyes in search of some peace, but what she saw was the confrontation between Sally Anne and her father. Then, she remembered a brilliant slashing wall of white light had incapacitated her. She recalled falling down the well then running through a thickening darkness being chased by demons that normally occupied the darker regions of her soul. Countless numbers of fiends jockeyed for position as they raced toward her each with their own sinister claim upon her. She glanced over her shoulder and discovered the number of demons had diminished, but they had grown in ferocity and size. They had merged their rage and coalesced into fewer but increasingly vicious threats united in their hostility to defeat her. She wanted to turn back and stand them down, but all the fight in her had been seized and incarnated by those hideous forms that were chasing her.

Then, she turned one last time and there was a single demon bearing in its aspect all the hell she had been carrying within her. Its eyes were fiery diamonds with jet black slits burning Tamara in their gaze. The serpent's sinister fangs glistened as they slashed within inches of her neck.

Tamara climbed up through the well toward the open air above. The night sky, seen through the mouth of the well, was flashing alternately between black and brilliant white. She emerged seconds before the serpent but was unable to slam the lid down upon it. In the next flash of lightning, she saw it encircle her father as he ran toward her. The serpent was twisting around his torso; then his throat. She grabbed the nearest thing at hand, a length of firewood, and she swung it with every ounce of deadly force she could find in herself. But the snake only grew larger in its rage. Then, in one of the most violent lightning salvos, a mighty hand grabbed the serpent by the throat and hurled it far out across the valley.

Slumped against the tree, Tamara buried her face in her arms and began to rock unable to lift herself up. Her head was throbbing. She tried to focus on the sound of the water, but the long, purplish serpent kept slithering through her awareness inviting Tamara to follow her up the path.

"Hey there," said a kind voice beside her. She felt a hand on her back. "Your mother and father are going to come have lunch with us at the church. Would you like to come, or shall we just sit for a while?"

Tamara lifted her head to discover a wizened, wrinkled old face only inches from her own. Wisps of white hair danced around her head in the breeze. All the wrinkles on her face seemed to emerge from her smile and formed a halo back around her eyes which were a dazzling baby blue much like her mother's. Her initial impulse was to retreat, but she couldn't resist staring in the woman's direction. Was she funny looking? She couldn't really say, but the woman's face, and the ease it offered Tamara, began to relax her mind.

Tamara didn't know how to answer the woman, but as she saw her parents walking back down the path talking with the preacher, she sensed the woman meant what she said. She showed no signs of hurry and was just as content to rest there by the stream with Tamara.

"Met your mother," she said. "She says you're up from New York."

The woman repositioned herself for a moment then said as she looked down into the water: "I can always tell when visitors come up here in search of something. What did you folks come up to find, I wonder?"

Tamara didn't absorb the question, but let it swirl and float with the water down the creek.

"I've often wondered," she said at last, "when God ran this stream through here, if he knew so much life would crawl up out of it. And by 'life' I don't mean turtles," she joked. "I mean new souls. Lord, I can't even begin to count how many baptisms we've had here. I remember my own like it was yesterday."

Tamara only stared and relaxed into the woman's comfortable presence. The long pauses the older woman took between sentences helped to settle Tamara's agitation. The woman's silences were just long enough to give Tamara room to ponder without letting her mind run too far afield before the woman gathered her back under her spiritual wing.

"My name's Barb, honey. Pastor Toby's my son. We've lived right over there for four generations, and all our people walked down these banks and gave their life to Jesus, right here."

The woman let the stream and rustling leaves fill a few more long stretches of silence. Any urgency Tamara may have had to chase after her parents evaporated, and she felt just right lingering there on the bank of the river. An unfamiliar peace settled into her mind for which she was grateful. Jolts of memory, images from the lightning, and the ruminations leading to another delusional episode took a pause for the moment.

"I never thought it would happen," continue Barb, "but there would finally come a moment in my life when this spot by the river stopped being the scariest place on the face of the planet."

That woke Tamara up, if she needed awakening any further.

"Every year, I tagged along with the congregation for these services. I dreaded them for weeks before, and every time we marched out here I would halt, right over there by that fence-post, and never set foot across the path. I was afraid if I did someone would grab me by the arm, yank me over the bank, drag me down, and dunk me under!" She giggled introspectively.

"They were all ready to do it! I was a bit of a hellion. My daddy was so desperate to have me saved I think he finally wore God out, and God decided he'd better get the job done or there'd be no peace from my father. So, God began to agitate me. And it took all God's doing to get me into that water. It sure wasn't anything I wanted. I was fine just as I was. And I never saw it coming."

Barb let all that hang out to dry for a while in the late morning breeze.

A Rest by the River

Tamara found herself on edge for the rest of the story and waited as long as she could.

"What happened?" she asked

"Well. I was as set in my life as I could be. I was miserable about it, but that was just my life. It was the way I thought it was always going to be. And the last thing I thought my life needed was the God who put me in the middle of it. I hated my parents, and I loathed Sally Anne – that was my sister – for being such a snotty goody-two-shoes, if you know what I mean. We fought like pit bulls day in and day out.

"And then, one day, I told my father just what I really thought about who he was, and all I thought he could do with his self. And the moment I did, I suddenly saw something I had never seen before. My father was terribly hurt. I had seen that face before, the hurt, and I usually chalked up another win when I saw it. But this time, it slammed back at me like a two by four across the head. Daddy was always beside himself most of the time because of me. And I just did not care, until that day.

"I realized that what I saw in his hurt was my all-aloneness, if you get what I mean. I felt a loneliness open up inside of me I have never known before. And I wasn't lonely for people. I had friends. I had a family, and though they had terrible faults they only wanted what was right for me. But my insides were grinding. My soul hurt, if that makes any sense. And that ache was becoming more than I could do anything about.

"So, when I saw how much I hurt my papa, I knew that was the day I was going to die and be damned to Hell. I saw Hell's mouth open up, and its flames were already burning me. I started having visions. At first, they were just nightmares, but the nightmares left such a haunting feeling in me there were times I didn't know whether it was real or if the boundaries between this world and the one below had been blown apart. Whatever should have been locked up down there was alive and well up here and giving me hell. The more my insides hurt, the more I wanted to hurt others. My daddy called the elders of the church to come to the house one night, but I wouldn't let them lay hands on me. I kept interrupting their prayers. Then, when old Elder William pulled out a little jar of anointing oil, I spit in his face, snatched the jar and dumped the oil!"

She shook her head as she recalled all this after so many years. The silences took her away for a while. Tamara squirmed hoping to catch her eye again. But Barb remained fixated on the flowing water. Only gradually did she ease back into her narrative though without breaking the spell she obviously cast on herself.

"A few nights later, I decided all the death inside me had finally killed any life left to me, so I went out to do myself in. And I would have, but my daddy stopped me. I ran away that night, and I was never going to set foot in that house again. I told myself if I ever laid eyes on him, I would kill him.

"I ran down the path over there and up the mountain to the overlook. When I got to the top, I was just going to keep running right off the edge. But my hate ran out of steam before I got there. Spent all night up there just looking out over the valley.

"Next day, as I was coming back down this path, all alone, trying to think it all out, I paused right over there. I wasn't really watching where I was walking, but suddenly I knew I had come to the baptismal pool. At first, I started to rush right by it. But I couldn't. I couldn't move. Just stood right there for the longest time, not wanting to look at it, feeling panicky. I closed my eyes, and I could see all my friends, all my family, all those church folk, one right after another, going down into the water. I felt like I was going to die, right there where I stood. I was all alone in this world.

"Everything grew so dark in my heart and I just wanted to die. If I could have screamed at the top of my lungs to let all that pressure out I would have, but I couldn't budge for anything. And then, I felt an urge I had never felt before. I had never, in my life, ever felt like praying. Whenever they did that in church, I thought about what I wanted to be doing instead. When daddy prayed in the evening at dinner, I just wanted him to hurry up and finish so we could eat. But there, that day, I had the strongest craving ever. And I wanted to run from it. I knew what that craving was, but I wasn't going to give in to it. All I could do was stand right there as this new hunger overwhelmed me.

"Finally, finally, when I permitted myself to believe I really did want to pray, then I had to talk myself into it! Kept resisting it. I remember looking down into the pool there and my urge to die and my urge to pray suddenly became an urge to drown. Plunge myself in. If I dived just right, I would never know it, and just be swept away, out into the sea. That would be my baptism.

"But I felt a mighty hand upon me, choking me, maybe, but pressing me just to say that first, "Dear God." Those were the hardest words I ever said in my life. Hardest of all. But you know, once I said them, once I choked them up from my gut, I couldn't stop. The dam had burst and I couldn't stop. I cried. I shouted. I heaved up more from my soul than I ever knew could be down there. Hurled it right up to God. I told him about my father and about all my hatred. I pleaded with him to heal my momma and shook my fist at him for making her suffer the way she did. I cursed him for the life he had given me and dared him to prove he could do better. I even prayed God would release me from this life. Take me out of it, I said. If this is the best he could do, then I didn't want any part of it anymore. I actually said all those things to God."

She shook her head and looked at Tamara with widened eyes.

"Then, after the hate, came the sorrow" she continued quietly. "There was more of that than hate, I believe. The remorse that moved through me then was unbearable. God showed me, I believe, the effect my life had on others. I saw their faces looking back at me and I realized why I was so lonely. I had pushed everyone out of my life. I was all alone. Right there be the river bank. All alone.

"Then, after all that fighting, and all that giving in, the words began to run dry, but my soul had a lot more it wanted to say. At that point, I paced in silence and agitation. I felt my soul saying things I couldn't put into words.

"At some point, I knew I had given it all up. After all that, the hardest word to say became, Amen. I just didn't want to let go of God at that point. And I guess I never have, if you think about it. God had caught up to me, and I guess after all that work he wasn't about to let me get too far out of reach again.

"My daddy called it being saved. So does my son. That's preacher talk, I suppose, but for me, it was more like being found. I had been running for so long I had lost track of where I was, or who I was. I was nineteen years old when I was baptized. Nineteen! Oldest ever in my family. Ten years late, and not a moment too soon, said my daddy, when the preacher finally laid me under. Oh, me.

"Well, that's probably enough rambling out of an old woman for one day. It just all comes flooding back whenever I see these young folk follow Jesus in baptism. It all comes flooding back."

There, she ended, and just sat beside Tamara, not expecting anything or saying anything more.

"I think I should find my parents," said Tamara, in the dullest of tones, though not moving a single muscle to make it happen.

"Your mother suspected you might not want to go back to the church."

Tamara looked at her with some amazement.

"I get the feeling that crowds are not your thing."

"You got that right," she acknowledged, looking back down at the water.

"Toby talked them into joining the others for lunch, but suggested to your mom that I might take you with me, and get a sandwich at my house, 'cause I don't like crowds much these days, either, tell you the truth. Then, we'll meet your folks at Nanna's a little later. What do you say to that?"

Tamara stared long and hard into this old woman's face, trying to decide why she wanted to go with her. Barb just let her stare as she looked right back into the coal black eyes of the young woman.

"You'll need to help me up," said Barb. "I don't mind sitting down on the ground, but getting up ain't what it used to be."

So, Tamara obliged her, and together they walked further up the path, away from the church, following the fence row until it made a sharp right. There, they joined a new trail that took them by a small pasture to a modest farm house. The smell of wood smoke welcomed them into the yard.

"Here we go," said Barb. "The old homestead."

They climbed the cinder block steps up onto an open, wrap-around porch, then passed through the kitchen door. A cast-iron cook stove stood to the left of a large, open-hearth fire place. Barb went straight to it, pulled on an old oven mitt, swung wide the door and began feeding small logs into it. She pulled a black skillet down from a hook on the wall and set it atop the stove then layered in several pieces of pink meat. The instantaneous aroma that filled the cabin caught Tamara by surprise, and her stomach churned with hunger. It was a smell from another world.

With equally fluid motions, a pan of small round white cake-like things went into the oven. It wasn't long before both aromas competed for which smelled best.

"Have a seat," said Barb, pulling a chair from the kitchen table. A glass of orange juice appeared from no-where. As Tamara moved toward the table, a black and white photograph of an older woman and two younger ladies, framed in simple wood, caught her eye. They were both wearing somber tones, the mother was in black.

"You're Nanna's daughter."

"Yes, that's right."

"Sally Anne?" asked Tamara, pointing to the other woman sitting beside Barb, evidently several years older.

"That's right."

"How old were you?"

"Seventeen, I think. That was taken at my grandfather's funeral."

Tamara shifted in her seat and made a tentative reach toward a ham biscuit. Barb pushed the whole plate in her direction, so she took one and tried a small taste. Her taste buds erupted in her dry mouth with a sensation she had not known in a long time. The food her mother made was usually rather bland, green or brown, and had a very healthy feel to it as you chewed it. When it was good, someone else had just delivered it.

"You like that, do you?"

Tamara nodded with solid affirmation. After taking another bite, she became aware of Barb's gaze and felt a bit self-conscious. The next time she looked up and met the older woman's eyes, they were moist and saturated with emotion. Barb quickly looked away, hoping to discover another purpose to pull her out of that wisp of memory. Tamara's own face flushed. She looked back to her plate and at the biscuit in her hand. She put it down, met Barb's eyes once more and waited her out as long as she could.

"You miss them, don't you?" whispered Tamara.

"That I do. Oh, I sure do. And, as life goes on, what I miss most is what I never got."

Tamara's look asked the question, but Barb answered with more sure-footed motion around the kitchen. Out from the cupboard came part of a cobbler, a small plate, and a pitcher full of fresh cow's milk. But Tamara wouldn't take a bite until she got an answer.

"What do you mean?"

Barb filled Tamara's glass with milk but when none of her efforts refocused Tamara, she relented.

"Well. When you get right down to it, a chance to make peace with it all. And, with them."

"They all died." said Tamara.

Barb nodded.

"I spent so much of my life hating my sister," Barb explained. "She was my father's little darling, and I was his little rascal, who became a big rascal. And it wasn't until she married Mark and began a family that I began to see life differently myself. I realized what kind of a sister she could have been. But then, it was too late." Her words trailed off and her mood grew increasingly introspective and melancholy.

"Why?"

"No," Barb answered, more firmly than she meant to. "No, honey. You didn't come here for all that. Enjoy your biscuit."

But Tamara set her biscuit down, and waited.

"Oh, me. Let me see. Where do you begin a story like that? My father, Nathaniel Slocum, was one of the most able farmers in the valley. He really was. He had one of the biggest dairy herds around, and he made a sharp cheddar that was out of this world. He was world famous for his butter, at least in our little world around here. He was big and brawny.

"He married momma – Nanna – when they were fairly young, but they had all their family's blessings. He wasn't perfect, by any means. Worked hard all week, but come Friday night and he was out of his mind drunk with all his old school buddies. Momma could never shake it from him, but so long as that was the extent of it, she came to accept it. But an accident with the tractor left him with a lame left leg. Now, that might have slowed most people down, but not my father. He determined to work harder than ever, not about to let a handicap 'un-man' him. But the pressure in him got worse, and he started drinking more.

"One night, he hit my mother. I was eight. Four weeks later, he was in such a rage he pushed her through the front door. He was throwing her out of the house for burning his dinner. Pushed her right through the screen door, and she fell down the steps, out there."

"Was she hurt?"

Barb lowered her eyes and clutched at the hand towel by her plate.

"Of course she was. We all were. She had been expecting, but miscarried the next day. Well, from that day...."

"You went down the well."

Barb's reaction was instantaneous. She buried her face in her hands and tried to shake the image loose.

"Yes," whispered Barb. She looked up and saw deep recognition in Tamara's eyes as she unfolded the story. "I've never wanted to think about it that way, but yes, I went down the well. I was so full of hate, they were so full of anger and despair. We all went down that well together, you might say."

"But then you were baptized," said Tamara.

"Well, yes. Several years later I was baptized, but even so, God had a lot of dirt to wash out of my soul. God keeps his own counsel, Tamara, and his own schedule about these things, and I think God wanted me to keep drowning for a while, and I suppose I did. There was a lot of hurt and anger in my family that didn't just go away because I found the Lord.

"No, daddy went on being daddy, and the drinking got worse. Momma became more depressed and withdrawn over the years. And me, well, you might say my soul got all dressed up with Jesus but had nowhere to go for a while. I started remembering a lot of the old Bible stories, and I began appreciating them more, but I was not a religiously minded person. No one ever thought to talk to me about that sort of thing. The whole church rolled their eyes when I said I wanted to get baptized, and if it weren't for Pastor Morley feeling a professional obligation towards me, I would never have gotten through the baptism classes. But I did, and he pronounced me fit to enter the waters of salvation."

"And Sally Anne?"

Another shade of sadness fell over Barb's face and she took a deep breath.

"Sally Anne. Well, honey. That's a story I may not be able to tell you much of. I don't mind digging up my own old bones, but some things really ought to remain buried and done with. And truth is, no one knows the whole story. She started sneaking off with her boyfriend and came home pregnant. Where they were sneaking off to, was up there on the mountain, near where your cabin is. His father had promised him that piece of land when he got married, and they went up there whenever they could just to sit and dream. But they got lost in their dreams. Mark never became much of a farmer, and his plans didn't pay off in time. They had their baby, and papa refused to acknowledge it. One thing led to another."

She said no more. That was enough for one day, anyhow.

"We should be getting over to the General to meet up with your parents," she said, looking up at the large clock on the kitchen wall.

Aimee and Terrance said their good-byes to Pastor Toby then left the church social hall to rendezvous with Barb and Tamara at the General. They got there ahead of their daughter and instead of going in decided to loiter on the porch to wait. The old screen door opened and Cindy stepped out beside Terrance.

"Afternoon," she said. "Sorry about your power," she continued. "We're hoping to get it back on later this afternoon. Power company said they had to make a few other calls first. They'll get up there as soon as they can."

With all the other events of the morning still swirling in his brain, Terrance just now remembered why they came down the mountain in the first place. He looked at Cindy with surprise.

"Tobias called me this morning to report it was out. Said he saw you on your morning walk."

Around the bend, Tamara and Barb came walking up the road. They paused and exchanged a few more words before Tamara left her. Barb waved from a distance, then turned and walked back toward her house. Aimee wanted to run and thank her, but resisted the impulse.

22

An Eternal Precipice

No one wanted to drive back up the mountain. The confusion of the morning left the family disoriented, and Terrance, for one, needed time to regroup. He had watched his wife and daughter engage in these experiences over the course of the morning, but he had been a complete bystander and now felt like an alien in their lives.

For their parts, Aimee and Tamara weren't ready to let go of the sensations moving around inside them. Something new was wanting to inhabit them, but neither could make sense yet of what that was.

"How about that hike you mentioned yesterday," suggested Aimee. "It is a beautiful day."

The mention of it made Tamara groan, and Terrance, who had walked the downward slope of that trail, had seen enough of the "great north woods" for one day. Besides, he pointed to the flats Aimee wore on her feet as a good reason not to risk a twisted ankle.

"Cindy carries some outfitting equipment," countered Aimee. "Let's go see what she has, just for kicks."

Tamara slumped in every aspect of her physical being, but Terrance was weakened enough not to challenge her, so he turned and led them back into Nanna's General.

Cindy had discovered that most up-scale weekend adventurers have a weakness for trendy new outdoor-wear, so she kept a selection of hiking sandals, walking sticks, water bottles, floppy hats, and a line of fleece outer garments. There is something about switching one's mental work toward making a new purchase that feels like relief to the weary of mind.

For them to be looking for shoes together offered a sense of momentary communion. They selected, then modeled, shoes they wouldn't be ashamed of wearing back in the city yet were rugged enough for their mountain trek.

"I see a hike is in store for the afternoon," said Cindy as they laid their shoes on the counter. "Where are you headed?"

"Well," said Aimee, "unless you have any other suggestions, we thought about the trail near the cabin."

"That's what I would suggest," she responded. "There are other nice trails within a short drive from here, but none of them will offer views as gorgeous as the one up there."

"How steep is it?" asked Aimee.

"It's not too bad. It is a steady climb, but there are plenty of places to rest along the way. Just take a couple of water bottles. I've got some trail mix here if you want to pack it along in case you need an energy boost. Otherwise, it is a very enjoyable afternoon walk."

They parked at the cabin and filled up their water bottles. Terrance was disappointed the power had not returned yet, otherwise, they didn't allow themselves much time for reflection. The cabin's environment continued to reverberate with thunder from the night before. They hit the trail.

The trail was well managed. It rose gently toward the east and bent back in the direction of town. There was little about the setting to pull them out of themselves, so after a few dozen yards they had spaced themselves out with Terrance in the lead, Tamara behind him, and Aimee pulling up the rear.

Soon, they came to a clearing, a small meadow bordered by a split rail fence, badly in need of repair. From there, they could take in the layout of the valley. Just below them was Nanna's General, and several farms filled out the landscape. A herd of cattle clustered on a small hill in the distance.

"Look at the sheep!" said Aimee, pointing south.

The church's blunt steeple was just in view to the far right. Across the street from that, the peak of a barn roof.

"That's where Barb's house is, I think," said Tamara.

"How did that go?" asked Aimee.

Tamara shrugged. "Good."

"She's nice, isn't she?" Aimee continued, hoping to open up her daughter a little. "How was lunch with Barb?" she asked. But her daughter chose not to respond as she searched out what she could of the barnyard behind Barb's house.

"Oh. She wants us to come for breakfast in the morning," Tamara said with little affect, but in truth she was hoping for a positive response from her parents.

Terrance's spirits plummeted again just as fast as Aimee's rose.

"That would be nice," said Aimee. "What time?"

Tamara shrugged, which left Aimee feeling a bit dispirited, but she didn't allow her daughter's attitude to get under her skin.

They turned up the trail and set a gentle pace until the grassy slopes gave way again to trees. The path bent noticeably upwards on the sunny side of the mountain, which was also much rockier. They passed through several large stone formations which bore resemblance to a tunnel with its roof removed. Here, the path became very narrow and required a lot more concentration to navigate.

When they emerged from the ravine, they found themselves on a terrace of sorts, a broad gravelly space with a few shrub pines, but otherwise the terrain was barren. The mountain proceeded up behind them, but the outer edge was a cliff guarded by a waist-high stone wall that overlooked the valley on the eastern side of the mountain. No one wanted to get more than a few feet from the wall. The view was just as impressive from where they stood. A burst of wind made them all rock back on their heels and Terrance had to chase his floppy white tennis hat as it took flight. Tamara retreated to the back edge of the terrace, found a large rock, and sat down.

Aimee stretched her vision as far as she could out over the White Mountains. She felt the urge to look down, so she ventured a step closer to the wall and bent her sight over its rim. The sudden drop in her perspective disoriented her. She had been atop the World Trade Center and looked over its ramparts, so she knew what "a long way down" meant, but the precious little that protected her from the plunge frightened her. Then, she noticed a small brass plaque affixed to the top of the wall:

> Stover
> Mark Sally Anne Tobias
> November 24, 1936
> Isaiah 25:6-9

She took in the data but resisted attaching any emotion to it. She knew the story too well from her study of the stock market and what it did to farmers when it crashed in 1929. She hoped to keep some academic distance from the truth pounding in her chest, but it didn't work. She shook off the implications and looked over the edge once again, but her eyes closed involuntarily and she was violently jolted by the sparks of insight that flashed through her mind. She turned her back on it and took several steps away from the ledge, then wrapped her arms around herself and tried to squeeze the sensations from her body. *God, what suffering must still torment these poor souls. Three more reminders of the turn a life can take when too much becomes too much, and the soul finally dials itself all the way back and shuts off the lights.*

She glanced over at her daughter and felt the wind slice through her. *Don't you ever...*

The reverberations of pain echoing through the generations now roared through Aimee's soul. Such an implosion does suicide make on the psyches of all its unintended victims. The collateral damage can't ever be accounted. And now, inexplicably, her family's personal tragedy has been absorbed into the family legends of complete strangers.

"I guess this is the end of the trail," said Terrance, breaking her concentration and adding the ironic punch to her emotional gut. "The only thing beyond here is down," he added, standing about a dozen yards beyond Aimee, peeking through some trees which were growing out of the side of an easterly facing wall of mountain top. "And no way up, either."

"I suppose it is getting time to go think about dinner." Aimee felt the need for food and the normalcy she hoped would return around the dinner table.

The sun was facing the other side of the mountain and the shade overtaking them was chilly. But as Aimee and Terrance turned toward the trail, Tamara resisted.

"I'm staying here," she said.

"Come on, baby," said Aimee, in her steadiest, motherliest voice, though she felt her emotional semaphore flags waving violently. "Let's go fix some dinner."

But Tamara wouldn't budge, and she wouldn't acknowledge her parents. Her face had turned sour, and her aspect darkened again. Her eyes were like coals, empty and without any emotion.

Aimee and Terrance looked at each other helplessly, though where Aimee felt fear, Terrance's frustration was brewing up anger. It had been too long a day for this, and he just didn't have it in him to wage another campaign of psychological combat with the two of them.

Putting up her hand to signal she would take this one, Aimee walked slowly toward Tamara. She stood for a moment beside her daughter, then sat down and rested her hand on Tamara's hand. Tamara allowed her mother's hand to remain, though Aimee could feel her daughter grow tense.

There were tears in Tamara's eyes.

Aimee fought every impulse to wrap all fifteen of her mother-bear arms around her and hold her. *Easy now, don't rush, or you'll lose everything you've just gained.* Instead, she clutched the hand she was holding, and while Tamara didn't squeeze back, she didn't pull away either. *That's it. Another step closer.*

"Honey. What is it?"

Tamara dropped her head. A stream of tears dripped from her cheek onto the rock. They were flowing profusely though Tamara made no sounds to accompany them. Her mouth was riveted shut and her brow so tightly furrowed. So many tears, and every one of them was cutting off the oxygen to Aimee's mind.

Aimee's heart was in shards, and her own eyes were burning. She fought hard to remain in control of her emotions, but her daughter's pain was scalding hot. Aimee let go of Tamara's hand and gave in to that bear hug, but her earlier instincts were better.

Tamara ripped herself away, rolled off the rock on to her feet, and moved rapidly toward the ledge.

The scream Aimee held inside her was primed and ready to explode, but Tamara halted at the wall, drew herself up straight, wrapped her long arms around herself and stood ramrod stiff. The only part of her body that showed any softness was her hair which responded lightly to the gentle breeze.

Her parents froze in terror. Terrance began to take a step, but Aimee waived him off. By mutual, unspoken consent, they both realized that the next step was all Tamara's. With her feet firmly planted about a foot from the wall and her gaze toward the horizon, Aimee calculated she was not actively talking herself into jumping. She figured that between herself and Terrance, she could not be seen by Tamara and so took as silent a step toward her as she could, waited, then took another.

Tamara remained still.

Aimee took another step, with her hand outstretched.

Then, Tamara glanced down and advanced toward the wall. Aimee strode four steps then froze again when her daughter bent over and placed both hands on the wall. Tamara was reading the plaque Aimee had seen earlier.

Aimee's breathing halted as she watched her daughter come to the same realization she had earlier and felt the same sledgehammer against her consciousness all over again. Aimee's time was up. She couldn't take it anymore, so she advanced toward Tamara, completely unsure of herself, yet determined she was going to make contact.

But as Aimee moved closer, Tamara fell.

Tamara collapsed against the wall then hit the ground. She lay still for just a moment, but then every muscle in her face contorted. She wailed, slashed at the air and lashed out at whatever fiends were now before her eyes. She pulled herself to her knees but then slammed her back and head against the wall as she thrashed against anything solid she could find. She rolled back to the ground, curled into a knot and wrapped her arms around her head. Her body convulsed as she wept.

Her parents were too stunned to react at first, but when Tamara began clawing at her wrist, trying to break the skin, Aimee grabbed her forearms. Tamara turned her ferocity upon her mother, who got herself smacked a few times and kicked in the side.

Again, Terrance couldn't find his way in to be of any use. But he found his voice.

"Tamara! Stop it, right this minute."

And, she did. She froze.

Aimee could feel all the violent energy evaporate from her daughter, and she let go of Tamara's arms. Tamara pulled her knees up to her chest and wrapped her arms around her head. There, she lay sobbing uncontrollably as she sought to purge the horror that so eviscerated her.

As Aimee watched helplessly, Terrance lifted his eyes and looked out over the mountains. He would never get used to feeling small, but it had become a very familiar sensation to him. The smothering sense of his personal nothingness knotted up in his chest. How alone could a soul possible be? And there were three of them there. Three souls with no hope or comfort in this world and no way of lifting them out of this. No cell phone reception, no road for an ambulance to rescue them, no emergency room within miles. He could run back down the trail but help could be hours in coming and it would be getting dark. He couldn't leave Aimee to tend to Tamara for that long. The only connection he knew how to make was with Aimee. There was no road leading in toward Tamara. So, he cautiously knelt beside his wife and rested his hand on her back. She rocked back on her haunches and rolled toward him, buried her face in his chest, and wept. He pulled her in and enfolded her in both his arms.

As Tamara lay there, now still as death, the three of them took a moment of emotional respite, though there was no illusion this was ending. Aimee embraced Terrance and recovered a measure of resolve, an emotional second wind, though she wasn't sure what to do with it. She gently unfolded herself from Terrance and pulled herself back onto her feet, paced for a moment by the wall, then circled back to where Tamara had been sitting earlier.

"Terrance," she said. "Bring her over here." It sounded like the simplest of solutions as she said it, and Terrance was slightly bemused she could utter such a statement with as little ease as she did.

"What!" He didn't actually say the word, just mimed it loudly at her.

"Pick her up." Terrance threw up his arms in disbelief.

"Pick her up, and bring her here," said Aimee, now speaking to the four-year-old Terrance suddenly felt like.

Shaking his head in disbelief, he bent over his daughter and took her up firmly in his hands. He pulled her back into a seated position, stood, and then hauled her up to her feet. He grabbed her quickly around the back then pulled her away from the wall. Her arms didn't have anywhere else to go but around his shoulders and neck. As they struggled for a moment to find their balance in a standing position, Terrance felt the closest thing he had had to a hug from her for far too long, and he was a bit unbalanced by the sensation of her grip on him. Even the illusion of affection was a powerful antidote to the helplessness he had been feeling. He let the embrace linger for a moment then, slowly, he walked her toward Aimee. The only resistance from Tamara came as she slumped against her father and tightened her forearm around his neck. Her legs wouldn't cooperate so they managed the several yards awkwardly but came at last to the large rock Aimee occupied.

"Tamara," said Aimee with calm conviction in her voice. "We have to walk back down the trail to the cabin now. We can't carry you. You will have to walk with us." Aimee left no room for negotiation.

Tamara's aspect grew darker. Aimee waited for a response, but she let it go and started to stand.

"I can't," whispered Tamara.

"Yes, honey, you can," reassured Aimee. "We will help you. But we have to go now."

"I'm not going back."

Aimee's reserves of patience had now run dry. She was about to take Tamara by the hand and physically roust her down the trail then realized that was not stubbornness but fear, even terror, in her words.

"Then where do you want to go?" asked Terrance, trying to avoid sounding angry but not doing a very good job at it.

"I want to go to Barb's."

"What for?" Terrance shot back, completely on impulse.

"Okay," said Aimee, firmly clinching Terrance's arm. "You can walk with us down the mountain, then we'll drive over to Barb's, okay?"

Her daughter closed her eyes and nodded, letting her relief show itself in fresh tears.

Aimee and Terrance exchanged a whole conversation in a series of looks at one another without ever saying a word: Well, okay, that's something, but then what? I have no idea, but we're taking this one step at a time. Then we'd best get to it. Agreed. Give me a hand.

Aimee pulled Tamara close to her and used the leverage of her daughter's weight to heft her into a standing position. Terrance stood on the other side of his daughter and wrapped his right arm around her waist.

The walk was slow because Aimee wouldn't release her hold on Tamara, and Tamara descended the hill as if she were riding her brakes all the way down. Terrance was constantly pulling out ahead, and then had to wait for them to catch up. Every time they stalled he felt a slight punch of impatience, and each time he fended off his frustration he considered just how apt a metaphor this walk downhill was for the last ten years: were they just about to finally hit bottom, and how hard would that slam be?

Twilight had come to the mountain by the time they reached their yard. The power was on at the cabin to everyone's relief. Terrance hurried in to turn on the porch lights. They drenched the yard with a harsh and glaring brightness, but it would be better than returning in the dark.

23

LIGHT IN THE VALLEY OF SHADOW

Night on the mountain was disorienting to Terrance who rarely saw the evening sky without skyscrapers decorating it. His evenings were always awash with the ambient glare of busyness that never went to sleep. But the mass of trees, illuminated by his headlights, haunted him. He struggled to keep the road in focus and felt little relief as they emerged onto Main Street and turned toward the farm.

A surprised Barb answered her door but assured them she was glad and, no, it was no imposition at all.

"Tamara said she urgently wanted to talk with you, and we couldn't get her to go back to the cabin until we promised she could. We are so sorry for the intru--"

"No, please, don't apologize. I would welcome the chance to spend some more time with your daughter," she said, focusing her smile on Tamara to communicate welcome to the young woman.

Tamara had pulled herself up stiff and hesitated to look the older woman in the eyes, but was visibly relieved she was being invited inside.

When Aimee and Terrance started to follow, Barb hesitated and said, "Isn't it a beautiful night? Why don't the two of you go rock on the porch swing for a few minutes while Tamara and I see what's going on here?"

Aimee and Terrance lingered on the porch, bewildered by Barb's hesitation to let them inside, then eased themselves onto the swing. It was the first moment alone they had had since their conversation on the porch swing of their cabin so early that morning.

Terrance took a deep breath and found some relief that their daughter had admitted herself into the care of a strange but assuredly able woman. He wondered out loud if all small-town folk were as eager to adopt total strangers as quickly as they had been adopted by this family.

"I don't think so," said Aimee. "I think there is a lot about this place that resonates in ways we would not have met with twenty miles up the road."

"Like?"

"I can't put my finger on it. But I don't think this was just a coincidence."

Terrance always went just a little postal at any suggestion of stars aligning, divine providence, God's eternal plan, karma, or universal vibes finally finding their harmonic resonance in our souls. So, his rational arsenal fought back.

"You don't think Samuelson set all this up, do you?"

"No," laughed Aimee. "I think we just had the good fortune of running into a woman who sees something in Tamara and has a soft spot in her heart for her, that's all."

They let the swing move them gently for a while.

"How are you doing?" Aimee asked her husband, but he could only shake his head and raise his eyes as if he were waving his white flag and surrendering his arms.

"I haven't been able to make heads or tails of any of it," he said. "But I want to." He became very introspective, and then he looked at his wife.

"I just don't know how," he continued.

Barb re-appeared on the porch, grabbed an old chair and dragged it over.

"Tamara wants to spend the night here," she said, "and I told her she could, if it's all right with you."

Terrance recognized that non-negotiable tone all his associates began with when they first laid something on the table, that impression she was not asking permission, just indicating she respected the parental protocols.

"You can come for breakfast in the morning and pick her up," said Barb.

Aimee was deeply troubled by the offer and openly resisted. With her daughter in the state she is in, they couldn't possibly leave her with a stranger who didn't understand what she was getting herself into.

But Barb looked her in the eyes, waited for her to use up all her words, and then quietly spoke.

"Honey. Children like yours are no mystery to me. We may seem a little 'back woods' to folk from the city (Aimee felt herself blush), but we have had to raise our children, tend our nephews, and look to our cousins in other ways. Troubles run deep in every family. Where psychiatrists and therapists aren't readily available, you learn other ways. And when you fail, you have God and one another to pick up and carry on. What you don't do is let down your duty to one another. Now, it seems, God has given me another duty, and I thank him for it. Let's just see what the night brings. The power is back on at your place I understand, so I can call you if I need to. Okay?"

Aimee nodded her head, but kept it bowed in humility as she considered the gifts this woman just kept giving them.

Terrance got ready to stand, but Aimee laid a hand on his leg and held him in place. They all let the pause deepen.

"Barb. I know it isn't polite to ask, but I can't get it off my mind, and after what you just said, I think I really need to know."

"What is it, honey?" Barbed pulled in close.

"Mark, and Sally Anne. And you named your son after theirs?"

"That's right."

"Please, tell me."

"Oh me," she said with a lot of breath draining from her. Barb was resisting, but Aimee's intensity wasn't simple curiosity. Barb understood where this was coming from and wanted to honor a young mother's search for assurances, but she knew that the story had few to offer. She would have rather spared them the hard look at this reality. She exhaled deeply and shut her eyes for the few moments it took to gain the strength.

"Depression hit, as you know. But it took a while to make it up to the mountains here. We were always poor in these parts. What a lot of people now call depression-era values were just what we did around here. Not a spare penny, ever, even when times were good. But, when it hit, it hit hard. Especially for farm-hands like Mark. He was working for his father -- next farm over -- when he and Sally Anne married. He had hoped to buy his own farm one day. In the meantime, he would plant trees for timber, up there on a bit of land his father gave him. He had a rough time of it.

"Well, when the price of milk dropped so far, the Stovers couldn't make it anymore. The bank foreclosed on their farm and the family had to move on. So, that meant Mark was out of work. My father saw it all, of course, and only set out to make things worse for him. When he saw all Mark's efforts collapsing, he offered to bail them out if Mark deeded him the land. They could live and work the land up there, rent free, but they would be tenant farmers. Mark was too proud for that. Time came when he had no choice and signed the papers. But as the fall wore on, even the help my father gave him didn't do any good by then. So, around Thanksgiving, Mark tried to count his blessings and he gave up. He walked up the hill and never came back down."

The tones of defeat had deepened throughout her narrative to the point she could scarcely articulate that last phrase. She looked off into the distance and seemed to forget she was with Aimee and Terrance. They waited for more, but it didn't want to come on its own.

"And Sally Anne?" Aimee asked as gently as she could, already bracing for what she didn't want to hear. Barb looked down at her hands and closed her eyes.

"My father had already disowned her and little Toby. Wouldn't welcome them home or offer any more support."

Aimee felt her heart racing and her maternal nature was in deep crisis, not wanting to hear any more, but she asked Barb to continue nonetheless.

"Well, my God. What was a woman like that to do?" said Barb, her voice rising with the last bit of unspent energy she had. "What could she do? And winter coming." Her voice trailed off and was content to let the obvious speak for itself.

Aimee felt tears burning her eyes. She would not have persisted, but by now she felt she had to hear this out. She drew near to Barb, took up her hand, and held it close to her own cheek as she looked deeply into the old, care-worn face, so beautiful in its age and wisdom.

Barb looked up, and their eyes met.

Terrance glanced back and forth between them. For the first time in his life, he was prepared to admit there must be something called eternity because he saw it gathering between them, its essence sparkling in the shimmer that moistened their cheeks and quivered on their lips.

"Please, tell me."

"It was getting close to Thanksgiving which they were going to spend all alone up there. This was before Mark left, but the way I see it, the closer Thanksgiving came, the more of a failure Mark felt. I got a note from Sally Anne asking if I could come up and see her. I was home with my parents. They wouldn't hear of me going up to visit, and they refused to invite them to our table. So, it was going to be a very cold Thanksgiving for us all." Barb was pleading for understanding, which Aimee freely gave.

"Mark just couldn't hang on any longer. And, I guess, neither could Sally Anne. A few days after Mark failed to come home, Sally Anne bundled up little Toby and took him out back. She dropped him down the well. Then she went in after him."

Aimee was choking. She still clutched Barb's hand near her cheek which Barb wrapped around the back of Aimee's head. She pulled Aimee into her bosom, and stroked her hair like she was her very own.

"I'm so, so sorry," was all Aimee could manage. And so was Barb, whose elder wisdom knew Aimee's tears were not born out of sympathy but a fear that has haunted these two parents for far too many years.

"So am I," she responded. "So am I."

Terrance, already feeling awkward before the conversation took this turn, now felt mortified that they had intruded so deeply into the tender places of this woman's life. But he couldn't figure out how to navigate himself away from this, as much as he wanted to.

Aimee found her voice again, instead.

"The date?" she asked. "There was only one date?"

"Honey. When Mark went off that ledge, they all went with him. So, that's the date I chose to remember."

"So, you put the plaque on the wall?"

"Yes. That's the only memorial for them. There's no spot in the church-yard for them. No headstone. I put that up after my father died so I could go up there and remember them and pray for children like yours."

Terrance felt his chest swell involuntarily and his eyes began to burn. He had no energy to resist the emotions running through him. Barb stood up and walked quietly over to him. She laid her hand gently upon his shoulders and closed her eyes lingering like that for as long as she had to.

As the emotional intensity of the moment began to calm, Aimee had one more question.

"Then you chose the quote from Isaiah. What is it?"

"It is a promise God made to heal the suffering we all seem to be part of." Barb closed her eyes: "On this mountain, the Lord of hosts will make for all peoples a feast of rich food, and well-aged wine. And he will swallow up on this mountain the shroud that is cast over all peoples, and the veil spread over all nations. He will swallow up death forever; and the Lord God will wipe away the tears from all our faces, and the reproach of his people he will take away from the earth, for the Lord has spoken. It will be said on that day: 'Behold, this is our God; we have waited for him, that he might save us. This is the Lord; we have waited for him; let us be glad and rejoice in his salvation.'"

She began with what little she had in her dry reservoir, but the words gave her strength as she proceeded and Terrance sensed her well was full and overflowing before she was through. Her hand still rested on Terrance's shoulder, and through it he could feel the power amassing in her as she spoke.

"You believe that," said Aimee, more as an affirmation that a query.

"With all my soul, I do."

"I wish I could," she confessed.

Barb nodded quietly and gave her all the room she needed. She had learned long ago not to answer too quickly, but let people listen beneath their own words and not assume that the first thing out of someone's mouth was what they really meant. Confessions like that usually rise up out of more faith than people realize they have. Most folk mistake their suffering for lack of faith, but she had known it to be the crucible for trust, since it was there one discovered how much grace was to be had from God.

"I have... such a small sense of who God is," said Aimee, almost imperceptibly. "He certainly isn't that God you just spoke about, and he doesn't seem ready to swallow up death anytime soon. You spoke of waiting, or Isaiah did, but I don't know who this God is I'm waiting for."

"Maybe not," said Barb. "But I do believe that before all this is over, you will."

She reminded them that Tamara was inside by herself, and they should probably all get some rest after so long a day. Terrance hesitated and acted as if he wanted to say something but then caught himself and said it could wait.

"Until tomorrow, then," said Barb, as if it were a benediction pronounced upon their need to look ahead.

"Oh. What time should we come in the morning?" asked Aimee.

"Well, what would be good for you?"

"Nine?" asked Terrance

"Nine!" said Barb. "Gracious me. I guess we can hold out till then," she said with a broadening smile.

Tamara was half way through the large cup of cocoa she was nursing, wrapped in a quilt and cuddled up in an old winged back chair in front of the fire.

Barb walked in without a word, stoked the coals and set on another log. She nestled herself into the other old chair and joined Tamara staring into the blaze that cast its warmth and light over them.

"Can you teach me how to pray?" asked Tamara.

Barb had imagined all sorts of conversations they might find themselves in, but that one was quite a surprise. Still preoccupied with those demons that wander down through the generations, she felt winded from her conversation on the porch. Barb knew Tamara was fighting many a demon. She was eager to listen, and even pray *with* her, but she was caught off guard by so direct a question from someone she wouldn't have suspected asking it. She rubbed her face with both hands and looked long into the fire.

"Oh, me. Teach you to pray? Well, let's see," she said. Her heart was palpitating, and she was listening hard to what Tamara really wanted to say. She didn't sense a primer on the methodology of prayer was called for, a topic she might address with her class at church, but not tonight with her young friend.

"Truth is, God is the only one who can really teach us that, since he begins the conversation." As Barb heard her own words and considered what Tamara had just asked, she sensed a conversation had already been initiated by God. Perhaps it was a matter of helping Tamara ease in to it.

"Is there something you feel like saying to God?" asked Barb.

Tamara's eyes went dark and her mind couldn't embrace the question. She needed more to go on.

"You pray a lot, don't you?" observed Tamara.

"Yes."

"Is it hard?"

"Well. Now that you mention it, yes. Often it is very hard," said Barb, who was struggling to think her way through a response that might make sense. She was often seized by the impulse to pray, and in those moments prayer felt like that essential next breath she had to take or drown. There were times when prayer offered her a deepening peace but only after long, pitched battles filled with confusion, heart-ache and loss. She sought solace in prayer, but it never felt very medicinal. Her prayer was more of an open wound that felt raw to the touch, and tonight that was proving itself to her all over again. Since her prayers were usually for those she loved, she felt their wounds and lingered in their heartache before God. So, the truth...

"It is hard to pray for those who hurt. When I really pray, and know others are in pain and in such need of God's help, I can't pray for them and not feel it. It hurts."

"Then why would you do it? If it hurts so much?"

"Because," she said, choosing her words with great care, "because God asks it of me, and when I pray, I see the way God means for us to love, and that brings me great joy. When I pray for someone to be healed, and I watch God heal, I am in awe, and that awe is a wonderful feeling. But when God does not heal in the way I have been praying for, I know he is holy and has his reasons, which I can't see, but I trust they are very good."

"I don't understand."

"No. But when you learn to pray, then I think you will."

"How do I begin?" she persisted.

"What do you want to say to God?"

As Tamara sat with that question, she began to sink within herself. She couldn't comprehend speaking with a being she couldn't see or understand, and she didn't know enough about prayer to imagine how that might be possible. But since that afternoon, it had come to represent a hope, one she could not articulate, but one that might displace the quaking in her mind and even heal some of the ravages her soul has endured for so long. All she faced was mystery. Was prayer a force she could make her ally? Was it a weapon she might use to defend her fragile psyche? Or, was it a kind of good magic that would ward off darker forces? What other forces were at work in her world, or in her, that she might still encounter? Were they good, or just more powerful? Were those powers for her, or against her? Could they be controlled, or was she already at their mercy? She became slightly agitated.

"Tamara, honey?" whispered Barb.

"How powerful is God?"

Barb could only stare at the girl, whose young, searching eyes were draining the old woman of spiritual vitality, leaving her feeling breathless and unsure how to address such big questions right out of the blue. Her own faith formation had come by fits and starts, through grinding emotional battles waged within her family and among the members of a rather bewildered congregation that didn't know how to guide her. She had asked her share of "imponderables," as she called them, only to receive blank stares from people, probably assuming she was wanting to challenge their beliefs, not develop some of her own. So, she felt the awful privilege she had been given, but didn't know what to do with it.

"How powerful is God? Nobody really knows, yet," was all she could muster, at least for starters. "God is powerful enough to create the world, and powerful enough one day to perfect it, powerful enough to save us from sin, and raise us from death. That's pretty powerful, I guess."

"But not powerful enough to keep us from suffering, or dying, or to give our minds any rest without it." Her words were in earnest and possessed an intensity that betrayed her despair.

Barb was jolted to the core. She felt a trembling within her, and her spirit grew dark, not with foreboding, but with remorse, then, rising anger.

"There is no rest in death, honey! It is not a peaceful end to suffering, no matter how bad it gets. Don't you ever let me hear you even thinking it, or so help me God..." Barb had risen from her chair and stormed across the floor. Her hands shook, and there were more words where those came from, words she had screamed at her dead sister for years still thrashed around inside her as she fought the impulse to take it all out on Tamara. Sally Anne's face had never left Barb; it was as fresh in her mind in that moment, almost superimposed on Tamara's body. She extended her arms to embrace Tamara, but to see the horrified look in the young woman's eyes as she drew near shocked Barb. She caught herself, adjusted her composure, and then sank down onto her knees beside Tamara.

"Tamara, honey, it is not death that brings us peace, and it certainly offers no peace to those it leaves behind. Death can only remind us of how fragile life is, and how precious. Your life is precious to God. And, to me." She buried her face into Tamara's shoulder and held her as tight as she could. "Don't you ever do that to your family, do you hear?" she pleaded. "And don't you ever do that to me."

The force of those words bore a new channel into Tamara's psyche, a channel still disconnected from the warren of subterranean tunnels already in place, but one that would soon find its way into regions of her soul which Tamara had never entered or knew existed.

Then, up through that channel came a whisper, a voice Tamara had never heard before, and it said: "Speak to me." Her eyes were shut, but many of the scenes that gave her such pain during her more psychotic moments, phantom images which she could never drive away were crawling out from the darkness into her consciousness: slashes of knives and eruptions of blood in her forearms; burning skin; babies with faces too much like her own split in two and their carcasses splayed open; her father smashing in her mother's skull with a tennis racket; her own wings, spread full and majestic against the city sky-line, so eager to test the currents beneath her, yet bursting into flame seconds after she launched herself into the air. All those images were forcing their vivid hell into her mind, and they were fleeing before an even greater, angrier beast who was storming up through the darkness behind them, herding those fiends into the field of her vision.

She saw the subway train bearing down on her. Her mother was now living with another family. She saw the earth, so far below her rising speedily to meet her with the ferocious sound of wind roaring past her. She felt the serpent slithering around her feet, encircling her torso, squeezing the breath from her lungs, staring viciously into her eyes, ready to strike.

Yet, closer still came the angry, spectral fiend. He came slaying, hacking and slashing at the beasts that scattered at his command. There was a great staff in his hand which he wielded like a sword, a flaming sword that scattered shards of darkness as he carved up the gloom and punished it with a word of power.

Blood-sucking stuffed animals that crashed her tea parties fled him; a mad rabbit, whose watch showed the time of her death scurried away. An ugly man in a wheel chair with a billy-club sped past her.

The great serpent, however, clung to Tamara's flesh and spit its venom into her face. The snake whispered to Tamara: "Say my name, and I will let you go. It's Thorafura. And I am the only mind you have. Thorafura. Say it, or I will squeeze the last breath out of you forever."

Then, thrashing his way fully into view, came this new Horror from below. Brilliant, machine-gun bursts of light ricocheted through her brain. With each starburst of new light the pitch-black background of her consciousness continued to brighten, as if she were watching a sunrise overtake the sinister creatures who thought they could wait around for darkness to return.

Thorafura spat in Tamara's face and said: "Don't trust him; he's worse than I am. But don't worry, I will never leave you to him. Look for my return whenever he gets near." Then, the serpent relinquished her grip on Tamara and slithered away. Thorafura followed the others into the dense forests of Tamara's subconscious, until Tamara felt herself standing alone, on a broad open plane, watching the horizon fill with the new light of a spring morning.

Tamara had no sense the fiends were gone, but they had submitted to this, their new Master, and were, for the moment, kept still by him. Her chest was heaving and she sweated profusely. For now, there was only the One -- haunting in his power, majestic in his terror, blinding in his lighted glory, fearsome in his aspect and gaze.

Barb was sure Tamara was having a seizure, and before it was over, Tamara was doubled over in her chair with her face in her lap, her arms wrapped across her head. Barb laid her hand on Tamara's back. Tamara's heart was pounding furiously, but her breathing was beginning to slow. Barb felt some relaxation begin to replace the tension throughout Tamara's body. It was a frightening few minutes, and Barb fully appreciated all Aimee and Terrance must have been through over the years. She kept her hand in place, sat herself on the arm of the chair, and closed her eyes.

"O God of mercy..." was all her lips found to say before a flood of emotions overtook her, not sobs, but the deepest of silences whelmed up and enfolded her, choking out the verbiage and defeating her ability to put any of it into words.

"God, help us, and defend us," came a few moments later. "Bring her light, and give her peace." Short, punctuated expressions of longing. "Heal your little lamb, and heal her family." Petitions separated by extended silences. "Set her free." Surges of hope were struggling against all the counterpunches of doubt pummeling her elderly faith. Yet, she persevered, trusting the Spirit to pray through her, unconcerned for how erratic it must sound to Tamara.

The disjointed words Tamara heard were foreign to her ears, and her conscious mind didn't know what to do with them, but she felt the warmth of Barb's hand and she found she was 'listening' to that, to the tactile assurance of a loving presence that was so near. She was absorbing sensations she never experienced in the concerns of her parents, teachers, or doctors. She never mistook her parents' concern for anything other than love, but it never felt like this.

"Speak to me," repeated the whisper in her mind, and again she was looking into his eyes, his staff in hand. She fought back, refusing to trust anything that would lurk within her. Her impulse was to slam the lid shut on the inhabitants of those cavernous realms. She wouldn't have said she could identify all her demons, so the fact that this was one she didn't recognize only confirmed how intensely haunted she was. But it meant one more battle she would have to wage, and she was so weary of never knowing what or who she would face every time her subconscious let something escape. She clutched fistfuls of hair and wrenched at her scalp as a groan rose up through her.

"Honey, honey. Look at me," said Barb, taking her by the shoulders, physically manipulating her body so they could be face to face.

"Tell me. You can't fight it out on your own."

Tamara's recoiled, and struggled to free herself, but Barb's hold on her was too strong. The look on Barb's face seized Tamara's attention. She stopped thrashing against the physical restraint, but fought back with her eyes. In the same way she had driven her mother out of her room on so many occasions, she met Barb's stare with a ferocious gaze of her own.

But Barb absorbed Tamara's intensity. She allowed Tamara to stare, then yielded her psychological high-ground by opening the door into her own excruciating pain and invited Tamara to look inside.

This, too, was different, thought Tamara: someone willing to join her in those infested caverns, unafraid of being hurt by what lay in wait. Every other soul in her life had learned to keep their distance. But she felt Barb diving deeply inside her where it scorched anyone who ever came this close. Everyone pulled back at this point. But Barb plowed into her as if this was the only thing that mattered willing to burn herself out if it could offer life to someone else. Tamara was jolted into a moment of clarity. She looked deeply into the woman's eyes, and in there she knew a sensation she had never known before: She was not alone.

"Speak to me." It was Barb's voice this time, not the one inside her head but the intonation was almost identical. Now, she knew it was real and not the serpentine subtlety of some psychic Trickster. Still, she hesitated, unsure of what answering might mean and unwilling to allow anyone else to invade her vulnerability.

"I think I need to go to bed," whispered Tamara.

Tamara glanced downward, and the connection was broken. Walls were going back up, but on her side, for the moment, it was fairly calm. She felt safe. And she was not alone. That was a lot for one night, and she did not let it go unnoticed. She would take that sensation with her to bed and be very grateful for it.

As Barb walked with her up the steps, Tamara passed more pictures and paused to consider one of them, taken at Christmas with three of the family gathered before a candle-lit tree: Nanna, Barb, and a young boy she took to be pastor Toby, who was the only one that seemed to be caught up in the glory of it. As the scene registered in her mind, so did a curiosity: Barb's husband. She let her eyes wash over the other pictures as she climbed the steps, and none of them answered her. Another absence no one had accounted for.

It would be Toby's room where she slept, the room of a young adult male frozen in that moment when he left to make his way in the world. The room was filled with all his passing interests: cars, airplanes, and a taste of military to give it an air of patriotism. There weren't many hints in this room that he would be a minister one day but plenty to suggest he had aspirations and lofty ideals. He was looking beyond himself at that age, and all the books, pictures, souvenirs and models were small portals through which he gazed out upon the greater world from this small valley nestled amidst the mountains of New Hampshire. His books said he loved mysteries, sports, especially football, astronomy, and there was some poetry.

As Tamara looked around the room, Barb watched her with fascination, mixed with pride in her boy, and an ache for the young woman who was so out of place here. Tamara completed her survey then turned silently and faced Barb with that 'what's next?' sort of expression on her face.

"The sheets are clean. I always keep them ready for guests," she said, as if that could make any difference at all. "The bathroom is directly across the hall, and you'll find clean towels hanging by the shower. My room is downstairs, and I'll use the bathroom down there, so this one is all yours. Just make yourself at home, and let me know if there is anything else you need."

That last statement froze them in place. Neither one of them wanted to move now that it seemed like someone should.

"Barb?"

"Yes, honey."

"I– " But nothing else could get out.

Barb let her search it out in silence. The weight had returned and the young woman's face was flush. The tempo of her breathing was accelerating again. Barb was growing increasingly uneasy watching her.

"I want to talk to God." She winced as she said it, equally unsure whether she could own the statement, or if she was treading where she didn't belong. She had just placed her sandaled feet on holy ground. Her request echoed back and slammed her in the chest, but she meant it. As the reverberations tolled in her mind like an ancient bell, the intensity of her desire firmed up her resolve. She looked Barb in the face for the first time since they left the living room, and the face Barb saw was filled with pleading: Help me do this, it said. It is what I need most.

"Then you will," said Barb. Her tone was gentle, but saturated with encouragement. "Do you want me to stay with you? Or leave you alone?" Tamara's instantaneous reaction said loud and clear not to leave her alone, and Barb was drawn into one of those ineffable moments of horrible glory. Seraphim were circling the Throne, their eyes and ears covered, and their proximity to the Holy threatened them with extinction. All her life she had used pious expressions like 'fear of the Lord' as if they were white bread gone stale, a phrase as common as could be among church folk but with little meaning left in it.

"I don't know how," Tamara said, as if she were drowning.

"That may be because you don't think you know God."

"I don't. Dad says he's a hoax, and mom gave up believing a long time ago. And with all that's happened to me, they say that's proof enough."

Barb knew precisely what she meant. She stopped believing for a while after Sally Anne's death. She kept hearing Job's wife snapping at her: "Why don't you just go and curse God and die your own self." She had been so bitter. All her former anger had returned when they discovered the truth about her sister. Barb's hatred for her father roared within her like a fire-breathing dragon, and she heaped it upon his head every chance she got. So, her sympathies were aligning with Tamara. That young woman and her haunted soul was all the evidence anyone needed that a loving and powerful God couldn't be both at the same time.

When Sally Anne died, Barb didn't want to expend too many more breaths sustaining her own little life either. But she was a daughter of Abraham now, a sister of Jesus Christ, and that meant the Lord had to keep his end of the covenant, to be her God, her savior. And by hook or by crook, she aimed to hold him to the bargain. She turned all her anger and remorse back onto God. For an extended season she dumped oceans of tears at his feet and held him responsible for every single one. And while remorse gave way to longer periods of inner calm, tidal waves of sorrow still rushed upon her. But in moments like this, when it really wasn't her time to be alone with her own feelings, she held the impulses to weep at bay.

"Sit down," said Barb. "And be still."

Barb led her to the chair she had just pulled from under Toby's desk. She walked behind Tamara and massaged her shoulders which were knotted with pain and anxiety. As she sensed Tamara's muscles relax, she asked her to close her eyes and repeat the words she said:

"The Lord is my shepherd."

"The Lord is my shepherd."

"I shall not want."

"I shall not want."

"He makes me to lie down..."

"He makes me to lie down..."

"...in green pastures."

"...in green pastures."

"He leads me beside still waters"

"He leads me beside still waters"

"He restores my soul."

"He restores my soul."

"He leads me in paths..."
   "*He leads me in paths..*"
"of righteousness"
   "*of righteousness*"
"for his name's sake."
   "*for his name's sake.*"
"Yea though I walk"
   "*Yea though I walk*"
"through the valley"
   "*through the valley*"
"of the shadow of death"
   "*of the shadow of death*"

Barb felt Tamara tense, but she squeezed Tamara's shoulders, laid her cheek next to the young woman's face and intensified her tone slightly as she leaned in to the next phrase without skipping a beat:

"I will fear no evil"

She had to wait a moment for Tamara to respond. It became clear she was no longer just mimicking the words. Barb repeated the words, this time with a tone of command in her voice as though to insist her young friend obey:

"I will fear no evil"
   "*I will... fear... no evil*"

Her words were halting and lacked conviction now. Was this the wrong approach? wondered Barb. She decided to push on, one more time:

"I will fear no evil"
   "*I will fear no evil*"
"for you are with me"
   "*for you are with me*"
"your rod and your staff"
   "*your rod and your staff*"
"they comfort me."

Again, Tamara halted. She saw the figure in her vision a few moments ago, swinging his staff. She assumed it was an evil wizard herding his minions through the courses of her soul, but now she was searching through that image with different eyes.

"They comfort me," repeated Barb

"*they comfort me,*" whispered Tamara, her words now barely audible.

"You prepare a table before me"

"*you prepare a table before me*"

"in the presence of my enemies"

"*in the presence of my enemies,*" and as she said it she saw her tea-parties being crashed by all those villainous rogues that used to come uninvited and push her dolls out of their seats and take over. She grinned, imagining this shepherd thrashing them with this rod and staff of his!

"you anoint my head with oil"

"*you anoint my head with oil*"

"my cup overflows."

"*my cup overflows.*"

"Surely goodness and mercy"

"*Surely goodness and mercy*"

"shall follow me"

"*shall follow me*"

"all the days of my life"

"*all the days of my life*"

"and I shall dwell"

"*and I shall dwell*"

"in the house of the Lord"

"*in the house of the Lord*"

"forever."

"*forever.*"

Barb let silence wrap around them once more as she gently massaged Tamara's shoulders. She halted and said she would be right back. She returned with a hair brush and pulled it through Tamara's long knotted black hair that had had more than its share of wind and fits of tugging for one day.

"That was beautiful," said Tamara. "What is it?"

"An ancient, ancient song," she said. All her well cultivated theological instincts prompted her to tell Tamara about David, who composed the psalm, then point out parts of it that were especially meaningful to her. But she simply added, without a shred of doubt in her mind:

"It's about Jesus."

"Baby Jesus," whispered Tamara, remembering something from long ago, a retrieved, repressed memory of sorts, but with no connection to anything else. Stories her grandmother used to tell her at Christmas, that was all.

"Baby Jesus," affirmed Barb. "Talk to him. I believe you know him better than you think. I'm convinced he knows you better than you will ever realize."

Barb was exhausted and felt it was long past both their bed-times, so she put down the brush, kissed Tamara on the top of her head and said good-night.

As Tamara fell asleep, she was enveloped in a mystery she would never fully comprehend. But for once, the mystery wasn't shredding her apart from the inside out. And that was huge.

24

A White Mountain Farm Breakfast

The morning light woke Aimee. She looked at the clock: 8:12. Her first impulse was to leap into gear in order to make their engagement, but the rustic decor of the cabin overcame any sense of urgency within her, so she rolled over and snuggled up to Terrance. As he stirred, she tightened herself against him and said good morning.

"It's time for breakfast," she whispered.

"A White Mountain farm breakfast?" he murmured into his pillow.

"I made reservations for 9:00."

Terrance opted for a quick shower. When he emerged from the bathroom he found Aimee standing on the front porch running her hand along the handle of the axe. Every muscle in his body seized up.

"I was thinking of having one installed by our front door at home," she said. "What do you think?"

For all that axe had come to represent in less than forty-eight hours, he was sure he couldn't make light of it without a lot of heart-to-heart conversation first.

"I'm sorry," she said. "I shouldn't joke. I was looking out over the mountains trying to imagine just how much they've endured and how much they've witnessed, and I saw the axe. I thought, given all we know about what happened, it is a wonder the family allowed them to keep this here."

"Well, the family doesn't own it anymore," he responded. "Maybe they didn't have much of a say in it."

"Maybe. But in such a small village, with all the sensibilities you'd run in to, the club would want to keep on good terms with them. So, if Barb's family wanted this axe removed, I doubt it would be here."

He looked away, but his mind was on fire with the imagery of the night before. He imagined that axe rolling slowly through the air, just missing Barb's father's head, striking home in the frame of their cabin. The farmer's pledge to love his wife mocked him as he saw himself running through the yard chasing Aimee with the very symbol of that pledge. Had it not been for Tamara's intervention, he might have killed Aimee.

What these mountains could bear witness to if words could be forced from their winds and lofty heights. But their silences were also their graces, and the sun peaking over the ridge testified to the mercy of a new day dawning all around them. They savored those silences all the way down the mountain.

When they climbed onto the porch and knocked on the door, no one answered.

"Hello?" Terrance shouted.

"Back here," came Barb's voice from around the house. As they stepped off the porch, they saw Tamara emerge from the barn wearing large baggy britches tucked in to knee-high boots. Her arms were filled with little tabby kittens. Three diminutive heads peeked out from the crooks of her arms.

"They were born last night," said Tamara. "We're taking them over to the shed. Barb has a small pen and a lamp that will keep them warm."

"How did it go?" asked Aimee, with an air of confidentiality and wariness.

"It went very well," said Barb, with her own air of introspection. "Very well. We've had a good time. Come on in. We're just finishing up a few barn chores."

As they entered the kitchen by the side door, Tamara kicked off her boots then went over to the fireplace and laid another log on it. Terrance was not sure who this young woman was, but she was not his daughter. However, when she turned around and stood face to face with her parents, a shadow fell across her eyes and she retreated back inside herself again. There she was.

"Tamara?" said Barb from the kitchen. "You were going to help me with this." She was standing by the counter with a large mixing bowl.

Tamara dutifully strode into the kitchen. She held out the eggs for her parent's inspection.

"Where did you get those?" Terrance asked.

"I got them from the hen house," she said.

"From the hen house?" said her dad. "You got those from a genuine White Mountain farm hen house?"

"Yes, I did," she said with triumph in her voice.

"Did you have to negotiate with the mother hen for the use of her eggs, or did you just snatch them right out from under her?"

"I politely explained the facts of life to her, and she told me I could have them."

"And just what do you intend to do with those eggs?"

"I plan to make you an omelet for your breakfast, sir."

"Just like that?"

"Just like that."

Actually, it wasn't just like that. Barb had to intervene numerous times, beginning with a lesson on cracking the eggs without getting shells in them and how to keep paying attention so they didn't burn in the skillet. So, the experience was largely that, an experience of trying to be friends and family around the breakfast table. It probably tried the old woman's patience a lot more than she let on as she nudged Tamara through some simple life lessons that might have been second nature for a lass in another day and time. But Tamara's world was not oriented in that direction.

"Do you remember where we left the herbs we cut for the omelet?" Barb asked Tamara, who nodded and ran through the back door.

Barb laughed when she saw the expressions on the two parent's faces.

"She has been up since five-fifteen!" said Barb. "I would have just let her sleep, but she was up with the dawn and had questions about every photo and every knickknack in the house, so I decided to direct her energy toward the barn. And she's done very well out there, I must say, for such a green farmhand as she is."

Tamara resumed her duties in the kitchen, and the omelet struggled to be born. Both Aimee and Terrance cheered as they watched it come to the table and gave it five-star rave reviews.

For Aimee, however, the last bite was more difficult to swallow than she imagined it would be, and she let the taste of it linger on her tongue too long. The flavor seeped over into her emotions, which she had not dealt with very well. For an hour and a half, Barb had absorbed their family in to this great and generous heart of hers, keeping the conversation light, salting it with old wives' tales, peppering it with mountain lore and a few well-chosen stories about her family's happier history. Aimee felt herself brushing up against something she had lost in their families.

Terrance's family history was always being burnished by the exploits of some uncle or other, but those epic tales served to further the family brand and firm up the family myth for the sake of the next generation who would inherit it. Barb's stories were more like the large quilt hanging in Nanna's General, memories a family kept wrapped around them to bring them warmth and remind them of who they are – not to determine who they will be, but to reassure them that they have a lot standing behind them if they want to make an honest go of it.

Aimee felt small and empty. She had been given a privileged tour of this woman's life and was humbled by that. She wanted more, and the awareness that they were about to step back out of it just as quickly as they had stumbled into it left her feeling very lonely.

"I guess we'd better head back to the cabin and pack up," said Terrance. "We've got to check out and be at the airport by two."

"I'm staying here," said Tamara, sending fresh shock waves through her parents.

"Now, what did I say about that?" said Barb, not scolding, but in a reassuring tone.

"Oh, yeah."

Both parents looked on clueless.

"Barb says I can come back this summer."

Aimee felt a cheer welling up in her, but she put on her negotiating face and stared at her daughter.

Terrance just sat in stony silence, remembering his own resolve never, ever, to set foot in a town that didn't have a Starbucks on every corner and ready access to the financial news. But, even he was watching this unfold with an eye he didn't know he had.

They looked to Barb to fill in the missing pieces, but she sat there looking at Tamara with a quiet confidence that wasn't going to rush anything.

"Well, we'll talk about it," said Terrance, breaking the conversational stalemate.

Recognizing the signs stewing on her daughter's face, Aimee straightened up and laid another hand on the table.

"I wouldn't mind bringing Tamara up again for a visit. I can check with Samuelson to see if the Club has anything for July. I'm sure I can get a long weekend in there somewhere."

"You'd be free to use the farm-hand house," said Barb. "The view isn't as nice from down here, but it's available anytime you want it."

It sounded heavenly to Aimee, but Tamara put her foot down.

"I'm coming by myself," she said, driving a stake in her mother's heart, but Barb was quick to intervene.

"One step at a time," Barb said to the young woman. "For right now, why don't you go change in to your own clothes and get ready. It will all work out, honey. Just trust, okay?"

Tamara slumped but did as she was told and slowly ascended the stairs. Now, her parents were sensing conspiracy and they looked intently at Barb.

"When she got up this morning," Barb explained, "she told me she didn't want to go back home. She wanted to stay here and live. I know. She's talked herself into some illusion of a sort which I did not encourage, believe me. I told her we would have to wait and see how the rest of her school year went. Then, if it was okay with you, she could come for a visit. I told her about the cabin, and you could all stay there, but she wanted to come alone and work on the farm."

"In a hundred years, I never would have imagined," said Terrance, more to the stratosphere than anyone in the room, not rejecting the idea, just dumbfounded by the thought of it.

"Honey," said Aimee. "Look around you. She has never lacked fodder for her imagination, and now she's surrounded by a fresh supply. Who knows what any of this means, but let's just figure out how we're going to take the next few steps in our lives first. I'm not even sure what those are, and all this could change in a few weeks. Who knows?" Then she turned to Barb.

"Whatever any of this means, you have been amazing," said Aimee, laying her hand on Barb's. "I can't begin to thank you enough for what you have obviously given to our daughter. Personally, I hope we do have the chance of seeing you again. This has been wonderful."

As hard as it was to break away, they finally navigated their way through the good-byes, got back into the car and climbed up the hill.

∽

As Aimee and Terrance scurried about the cabin collecting their belongings and tidying up so they could leave, Tamara sat on the couch with her satchel beside her completely withdrawn.

"How're you doing, honey?" asked Aimee.

Tamara shrugged, looking as if she needed to speak but didn't know how, so Aimee put down the grocery bag and waited.

"Mom. Can I get baptized?"

Aimee had heard plenty of astonishing things come out of Tamara's mouth, many of which were either delusional or weapons to knock the wind out of her parents so she could bounce on their emotions for a while. But Tamara's face flushed. She cringed at her own words as if embarrassed by what she had said.

Instead of ramping up her defenses, Aimee went flat involuntarily. She didn't have a religious bone in her body that knew to respond to this positively. What she had was a therapeutic world view that wondered at the fantasies her daughter was concocting about the power of faith and how this would complicate any return to reality as they headed home. So, Aimee said nothing and stewed in her uncertainty.

"I think that would be fine," came Terrance's voice from the hallway. He had overheard the question and watched his wife's perplexity. It may have surprised him as much as the others to hear those words coming out of his mouth, but hearing them firmed them up in his mind.

Tamara looked conflicted, and her face became ashen. She was't sure what she had started and wondered if she should retract it. She looked up at her father and hoped he would say something quick. So did Aimee, for that matter.

Terrance nodded. "I think you should look into it. Don't rush into it, but if it is what you want, then I will support you."

The women stared at him in stunned silence.

Tamara stood up, unable to calm her inner agitation. She tried to look at Terrance and struggled mightily over words she couldn't articulate, then she slipped out the door to the front porch.

Husband and wife stood alone in a stalemate of confusion.

"Honey..." Aimee began tentatively. "I..."

"What? Are you worried this is just something she's grasping at?"

"Yes! Exactly."

"I know. That certainly bothers me. I mean, you know me, that's the only reason I can imagine anybody goes in for religion in the first place."

"I just don't want her to get hurt anymore," said Aimee, "and I don't want to go chasing her down any new rabbit holes that will end up burning her worse than she already is. If this is some kind of false hope she's picked up around here..."

"The higher she climbs, the farther she falls," whispered Terrance, evoking in Aimee's mind the eternal expanse that lay beneath the ledge up on the mountain behind them.

"Yes."

"But what about you?" said Terrance. "You seem to have drunk quite a bit of White Mountain cool-aid this weekend yourself."

The words stung, but as she searched out the truth of them, she knew he was right. She had been challenged to take a hard look at their lives and nothing was coming into focus. Yet this morning she felt a new

A White Mountain Farm Breakfast

grace at work amongst them she couldn't identify but wanted to ponder long and hard for a while. She had hoped to carry those sensations home with her, but now she felt embarrassed by them. She slumped in her emotional demeanor, and Terrance took a step toward her.

"Look," he said. "There are no illusions here. I realize that we are in for a very long haul. This will be our life from now on. I don't know what any of this means, but for now, this is where we are. Aimee, if this is bringing our daughter any peace, even a momentary vacation from the hell she has endured for so long, then my sense is that her heart and mind need it. No illusions."

"Thank you," she said. "I'm very proud of you. Are you sure you didn't drink a bit more of the cool-aid than you're letting on, yourself?"

"Not so fast!" he said with a playful grin. "But I did lie awake quite a while last night thinking about everything that has happened. Seeing the effect Barb had on Tamara this morning was no small thing. I haven't figured any of it out, but it wasn't just skin deep. I've never seen Tamara impacted like this before, even if it is temporary. We can only wait and see. But for now..."

"So. Okay. But how in the world do we proceed?" asked Aimee. "Are you going to start taking her to church? Last I heard, you don't just walk up to a local priest and say, I want to get baptized."

"Why not?" he joked, then sat down on the couch. "Not long after Tamara was born, we had all those fights with our folks about Tamara's christening and religious education. Do you remember what we told them?"

"No."

"I told my parents I wasn't going to force religion down my daughter's throat, especially since I didn't believe in it myself. I insisted that it was going to be her choice. And, I guess, it's time to eat my words. Or, stand behind them."

"So, do we ship her off to your parents to complete her religious up-bringing?"

"Good God, no!" he said. "If this is real, we don't want to kill it that quick! My parent's faith is a sham. It has never been anything more than an ego boost for my dad, a social security net for my mom, and a lot of bother for us kids, for whom all Ten Commandments were rolled into one: don't embarrass the family."

Terrance stood and embraced Aimee, then he held her shoulders as he looked into her eyes. "I think we ought to talk it over with Samuelson for starters. He seems to have some insights there. But then…" He hesitated to make sure he really wanted to say this: "Then, I think we ought to talk about sending her to stay with Barb for a while, if Barb sincerely meant it, and if Tamara is doing fairly well through the spring."

Aimee's heart was soaring. She pulled Terrance close and held him, then she let him resume his packing.

Out on the lawn, Tamara had taken up her post, ram-rod stiff against the wind, her face lifted to the sky, her eyes closed. Aimee's soaring heart was drawn downward again as she stared at her daughter. *Where are you now?* She took a step toward the door then halted fearing the spiraling descent such a demeanor often betrayed. *Into what cavern have you fallen, and through what tunnel are you running? Or, are you flying? Soaring onward to that great Faraway? And how long must we wait for you to return?* Aimee closed her eyes, unable to watch, anticipating her daughter fighting with them all the way home. *What does 'going home' mean for you, now, anyway? And, will you go?*

"Can I take this out to the car, now?" asked Terrance.

"Oh, yes. It's ready." She was disoriented by her ruminations and struggled to remember what she was doing before they got lost in this conversation. The mountain's gravitational pull seemed to increase, slowing them all, but they managed to pack their bags, and their lives, back into the SUV for the drive back to the airport.

As they re-entered the woods and began their descent, Aimee saw Pastor Toby striding up the path.

"Stop," she said to Terrance, and then rolled down her window to greet him.

"I see you folks are all ready to go," he said good-naturedly.

"Yes. We hate to go, but we sure are grateful for all you have done for us this weekend."

"It's been our pleasure. But I'm glad I caught you. Mom wanted you to have this," he said, as he handed Aimee a parcel wrapped in brown butcher paper with twine for a bow.

"She shouldn't have..."

"You oughta know you don't tell my mom what she should or shouldn't do!" he laughed. "Anyway, I'm glad I got a chance to say good-bye myself. Hope you folks have a good trip home."

"Can we give you a lift back down the mountain?"

"Thanks, but I always hike up to the overlook on Sundays for prayer, and it looks like a beautiful day. Well, have a nice flight, and God bless you all!" He patted the hood of the SUV, then continued his climb up the trail.

"What is it?" asked Tamara, reaching for it, but Aimee held it out of her reach long enough to unfasten the twine and slip it out of its wrapping. There she sat, face to face with the dirty blond teenage girl with the chameleon expression on her face, still locked in combat against her clinging father. Aimee held it for everyone to see, and as she tried to decide what the girl's expression said to her now, Tamara spoke from the back seat.

"I think the girl is going to win."

"I sure hope so, baby," said Aimee. "I sure do."

25

Final Descent

"Ladies and gentlemen, in just a few moments we will begin our approach to LaGuardia. Our stewards will be coming through the cabin to collect any trash you may have and to prepare the cabin for landing."

There were more surreal images still inside of her to get out, but precious little room left on the page, so Tamara stuffed her notepad in the seat pocket. She unbuckled her seatbelt and started to climb over Terrance, then she sat back down again.

"Going somewhere?" he asked her.

"Not anymore."

"Did you need something?"

"No. Just bored."

"Sorry. That club is too exclusive for us Baxters. They won't allow us to join. Besides, the waiting list is too long. You'll have to find another purpose in life." Aunt Tamara had spoken.

So, daughter Tamara retrieved her pad and began a rough sketch of a farm scene, but became bored.

"Wouldn't it be cool if we could get some chickens?" she said.

"That would be cool," sang Aimee.

"And some lambs."

"Even better!"

"We should buy a farm in New Hampshire," said Tamara, encouraged by her mother's tone of voice.

"With a barn and some cows!" chirped Aimee.

"And pigs."

"Oh, sure," said Terrance. "You can just send me some cheese you make with the cream from the cow you have to milk at four every morning before you gather those eggs from those chickens you so desperately want. And don't forget the wood you'll have to chop, the pigs you'll have to slop, the sheep you'll have to shear, and the shit you'll have to shovel."

"Terrance!" shouted Aimee.

"Then, we'll have lunch," said Tamara.

"Oh, and look," said Terrance pointing to his paper. "I see hog futures are up, so you should get that old swine to market before dinner."

"Sold," said Aimee.

"Hey!" shouted Tamara. "That was my pig!"

"Just another commodity," he parried.

"I also want to have a horse on our farm," said Tamara.

"We'll need at least two, or three, if your dad is going to ride with us."

"All the way to the glue factory," he said. Tamara elbowed him in the ribs.

"Hey! It sounds like you two are already moving out to the country. With that kind of menagerie that's not just a getaway in the mountains anymore," he said.

Aimee was in no mood for reality at the moment. The banter exhilarated her spirits, and she didn't need Mister Business Sense poking a hole in their fun. The fun was too rare. She became introspective again, and Terrance registered the change in her aspect.

"We could buy a share in Samuelson's outing club," said Terrance, then retracted the thought. "I take that back," he said. "I just handed in the keys to the Rusty Axe Lodge and have no intention of asking for them back any time soon."

"I'll second that," said Aimee, as she withdrew further into herself.

"We could go live with Barb," said Tamara. "She has a great big house and needs help on the farm."

I'll second that one, too, thought Aimee, as she yearned for the simple home life she rejected as a young adult. *Was there ever a time when we just wanted to be a family?* She looked at Terrance and considered the clan she had married into. *Right now, all I want is a family whose existence means more than the empires we think we need to build or the influence we* have to exert on others to give our lives significance. Is that so ridiculous?* She fingered her wedding ring. *It is so long as my last name is Baxter.*

The emotional pull exerted by that little White Mountain village was too strong, and Aimee got lost again. Her heart was still hidden somewhere in that woman's home. Barb had mothered them with a simplicity and ease that strengthened Aimee. She had reached into Tamara's soul in ways they had never thought possible. *Could I ever be that for Tamara? Or, for anyone?*

Just that morning, for a short but precious moment in an old woman's kitchen, Aimee had witnessed a metamorphosis. Her daughter was no longer her own but had been adopted into a larger world. *Or was it a tinier world? I never thought it could get any bigger or better than New York City! Before this morning, I was sure small towns could only shrink people, diminish their minds, and narrow their perspectives on the world at large. Yet, in that humble country kitchen, Tamara expanded. It was like she became finally real. Then what are we doing to her now? Forcing her back into her confinement, clipping her wings, pulling her cocoon back over her head?*

Tamara turned the page in her sketch pad and stared at the white space before her. Her face grew serious.

Here we go again.

"Honey, we're almost home, just sit tight," said Aimee. But Tamara ignored her.

Something new, molten and mysterious was moving through Tamara, a liquid fire and the colors of heat and flame, but the images cooled and the lines of another drawing formed in her mind. She was enjoying the stillness this new image brought her, however, so she wasn't ready to do the physical work of drafting it out. She wasn't sure how to sketch the swirling images of running water now so fluid in her. How do you convey the gurgles of a stream, liquid sounds that don't quit and never repeat, yet blend into a chaotic unity of wet intensity? How do you depict that part of the water that does the cleansing and refreshing when you are so dirty, sweaty, and hot? And how do you draw something so wet you can swish the colors around in your mouth, or hear the splash as you dive beneath the surface with your eyes? She didn't want to draw the wateriness until she was sure she could perfect it, so she let the streams flow unhindered and watched them glisten beneath the light of her inner mood to see if they would give up any clues for capturing them.

The pen hovered centimeters above the paper waiting in obedience. Her hand began to tremble drawing Aimee's gaze.

What now? Haven't you shown us enough? Just… put your pen away and give us a break. Aimee braced for what was about to emerge. *I can't watch this anymore. I have got to get off this plane and figure out some way to cope with what is going on insider her.*

Then, Tamara's pen began writing words instead of drawing, fluid words that rippled across her mind and made sense only in the way they made her feel.

Awashening.
Waterfallen.
Showerful.
Moistmushened.
Puddlepondering.
Swishmorish.

Awashening through a waterfallen wondermoat,
    a moistmushened Molly was puddlepondering
        her boatwayish upandonder the strealaream.
She was castarounding her streamthrimmer for swishmorish fishmashish,
    when, slowering came a horrish downpuddler
        with a smashacrashamer and a puddlunderer.
Then suddenlundelly…
    Swomedown!
    Splashlander!
    And plopunder!
    Spillherover and thrashathunder!

Molly swashelovered in her boatwaying skifferloafer,
    underpuddling, she gurglepindered

> *and spewthrew her swishmorishing fishmashishes.*
> *Rollashoren, she washerendered*
> *where the seashellers spittledribbled their susher*
> *and swalluped their stewslurp in vats of icescrimshander*
> *and cherries upanonder the sweetletweet.*

The watery words her mind made up freed Tamara to listen to the sounds of other currents moving through her depths. The white cloud vapor through which they flew, and the many tears she had wept over the course of the past few days, had been to her one and the same, an atmospheric mystery that her existence had disturbed. There were no still waters where she existed, no calm eddies, reflecting pools, or gentle streams that irrigated green pastures where people could find rest near her. Tamara was a cascading waterfall over which her torrential emotions hurled whatever hope or happiness she ever had. And the mountainous heights over which that river plunged disoriented her. How much of her life had disappeared over that cresting rush of water? What had spilled that was now forever lost?

A slurry of memories she never paid attention to before roared through her with such emotional volatility that her mind revolted, and she held her breath until she could regain control. She closed her eyes and clinched her fists, then she glanced involuntarily at her mother and saw what she never wanted to see: the impact her life had been having on those around her.

The waters that had been running through her imagination now filled her eyes, but this time she didn't want her tears to be seen. She had never been self-conscious of them. She had wept rivers of remorse, anger, self-loathing, and indiscriminate pain without a moment's thought. The tears never *meant* anything, they were extensions of her inner eruptions that had nowhere else to go.

Tamara became acutely aware of her parents in that moment and of her proximity to them. She was *with* them. That sense of *being with* them was washing something up onto the shores of her mind she couldn't recognize. They were always with her. They never left her alone. But she was being with them in a way she had not been with them until now.

Her pen was shaking in her clinched right fist. She had never thought thoughts like that before.

Please, God, get us on the ground in one piece. Aimee massaged her tired eyes. *Then, whatever it is we need to do just help us take that one next step. This can't go on.*

"How much longer till we're home?" asked Tamara.

Her daughter's voice jolted her, and she couldn't respond.

"Oh, still about twenty minutes until we land then the taxi ride home, however long that takes," answered Terrance.

"Then what?"

Coming to herself, Aimee said weakly: "We'll get something to eat, then it will be about bed time."

Tamara stared at her mother, needing something more.

"Then, school in the morning," stammered Aimee.

"I'm not going to school," said Tamara, staring with deeper intensity at her mother.

Aimee took a deep breath and struggled to maintain eye contact.

"I want to stay with you tomorrow," said Tamara.

There was something in her daughter's eyes Aimee had never seen before.

"I have to work tomorrow," said Aimee, who grieved every one of those five words.

Tamara pressed her head back hard against her seat, folded her arms and slammed shut her eyelids.

What have I done to you now? Aimee wanted to put her arm around Tamara and pull her back, to connect, but she spared herself the rejection. A deep-seated loneliness overtook her.

Then, Tamara went back to her bag but this time came up with an old burgundy book.

"Where'd you find that?" Aimee asked, trying not to sound alarmed that her daughter was thumbing through a rather tattered old Bible.

"Barb," answered Tamara, as she lay it open on the tray table in front of her.

Tamara flipped through the pages, unable to comprehend what she held in her hands. Near the center, she noticed a red ribbon then turned to the marked pages. There, she found the psalm Barb had quoted to her about a shepherd leading a distressed soul through a valley dark with shadow and death. She scanned the page which contained other poems. Her eye settled on the one before her shepherd psalm. It began, "My God, my God, why hast thou forsaken me…" and she saw, vividly, this valley of hell from which she needed deliverance. Where was her shepherd?

"Ladies and gentlemen," came the voice of the steward, "we have begun our descent into LaGuardia. The captain has turned on the seatbelt sign, so we ask all passengers to return to their seats. As always, we want to thank you for flying Gateway Airlines. Stewards, please prepare for landing."

Aimee had not yet felt the descent in her inner ears, but everything else within her was tumbling toward earth. As she stared out the window she strained to get a look at the skyline but decided she didn't want to see it. This short flight wasn't enough for the decompression she sorely needed. Surely, they had seen their worst on the mountain, but her intuition warned her the worst was still ahead of them in the city she had grown to love and call home.

Aimee felt the plane lurch beneath her as its nose poked downward and began to fall. Her stomach rose within her and she reached for the bag in front of her, but the view out her window caught her attention and pulled her out of her nausea. The solid mass of white became a thickening dark swirl of stormy gray. Its density dissolving, the wispy curls of cloud permitted shapes to emerge through them. Then, there it was: in all its ugly beauty, a city where more wealth and power, glamour and glory was aggregated than anywhere else in the country if not the world. It had been hers to master, but she was now afraid of it. About ten hours had passed since she woke up to a day that signaled a hint of hope. Yet as the majesty of the New York City skyline filled her horizon, all it evoked was dread. She had left the mountain too soon.

As the taxi made its way through mid-town traffic, Aimee fought with the images creeping past her window. She wasn't ready for the city yet. The rush of adrenaline she usually felt was replaced with sludge clogging her veins. She tried to close her moistening eyes against it and reached for her carry-on bag for a tissue. The small picture of a girl and her father, still partially wrapped in its brown paper, had been quickly stuffed inside as they prepared to board the plane. The parcel caught Tamara's eye and she reached in and snatched it out to take another look.

The Prodigal Daughter

As Tamara studied it, Aimee fought several associations that collided in her mind. *How many times have I seen that expression on so many young women in these streets? Young, haunted women, needing to pull away from whatever savage grip held them in slavery to an animalistic existence. Displaced, soul-savaged women, each wishing such a hand could hold her in love, instead.* She shivered as she saw her daughter among them, with a vapid look in her eyes, her mind eviscerated by years of neglect. Aimee saw Tamara's face beneath her long, snarled hair. She was wearing a tattered dress as a man twice her age clutched her, not in love but in the wake of a vengeful lust unleashed where it never belonged. She fought away the impressions and looked instead at her real daughter, the one they were bringing home.

"She's pretty," said Tamara.

"You think so? Really?" asked Aimee.

"Yeah. She reminds me of Barb, in a way."

"Oh? How so? I'm not sure I would have seen a resemblance."

"Look at that soul," said Tamara.

The answer quickened Aimee's heartbeat. Yes, there was plenty of soul to be seen in that young girl, and for her daughter to see in that face an expression of promise, instead of defeat, stoked a silent awe that overwhelmed Aimee. Her eyes couldn't contain her emotions, and they let go. She resumed a frantic search for that tissue.

"What is it, honey?" asked Terrance.

Aimee was trying to control the flow of tears but clasped her hand over her eyes instead, as though she could build a dam around them.

"Hey," he said. "We're okay here."

Aimee forced her head to nod, but put no conviction behind it.

"I hope so. God, I hope so," she moaned.

"Where is this coming from?" asked Terrance, now slightly frustrated by this sudden show of anxiety.

"I don't know. I just don't know anymore," she answered. "But I'm still so afraid."

Terrance reached across Tamara and took Aimee's trembling hand.

"Wanna hear what Barb told me?" asked Tamara.

No one answered her, so she assumed a slightly affected imitation of the older, wiser woman, in order to get their attention.

"She said, 'There are those frightening things you should run from. There are those frightening things you should stand up to and defeat. And then, there are those frightening things you should let win.'"

As both parents absorbed that bit of New Hampshire wisdom, it was Terrance who responded most unexpectedly. He looked hard at Tamara and let Aimee's hand fall free. He wrapped that arm around his daughter and drew her tight to his side, buried his face into her hair, rubbed his cheek across her scalp and held her there. Then, for the first time Aimee could ever remember, his eyes grew wet and he tried to shut them against the flood.

"What has gotten in to you?" asked Aimee.

It took him a moment to compose himself enough to speak and then whispered, "That's just the sort of thing my aunt would say."

Author's Note: The story continues in *Those Frightening Things You Should Let Win*. Tamara Baxter is growing up and decides she needs to reclaim the initiative for her healing from her mother. Determined to return to New Hampshire to help Barb on the farm, Tamara's mental state initiates a chain of events that leads her back to the mountains where she seeks to begin a new life.

Acknowledgments

As the impulse to write this novel gained momentum it became a personal mission to encourage families to claim hope in the midst of their suffering caused by mental illness. I want to thank those who taught me how essential it is to find a community of care that will walk with you in healing ways. Appropriately, this novel has been a community effort and was partially inspired by the gracious souls at Gould Farm in Monterey, Massachusetts. This therapeutic farming community provides a holistic environment dedicated to recovery and healing. They live well into their motto: "We Harvest Hope." I encourage you to investigate and support the care they give to others. (gouldfarm.org)

As I was finishing this story I learned of a fledgling project in Rhode Island, Harvest Acres Farm, run by Cindy and John Duncan. With a deep and personal interest in encouraging those suffering from mental illness, they have dedicated their farm to become a haven of healing for those struggling to find a path toward mental and emotional wholeness. Their effort is truly worthy of your support (harvestacresfarm.org).

A portion of all proceeds from the sale of this novel will be donated to these essential organizations.

Numerous friends and family cast a critical eye on this project and offered meaningful feedback. I am most grateful to my supportive and long suffering wife, Beth, and my mother, Judy, both of whom read multiple drafts; to Sandra Lindstrom, Kathe Jaret, Tripp Reade, and Walter Cole, each of whom helped polish the story. Special thanks to Captain Dominic Zachorne, founding member of the Wickford Shipyard Literary Society, who lent invaluable encouragement.

Quotations from Scripture are my own modernized adaptation of the King James Version of the Bible. The hymn, "*Come, Every Soul by Sin Oppressed* was composed by John H. Stockton in 1874.

About the Author

Clay Berry lives with his wife, Beth, in Wakefield, Rhode Island where Clay has served as pastor of the Wakefield Baptist Church for over twenty years.

Clay was recently awarded the Doctor of Worship Studies degree from the Robert E. Webber Institute for Worship Studies. His thesis examined connections between worship and healing. *Through a Shattered Looking-glass* is his first work of fiction, and the first in a series of novels that will explore issues of mental suffering and the restoration of hope.

www.ingramcontent.com/pod-product-compliance
Lightning Source LLC
Chambersburg PA
CBHW071654090426
42738CB00009B/1524